# EMPOWERED

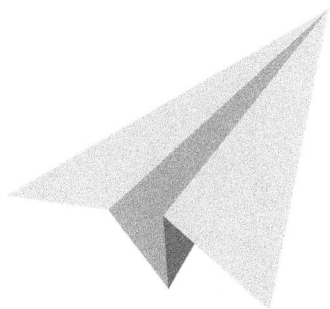

# EMPOWERED

## a new generation of leaders

### AVIV PALTI

First published in 2024 by Aviv Palti

© Aviv Palti 2024
The moral rights of the author have been asserted.

A catalogue entry for this book is available from the National Library of Australia.

ISBN: 978-1-923225-04-6

Printed in Australia by Pegasus
Project management and text design by Publish Central
Cover design by Pipeline Design
Graphics by Jessica Palti

To the dreamers who become change-makers and tomorrow's social leaders.

To the followers who become leaders, and the leaders who become mentors.

To those who believe in others before they learn to believe in themselves.

And to Mich, Jess and Steph, the wind beneath my wings.

# Contents

# Introduction

This book is not about world leaders, or corporate leaders; it's not even about social leaders. This book is about all of us and about you, and the leader within you. The leader you want to be, the leader you can be, the leader you are afraid to be. Leaders are made, they are not born – they are moulded from life experiences and life skills. The best leaders are the ones who don't even know they already lead, yet they share their life with others in an empowering and inspirational way, causing the tide to come in so that everyone around them is raised.

You are such a leader already – otherwise, you wouldn't have this book in your hands right now. You know you have the key in your hands – you know you want to unlock more knowledge, so you can lead by design, not by default. You know there is more to learn, and that's a great place to start.

This is the story of turning a lemon into a lemonade factory, and then giving away franchises for more lemonade factories. Forget 'If you give a man a fish, you feed him for a day. If you teach a man to fish, you feed him for a lifetime'; imagine teaching a new generation how to catch the fish and how to breed the fish!

## Whose story is this?

This is the story of the Cambodia Rural Students Trust (CRST), a non-government organisation (NGO) in Siem Reap, Cambodia, which has become a leadership factory. As an NGO, CRST is registered with the Ministry of Interior in Cambodia, but operates independently of any government. Our mission is to 'Break the poverty cycle through education by educating future leaders'. Using education as the spine of CRST, we address critical social issues through our projects, including empowering women, protection of the environment, WASH (water, sanitation and hygiene), energy poverty and the alleviation of all poverty.

CRST is entirely led and managed by our 100 students, who embrace the NGO's three pillars of Education, Empowerment and Inspiration. Providing formal education as well as soft-skills education while balancing skill sets with heart-and-head mentorship, we empower some of the poorest young adults on the planet to become bright stars, lighting the way for others to follow, amplifying our impact to reach hundreds of thousands of rural Cambodians.

Using education to break cycles of poverty is not a new concept. What sets this story apart is that the education extends well beyond formal high school and university tuition. We educate future leaders by mentoring our students to develop the skills they need to manage and lead both CRST as an NGO and our social enterprise projects.

Our students are mentored that as Cambodia's future leaders, it's their responsibility to become empowered and help develop their nation. As they lead and manage the NGO and its educational social enterprise projects, they gain vital life skills in effective communication, leadership, management and social responsibilities. They discover that there is no magic moment in life to become empowered and create social impact, the moment is now!

As they learn, practise and hone their management and leadership skills, they become empowered and inspirational leaders. By the time they graduate from university, they are high-impact social contributors who enter 'the real world' life ready.

At the end of the day, business is a matter of three simple steps:

1. Ask people what they want.
2. Go get it.
3. Give it to them.

But business is also about people, and I've been part of our family business for over 40 years, helping to build it up from a simple photo shop selling photo frames to an international lifestyle and homewares business. I've learnt that when we take care of our team, our team takes care of our retail partners. When we take care of our retail partners, they help take care of our business, allowing us to take better care of our team – it's this cycle of value adding that underpins our longevity and success.

## 3 SIMPLE STEPS

ASK THEM WHAT THEY WANT

GO GET IT

GIVE IT TO THEM

## ADDING VALUE

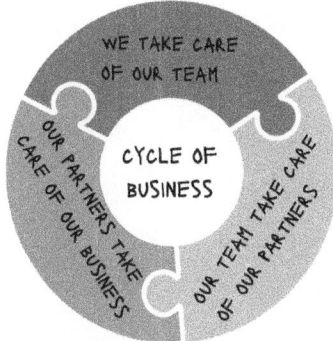

WE TAKE CARE OF OUR TEAM

OUR TEAM TAKE CARE OF OUR PARTNERS

OUR PARTNERS TAKE CARE OF OUR BUSINESS

CYCLE OF BUSINESS

It was these learnings that my family and I took to Cambodia, as we worked to support the long-term development of students there and help them become the leaders of tomorrow. But this learning was never a one-way street. We learned – and continue to learn – as much from the students we work with as they learn from us. We listen to what they need, and develop our programs around what would support them best over the long term. Their stories matter, and I've included these stories and the conversations I've had (as I remember them) throughout this book. I've also reproduced, with their permission, emails written by our students and presentations they made as part of our Ambassador Program.

I use the word 'we' a lot in this book, because I do nothing alone. Our Cambodia journey commenced with our youngest daughter, Steph, and these days it's our eldest daughter, Jess, who mentors our students and provides much of the critical inspiration and vision for the NGO. She puts in countless hours alongside me, dedicating much of her time and life to leaving the legacy of education, hope and inspiration in Cambodia. Our NGO would not be what it has become without Jess's tireless contributions. My wife, Michelle, and I are blessed to have the common thread of our activities in Cambodia bind us as a family, enriching our lives.

This is the story of young adults breaking their families' poverty cycles and empowering themselves from poverty to middle class in just a few years. It's the story of humanity converging on our commonality, not our differences, as we inspire the next generation of future leaders to lead with vision, passion, compassion and commitment. So let's get started!

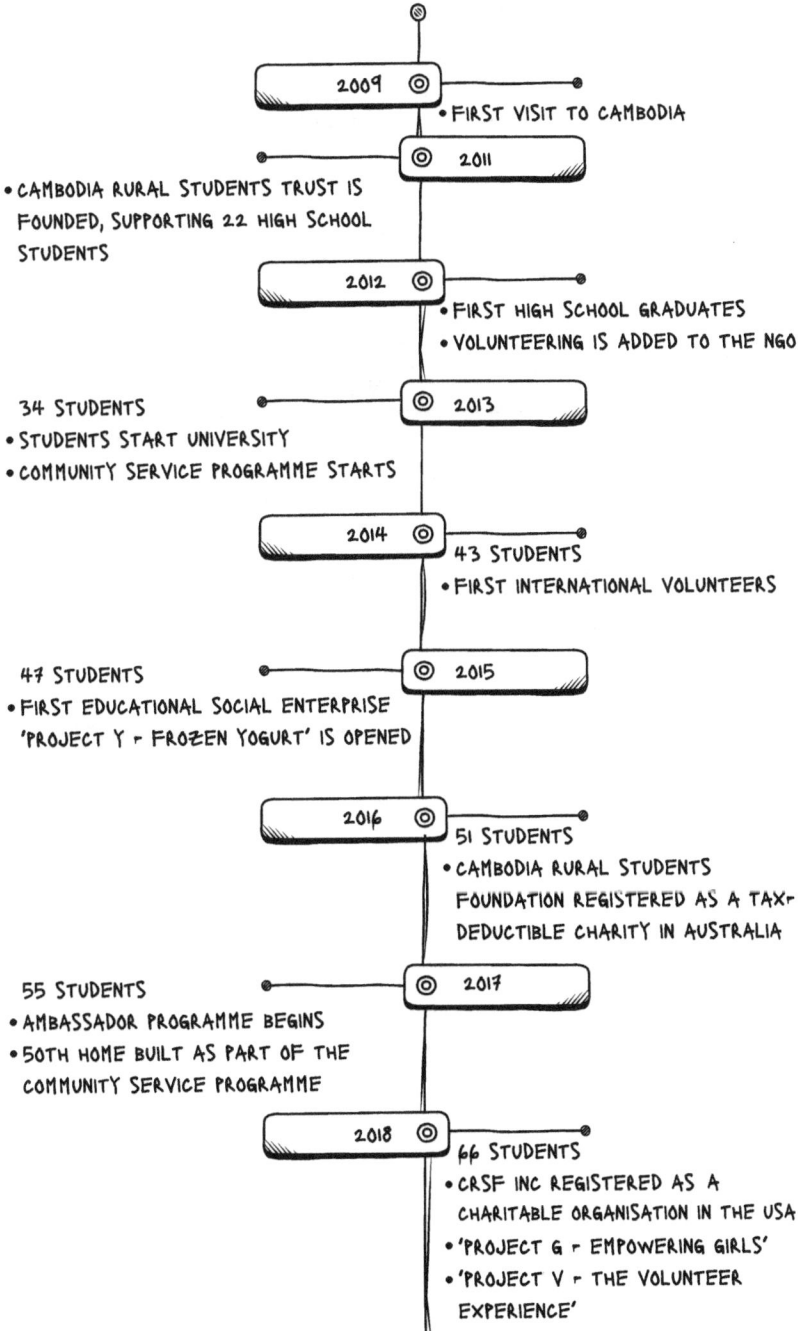

# TIMELINE

**2009**
- FIRST VISIT TO CAMBODIA

**2011**
- CAMBODIA RURAL STUDENTS TRUST IS FOUNDED, SUPPORTING 22 HIGH SCHOOL STUDENTS

**2012**
- FIRST HIGH SCHOOL GRADUATES
- VOLUNTEERING IS ADDED TO THE NGO

**2013**
34 STUDENTS
- STUDENTS START UNIVERSITY
- COMMUNITY SERVICE PROGRAMME STARTS

**2014**
43 STUDENTS
- FIRST INTERNATIONAL VOLUNTEERS

**2015**
47 STUDENTS
- FIRST EDUCATIONAL SOCIAL ENTERPRISE 'PROJECT Y ⊢ FROZEN YOGURT' IS OPENED

**2016**
51 STUDENTS
- CAMBODIA RURAL STUDENTS FOUNDATION REGISTERED AS A TAX⊢DEDUCTIBLE CHARITY IN AUSTRALIA

**2017**
55 STUDENTS
- AMBASSADOR PROGRAMME BEGINS
- 50TH HOME BUILT AS PART OF THE COMMUNITY SERVICE PROGRAMME

**2018**
66 STUDENTS
- CRSF INC REGISTERED AS A CHARITABLE ORGANISATION IN THE USA
- 'PROJECT G ⊢ EMPOWERING GIRLS'
- 'PROJECT V ⊢ THE VOLUNTEER EXPERIENCE'

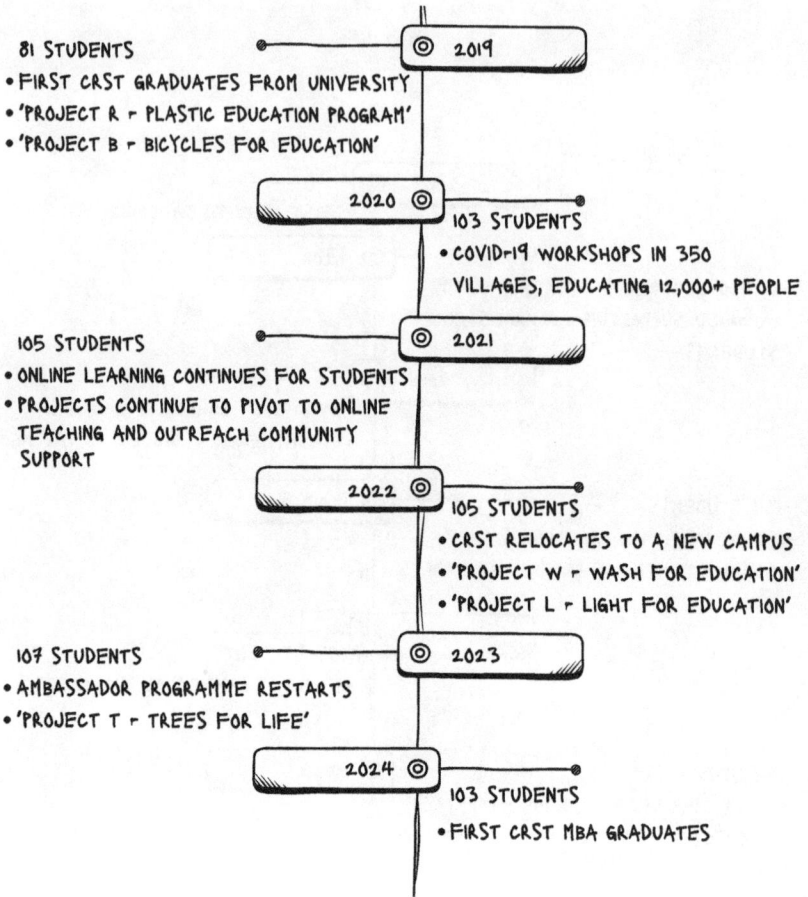

**81 STUDENTS**
- FIRST CRST GRADUATES FROM UNIVERSITY
- 'PROJECT R ⊢ PLASTIC EDUCATION PROGRAM'
- 'PROJECT B ⊢ BICYCLES FOR EDUCATION'

**2019**

**2020**

**103 STUDENTS**
- COVID-19 WORKSHOPS IN 350 VILLAGES, EDUCATING 12,000+ PEOPLE

**105 STUDENTS**
- ONLINE LEARNING CONTINUES FOR STUDENTS
- PROJECTS CONTINUE TO PIVOT TO ONLINE TEACHING AND OUTREACH COMMUNITY SUPPORT

**2021**

**2022**

**105 STUDENTS**
- CRST RELOCATES TO A NEW CAMPUS
- 'PROJECT W ⊢ WASH FOR EDUCATION'
- 'PROJECT L ⊢ LIGHT FOR EDUCATION'

**107 STUDENTS**
- AMBASSADOR PROGRAMME RESTARTS
- 'PROJECT T ⊢ TREES FOR LIFE'

**2023**

**2024**

**103 STUDENTS**
- FIRST CRST MBA GRADUATES

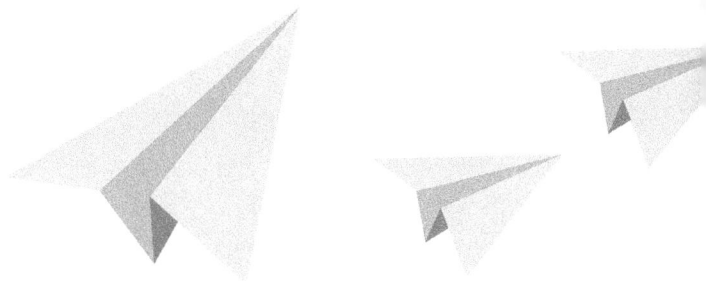

# Chapter 1

# Everything happens for a reason

In April 2009, our receptionist Julie put through a call to my desk – 'I think it's Steph, but I'm really not sure,' she said.

I picked up the extension with my usual 'Hi, this is Aviv.' It was indeed Steph, our 14-year-old daughter, on the other end of the line, but her voice was hardly recognisable.

'Dad!! Help me!! Help me!! He won't let me go!!' she yelled and cried hysterically. I felt a chill down my spine and stiffened up in my chair, pressing the phone hard into my ear as panic set in, my face reddened and I started to sweat.

'Who won't let you go? Who's got you? Where are you? I'm coming – where are you??' my panicked voice screamed into the phone.

'He won't let me go dad!! Help!! Please help me!!' She continued yelling and crying hysterically, but I couldn't really make out what she was saying. I stood up at my desk, reaching for my car keys and shutting down my computer in a frenzied hurry.

'I can't understand you!! Just take a breath!! Slow down – tell me where you are!! I'll call you from the car – where are you??' I yelled into the receiver. A few colleagues gathered at my office door, sensing something was terribly wrong.

'No!! Don't come!! Ring him dad, you've got to ring him!!' Steph was now crying in anguish.

'Honey, take a deep breath – slow down. Are you in any danger right now?' I asked her.

'No, Dad!! No!! It's Kennard, he won't let me go!!'

## Turning disappointment into opportunity

James Kennard was Steph's school principal. A stern, bearded, bespectacled middle-aged English pedagogue who emigrated to Australia to take up the position as principal of Melbourne's largest Jewish day school, with over 1000 students. He was a qualified Rabbi and commanded respect by using deliberate, articulate language and calculated gestures.

Kennard had a role to play and he played it well – including when dealing with some very wealthy parents and impressive power brokers. When it came to school matters, he was the ultimate authority and he wouldn't be challenged. He succeeded in maintaining the school's academic record, but when it came to turning out empowered and inspirational young adults, in my opinion the school failed miserably. Graduating students were academically often top of the state, but rarely leaders of sustainable social change and social justice.

So when the school decided to organise a grade 9 volunteering trip to build houses in rural Cambodia, my wife, Michelle, our 18-year-old daughter Jessica, who was attending the same school, and I all thought it was a great idea. Wow! Travel to a developing country, build houses for poor rural villagers you've never met – now that's impressive!

Steph wasn't so sure … You need to understand that Steph's got the biggest heart, but she's a free spirit, taking all the time she needs to consider what to do because she just doesn't want to do the wrong thing. Timelines are an artificial construction – time can wait. Steph is the sort of person who can think and overthink crossing a bridge – should she cross, should she not cross, what could happen while she's crossing, what might happen on the other side, what if she doesn't like the other side, can she come back from the other side, what if she wants to go back and forth? I, on the other hand, like crossing bridges. I'll plan the crossing and get going – life is too short to stick to what I know, and I know that life begins at the edge of my comfort zone.

So after a lot of thought and a lot of discussion, Steph finally decided she would join the school trip to Cambodia – a country she knew little about, full of people she had never met, far from home. It was a big decision for any 14-year-old, but she had made it. The only problem was that the closing date for the trip was the previous Friday, and she'd needed the two extra weekend days to decide, so she only took the signed paperwork to school on the following Monday.

I was hardly surprised when the esteemed principal advised Steph that her paperwork was late and she would miss out on the school trip to build houses for destitute people in a developing country she hadn't heard of until recently. 'The students have to learn that in life, when your paperwork is late, you miss out,' he told me when I rang him that afternoon.

Despite my best efforts to persuade him otherwise – including pointing out the lessons of charity and service, and that the trip was far from fully subscribed – Rabbi Kennard would not be swayed.

To Steph's credit, she also made an appointment and went to see her principal that afternoon to plead her case, but he flatly turned her down.

## Raising leaders – through education and by example

To me the sign of any good leader is their ability to adapt to their team and situation, so they can lead from within, not flog from behind. Real respect is earned, not commanded.

The focus on academic results at Jess and Steph's school was not entirely the principal's or the school's doing – much of it was due to the system, as in so many developed countries. Too many educators still think the 'best way' to measure the quality of education is to instil in the next generation knowledge of sine, cosine, tangents and Pi, to teach them to skim read for concepts rather than deep read for meaning and that history is full of facts, not research and perspectives.

Our schooling system is not designed or measured to empower us as beings of social change – few classes focus on teaching students to respect themselves, so they can respect others and be respected. While the curriculum is slowly changing, we still need more measurable classes teaching life skills, communication skills, understanding who you are, loving, owning and developing who you are, managing your inner voice to uplift rather than limit you, breaking the ice with strangers, learning to accept, love and respect others because they are different from you, learning to contribute and to lead, to manage and to report, to work as a team of equals so that everyone rises and benefits. Too often, students are still being taught that they need to work within the system, not that they *are* the system – the education system should support them to become the most 'life-ready' they can be, instead of just being a statistic in the grading system.

Steph came home that night angry and emotional about the injustice of it all – and distraught at the thought of what those poor Cambodian families would do now that she wouldn't be able to help build them a home. Where would they live and who would help them? Only six students out of over 100 in her year had signed up. There was still space, there was still time – how was this fair? The world was just a big black blotch.

The four of us discussed the whole day's events over dinner that night, as we often did when we sat down together to exchange our daily happenings. Of course, the mood was flat and the dearly beloved school principal copped a lot of heat. By the time we finished dinner, we all agreed that Steph's paperwork was undoubtedly late, but her desire to contribute to the poor people of Cambodia was a higher calling than timely paperwork.

'What if we make our own trip to Cambodia? What if you and I go, and we'll build houses together?' I asked.

'Dad, what do you know about building houses? You have a tool kit with one hammer and two screwdrivers, and even when you assemble Ikea furniture, we need to do it together so you don't skip any steps.' She stung like only a 14-year-old knew how.

But she was right – I knew nothing about Cambodia, or building houses, or how to even start on the subject of volunteering in Cambodia. 'Well, hon, you're right – I know nothing about volunteering in Cambodia, so why don't we google that after dinner?' I asked.

After dinner Steph and I googled '14-year-old volunteer Cambodia', and of course multiple sites came-up. We sat there reading through many of them and emailed six to request more information. By the next morning, four had replied and Steph went to school with a fresh attitude – she and her dad were going to Cambodia to volunteer for two weeks, we might not even build houses, we might be teaching English at a rural school.

And so it was that a few months later, six of us turned up in Siem Reap, Cambodia – Steph had agreed to expand our mission to include my wife, Michelle, my mother, Nili, my nephew Mikki and Alexandra, a friend of hers. Our eldest daughter, Jess, was unable to join us because she was preparing for her final high school exams. For the next two weeks, we were going to be volunteer English teachers at Savong School, a small rural school, teaching the students from nearby villages. My mother was an educator (at age 27 she was appointed principal of a school for special education) and Michelle was a qualified teacher (although she gave up teaching after just two weeks because she hated it), so we had some great fire-power. For weeks before our trip, we had been in contact with the school we would teach at, finding out what they had, what they needed and what we should be teaching – basically they had nothing, they needed everything and we could teach whatever we thought best.

## Getting started

Steph and I arrived ahead of the rest of our team, so she could get the sense that this was her volunteer mission, with the others joining a couple of days later. We were met at the small single-storey Siem Reap airport by Savong, who was the 27-year-old school director of Savong School. Savong had a smile that could conquer the world, and a warm and welcoming demeanour of a friend who has known you for a lifetime. A few years earlier, he had been a monk who was teaching English for free to students from poor rural families. He met a couple of tourists from Japan and New Zealand and they offered to give him some money to build a small school in the countryside. Savong's Free English School was the result.

Our first impressions of Siem Reap were that it was a dusty township, straight out of *Good Morning Vietnam*. It seemed to be a place stuck in a 1970s time warp, with simple one- to two-storey buildings, few cars, some motorbikes, numerous tuktuks and bicycles, dust, some piles of trash, skinny dogs and tailless cats. The people were warm and friendly, and grateful to meet foreigners who came to spend some time with them. We stayed in a $25 a night guest house ('the rooms need air-conditioning and private facilities – and there needs to be a pool' were the only conditions Michelle insisted on) and at night we walked down the road to Pub Street. This was the town's restaurant and nightlife precinct, complete with $3 foot massages and the super-weird fish foot treatment, where small fish nibbled at your feet cleaning away dead skin while you sat at the edge of a huge fish tank.

Of course, Siem Reap has been hosting tourists since the mid-1800s when the magnificent ancient temples of Angkor in the nearby jungles were visited by French explorer Henri Mouhot, who then popularised the temples in the West. Upscale hotels were available for hundreds of dollars a night, but we were here to volunteer, not holiday, and our mission was to minimise costs so we could give more to others.

Savong picked us up the next morning at 6 am for the 30-minute drive to his school in Bakong Village, getting us there well in time for the first class at 7 am. The school consisted of four main classrooms, an office, a library and a small computer classroom with seven old desktop computers. Each classroom had enough wooden desks for 50 students, who sat three to four to a desk, with their ages making no difference at all. The classes were based on ability and English level, so while some students seemed to be six or seven years old, others were 16 or 17. There was no shame and no discrimination – they were all eager to study and age was irrelevant. Of course, the older kids had a sense of urgency and commitment, while the younger ones were more playful. Overall, the system of older and younger 'brothers' and 'sisters' seemed to work.

Steph and I were introduced to the permanent teaching staff at Savong School – these were young villagers who lived nearby and supplemented their farming incomes by teaching. Teacher Kimhey was in his mid-20s, living with his mother while studying his bachelor's degree in town, teacher Sopheak was also studying for his bachelor's degree, teacher Salas had graduated from high school and planned to go to university, and teacher Sovanarith was studying for his master's degree. The computer teacher, Voan, knew a little about computers, so he took on that role. What they lacked in formal education qualifications, they more than made up in enthusiasm, commitment and camaraderie with their students.

All the students also attended nearby government primary and secondary schools, and supplemented this education at Savong's Free English School. In an area as heavily dependent on tourism as Siem Reap, English is a great asset to increase your earning capacity. Guesthouses, restaurants and tourism businesses all needed staff with at least basic English – and the steady income these businesses offered was the Holy Grail for rural students who came from poor rural families, where income was derived from long days working under the heat of the sun and a heavy dependence on the rainy season for growing crops.

As Steph and I entered the class, the students stood up in their navy-blue pants or skirts and white shirts and in unison recited,

'Goooood mooooorning teeeeeacher' – we were a little taken aback. In our Western classrooms, teachers often walk into classrooms unnoticed and need to take some affirmative action to begin the class – at the very least staring down pupils, but all too often resorting to raising their voices. Steph and I replied, 'Good morning students' and everyone giggled. Great. That was the ice-breaker. We turned to the whiteboard to write our names in big blue letters – and when we turned back to the class, the students were all still standing. We looked at teacher Kimhey and he said, 'You have to tell them to sit down.'

'Please be seated,' I said, and they all laughed as they took their seats – needless to say, we knew we were in for a super-fun two weeks!

## Jumping straight in

By the time Mich, my mother, Mikki and Alex arrived, Steph and I had been at the school and nearby small orphanage for a couple of days, so we had 'the lay of the land'. Savong operated the school and orphanage using donations from visiting volunteers and tourists – we were happy to volunteer and buy things we saw they needed, but we weren't going to make donations. We knew from our research that numerous local non-governmental organisation (NGO) directors or owners ran these organisations as their own money-making businesses. While part of the donations was used for the organisations' needs, the rest of the money was their private income or profit. Savong was okay with us not donating – he was very grateful we were prepared to spend two weeks volunteering.

The school had two sessions, 7 to 11 am and 3 to 7 pm – these reflected the government school times. Due to the limited number of classes and teachers at government schools, students were assigned to either morning or afternoon classes. The students, therefore, filled in the rest of their days with extra classes, working in the fields with their parents, or coming to free English schools like Savong School. Most volunteers taught either in the mornings or the afternoons, leaving them the rest of their days to relax and be tourists – but we came for a purpose, and so Steph and I were determined to volunteer for both sessions at the school.

Our days started at 6.15 am when Savong or his brother, Theavy, would pick us up from our guesthouse. We taught four classes until 11 am, drove back to town to take shower number two, have lunch, maybe a swim, send some emails, and return to the school by 3 pm. After finishing at 7 pm, we would often hang around at the school chatting with the students who wanted to practise their English. We then returned to town for a late dinner, maybe a foot massage, shower number three and a solid night's rest. The tropical humidity was impossible to avoid and I was sweating right through to my underpants from morning until night. No sooner had I wiped my face with a handkerchief in class, and I would start perspiring again as I hung it out to dry on the window ledge – of course the students found that hilarious.

The days were full and fulfilling, and the lesson plans we prepared were pretty exciting – because teaching and learning should be exciting! – and we had different themes for each day. On 'colours day' we taught about the names of the colours, what new colours could be created by mixing two colours together and we played games using the new words our students learned. For 'fruit day' we stopped in the market on the way to school and bought colourful tropical fruit, so we could teach the fruit names, reinforce the names of the colours, and feed the students. 'Sports day' included an egg and spoon race, sack races, tunnel ball – and of course everyone got a ribbon and icy poles. For 'craft day' we tie-dyed t-shirts, so each student went home with another piece of clothing. On 'slushy day' we taught the words associated with making ice slushies and then shaved ice on two ice-shavers we bought in the market, topping the slushies with colourful syrup. Mikki played his guitar as we had class singalongs to 'Heal the World' on 'music day' after teaching students the lyrics and meaning of the song – and on 'photo day', we brought in our digital camera and the students were amazed to see their own faces, and their friends' faces on the back screen, as if it were magic. We took photos of more than 400 students and printed 4 × 6" photos in town. The next day, the students used A4 colour sheets of paper as 'frames', stuck their photos in and took them home. For many of the students, this was the first photo of themselves they had ever seen.

And we saved the best for last – 'pancake day'. We taught the English words associated with making pancakes and then, using camp stoves and frying pans bought in the market, the students made hundreds of pancakes, and filled them with Nutella or honey. They stood outside the classes well after nightfall, making, flipping and gobbling pancakes under torchlight, surrounded by countless bugs attracted by the light, and landing in the Nutella and honey for a bit of extra protein!

Each day, the first morning class was filled beyond capacity – over 60 kids sitting three or four to a desk and on the floor in front of the first row, with more even looking in through the window bars. Word spread through the nearby villages that an Australian family was at Savong School and running some fun classes – and that each class had snacks. As well as the classes, my mother was usually doing art-and-craft activities in the school library, always chatting with the students, letting them practise their English and learning more about them and their family lives.

## Learning from initial impressions

Each night over dinner, the six of us would debrief – discussing what we saw, what we felt, what we did well and what we'd do better tomorrow. What we saw was poverty, extreme poverty – skinny, skinny students, teenagers the height of 10 year olds back home – but also pride in their appearance, from their hair to their clean hands and neat uniforms. We saw the biggest and most genuine smiles we've ever seen and we saw deep brown eyes that were so grateful for every little thing we did, and eager for so much more. What we felt was unconditional love – complete acceptance, no judgement. Our Cambodian students embraced us as we were – tall or short, tanned or white, overweight or underweight, young or old.

At one of our first dinner-debriefs I got choked-up, humbled by the love of some of the poorest people on the planet, who accepted us just as we were and were so deeply grateful that we had come to spend a few days with them. My mother was also extremely emotional – she couldn't even eat, the social injustice of it all was eating her up so much. How could these beautiful human beings be starved of food, education and opportunities, as we sat in our comfortable Western homes with over-stuffed pantries and fridges, throwing out any food that was past its use-by date?

As most Jewish mothers, she wears her heart on her sleeve – 'just so you know that's what I feel'. Her being is best described as deeply emotional, and tenacious for social justice and fairness. She's also a great travel agent – for guilt-trips. Her pain on that night was visible, and despite us telling her that here we were, bringing joy and lessons to our Cambodian students, she was inconsolable. She told us that our efforts were valuable but, like the passing rains, would soon be forgotten, leaving nothing behind.

At another dinner debrief we discussed how it was possible that Australian students would whinge at being woken up at 7.30 am to be at school by 9 am, while our Cambodian classes were filled with 60 to 70 students at 7 am, all smiling and eagerly waiting for the teacher. Why did students in Australia complain at having to sit on the school bus for 45 minutes to get to school, while students in Cambodia happily walked to school for over an hour in the scorching sun or the tropical rains? Why did our Cambodian students ask us for homework and hand it back to us to check the very next day, while in Western countries debate continued as to whether homework was even acceptable.

We also discussed the extreme cost of living differences between Australia and Cambodia. At home, a bottle of water was $2 to $3 and a cup of coffee was $4 to $5; in Cambodia the bottled water cost $0.10 (ten cents!) and the beer was $0.50 (fifty cents!!), not that we drank any. In rural Siem Reap, families lived on $50 to $100 a month, while in Melbourne that would be the price for a family dinner at a restaurant.

Our two weeks flew by and some of the students accompanied us to the airport to say goodbye. While the six of us had our comfort-zone-life to return to, it was still hard to say goodbye. Steph was crying uncontrollably and many of the students also broke down. No-one wanted to say goodbye, and I remember Kadeb, one of our students, tearfully saying to me, 'I know we won't see you again, I know. I'm really, really sad.' He burst out crying. I put my arm around him to console him and said, 'This is not goodbye, we'll be back – of course we'll be back!!' He looked me in the eyes and said, 'Everyone always tells us that, but no-one ever comes back.'

## What next?

A couple of weeks after returning to Australia, we had an extended family dinner with my parents as well as my brother and his family. I asked my nephew Mikki whether he enjoyed the trip, and he flashed his trademark smile and said 'It was awesome!!' I took the opportunity to thank Steph for allowing Mich, my mother, Mikki, Alex and me to join her volunteer trip to Cambodia. I thanked her for allowing us to share the experience, which had changed me as a person, forever. I had left a part of me in Cambodia, and came back with Cambodia under my skin.

We pondered how it was possible that we had nothing seemingly in common with our Cambodian students, yet we felt such a strong connection. We had no common history, heritage, nationality, culture, religion, language or food – and yet we felt a kinship. 'Maybe this is "humanity"', I said. 'Maybe we are all members of the same species, all human beings, rising above artificial barriers of nationality, culture, religion and language, and connecting on a higher level – because, on a higher level, we are all the same. We are all members of the human family.'

Over the next two years, our family returned to Cambodia three more times, always volunteering at Savong School, fulfilling our promises to return and teaching our students that perhaps we were not like the other volunteers they had met in the past.

## FOUNDATIONS OF LEADERSHIP TAKEAWAYS

- When life gives you lemons, don't make lemonade; make a lemonade factory.

- Create your own sunshine.

- An open mind and an open heart go hand in hand.

- No-one has the exclusive right to be right – 'right' is a matter of perspective.

- Be your team's cheer squad, no matter the circumstance; support their growth.

- Most barriers are in our heads, not in our reality.

- Give without expecting to receive and you will receive more than you ever expect.

- Be prepared, and be flexible.

- Everything happens for a reason, and that reason is here to serve you, to make you better, to make you the best you can be.

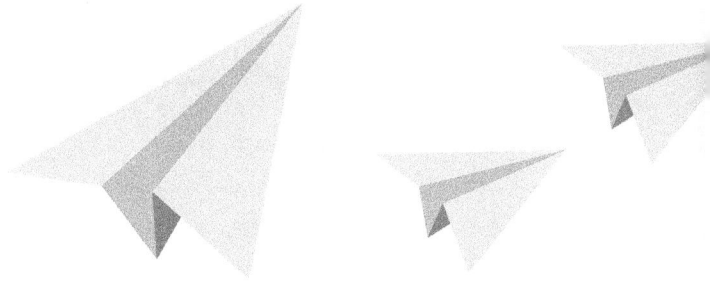

# Chapter 2

# Dream big, plan, act, correct, continue

Each time we returned to Savong School, we gained new insights into the lives of the rural students we were teaching. We knew their families were poor, but we learnt that their spirits were generous – the less they had, the more they shared.

We often distributed cut-up fruit in our classes, and the students who volunteered to walk around with the plastic plates carrying the fruit always ate last, hoping some would be left for them. When we played games such as bingo or hangman, the prizes were popular Khmer snacks in little packets – students always loved getting those little packets and holding them in their hands during the class. At the end of class, we often noticed students put the snacks in their school bags and we asked whether they planned to have them later.

'I'm taking these to my family, we'll share them tonight,' one replied smiling shyly. And that was the norm – when you get something special, you bring it home to share.

## Building our understanding

To understand Cambodia better, we spent time learning a little about this beautiful but desperately poor country's history. We learned that over 1000 years ago, the Khmer empire stretched across most of Asia – from today's western China, across Myanmar, to Laos, Vietnam and Thailand. The impressive temples of Angkor were built at that time – in fact, numerous temples and structures dating back to those times were all over Cambodia. Most were destroyed by invaders, stolen by occupiers or simply crumbled over the centuries. What makes the Angkor Wat temples so special is that for hundreds of years they were 'lost' to most people – although locals knew they were there, they were protected by the tropical jungle that grew around the structures.

Intricate carvings in the stones pay homage to victories, nobles, deities and daily life. Some of the structures are surrounded by moats, others are high up on hills, featuring massive staircases, or with trees uprooting the ancient stones. Wall after wall, pillar after pillar, miles of stone floors, all with stories to tell. These stories outline the magnificence of the Khmer empire with its thriving culture and wealth based on agriculture, trade and war, led by iconic kings who headed a nation that over its 600 years worshipped both Hindu and Buddhist religions. The Angkor Wat temples are considered by *Guinness World Records* as the largest religious structure in the world and are a UNESCO World Heritage Site. Angkor Wat is proudly featured on Cambodia's national flag.

That's the Cambodia that most tourists come to see – but actually much more of the Cambodia they will see has been shaped by more recent history. A mere 50 years ago, in the 1970s, historians estimate the US indiscriminately dropped around 500,000 tons of bombs on the people of Cambodia as part of their Vietnam War campaign, killing as many as 150,000 civilians. The Vietnam War provided the cover for the Khmer Rouge ('Red Khmer') to overthrow the Cambodian government and begin a brutal reign that saw a quarter of the country's population, by many accounts around 2,000,000 people, exterminated within a few years, mostly through ethnic and political cleansing, starvation, disease and summary executions.

The Khmer Rouge's version of communism was based on an agrarian society, which required all citizens to live in rural areas and work the land. Schools and universities were closed and cities were emptied, with educators, artisans, intellectuals and monks particularly targeted. Families were split, and people were encouraged to report any 'anti-social' behaviour such as sneaking food or helping others. Citizens were tortured and killed by the most brutal means possible. Many people escaped to the forests and survived by eating plants, crickets and frogs – and many never returned.

Following the atrocities of the Khmer Rouge, the country plunged into civil war, leaving its shattered population poor, scared, illiterate and lost. As some generals and politicians carved up the spoils, ordinary people were left with nothing to restart their lives.

## Cambodian education in context

It's against this backdrop that we need to see education in Cambodia – until relatively recently, the educated were executed, schools were closed and books were forbidden. Our students' parents never went to school – there were no schools and they were too busy focusing on survival by catching frogs, spiders and grasshoppers while foraging in the forests. At the end of the turmoil, our students' parents had no choice but to pick up whatever was left around them and start their lives again. Too often, all they had was their hands, so they slaved over inhospitable land that was parched in the dry season and flooded in the wet. If they had a good season, they traded some rice and bought some clothes or other essentials. If they had a bad season, they would rely on the generosity of others to survive. No-one in the countryside had plenty; everyone was just doing their best to survive and live to the next day.

When we visited some of our students' families, we were humbled in their presence – they lived in homes made from wood, bamboo and palm leaves. The homes were one space, about 10 m², where everyone sat and slept together. They hung the few spare clothes they had on the inside of the palm leaf walls of the house. A single light bulb was powered by a car battery, which had to be taken to the local market to swap or recharge. The kitchen was an undercover area outside the house, with people cooking over wood or charcoal. Water was pumped from a nearby well and, of course, had to be boiled if it was to be drunk. A shower was taken by using a ladle or small container and pouring the water on your head, so it would run down over your body. The toilet was any outside space you could find, preferably near bushes.

All houses were raised off the ground to avoid the heavy rains and frequent flooding in the rainy season. If the family had enough money, they built the house high enough so they could create an open living space under the house – it's in this space that we met our students' families. We'd sit on concrete benches or plastic chairs and our students would translate the conversations between us and their families. Many parents were emotional when they hosted us, feeling so proud of their children conversing with us in English. They were grateful that we had come to spend a little time with them, cupping their hands to thank us for teaching English to their kids. They knew the value of education, and they knew that without education their kids' lives would be as tough as their own, struggling to survive.

As little as they had, they still offered us water or a can of soft drink. On one occasion, a host even climbed a palm tree to pluck a fresh coconut for us to drink. Some even invited us to eat with them. We always politely declined. How could we possibly take the food and drinks they so desperately needed?

As poor as they were, their smiles were deep and genuine, and they had dignity. We couldn't help loving them and respecting them.

## Greeting and gratitude in Cambodia

In Cambodian culture, cupping both hands and raising them in front of the body is used for greetings and to show respect and gratitude. Known as 'sampeah', this action has five levels, each represented by the level of the hands, as shown in the following figure.[1]

SAMPEAH

CHEST   MOUTH   NOSE   EYEBROWS   FOREHEAD

The levels are used in the following ways:

- For friends who are of a similar age, place both palms together at the chest level.
- For older persons, bosses or higher-ranking people, place both palms together at the mouth level.
- For parents, grandparents or teachers, place both palms together at the nose level.
- For the king or monks, place both palms together at the eyebrows level.
- When respecting Buddha or sacred statues, place both palms together at the forehead level.

## Looking further

We knew that Savong School was doing a good job – the students got better and better between our visits. The older students brought their government school assignments and reports to share with us, proud

---

1   This figure was created by Ney Shen, a CRST student and talented artist.

of their achievements. Conversations often led to what they planned to do when they finished school, with many saying they weren't sure they would graduate – their families wanted them to drop out and start earning money to help support the family. Many were already working on the land as well as studying. If they were to get a job, everyone wanted to be a policeman, a teacher or a doctor – literally everyone! When we asked why these were the only three choices, the replies were always the same – these were the jobs that allowed them to live in the village and earn a steady salary. These were the only role models these students saw.

We grew to understand that our Savong School students didn't believe they would ever leave their 'hometown', as they called their village. They were the children of poor farmers and their destiny was to be the next generation of poor farmers. Even if they had a little bit of education, they could never compete with those city kids, whose parents sent them to city schools, with better teachers and better employment prospects, often through connections. We knew that being poor didn't mean being dumb, but we learned that being poor did mean being pigeonholed, with few opportunities.

When saying another goodbye at the school one night, Nak, one of our Savong School students who was in grade 10 or 11, came up to me and handed me a letter. It was beautifully handwritten with neatly spaced words. The note from Nak said that he so loved having us teach him English and that we opened his mind with the many subjects we had discussed, from life in developed countries to the solar system. He told us that he came from a poor family, his father worked long days as a tuktuk driver, his mum stayed at home to raise him and his siblings and looked after the two pigs the family owned. His father only studied for two years before he had to give up his schooling when the Khmer Rouge took power, and after he married Nak's mum, he taught her how to read. All of Nak's siblings went to school – his parents never wanted their kids to give up on education because they knew that life without education was a life of poverty and misery. The letter went on to say that he would like our support to graduate from high school – and he told us that if we could possibly be his sponsors, he promised he would never drop out, never quit, always do his best and make his parents and us proud. 'Please trust me. I will not let you down.'

I thanked Nak for his letter and told him that maybe we'd consider sponsoring him when we returned on our next trip – he looked at me quizzingly and said, 'But how will you find me?'

'We'll find you,' I said, with a big grin on my face. 'You'll be here at Savong School.'

## Setting off on our own

Actually when I read Nak's letter, the first thought that entered my cynical mind was, *I wonder how many of these he had written and handed out to volunteers over the years*. I'm ashamed of that thought now, but I own it.

I'd learned to be cynical because on this volunteer trip, I'd discovered that Savong was building a guesthouse on the edge of town, and had upgraded his scooter to a used Lexus. His free English school was helping hundreds of students and supporting five to six teachers, so perhaps he thought it was okay for him to pocket 'surplus donations' to enrich himself.

I asked to meet with him so I could offer some suggestions on transparency and accountability to help ensure donors continued to support him. He thought this was a good idea and arranged for me to meet with his younger brother, Theavy, who could learn from me. I met with Theavy and within an hour it occurred to me that I was barking up the wrong tree – this was Cambodia and Savong School was a Cambodian business. Part of the business model was to generate a profit for the owner. If visitors and volunteers were willing to give money without requesting accountability, why would Savong or Theavy want to allow me to interfere in their business?

I love Savong, he has a good heart, but I couldn't condone his business ethics – it didn't make me right and him wrong, but it meant we were no longer aligned. To be sure, Savong is a good guy and he's helped countless students by operating the school, yet I was bothered that by volunteering at the school, we were condoning his business ethics – and that didn't sit well with me at all.

And so it was that when we returned to Australia, I told Michelle and the girls that if we wanted to continue volunteering in Cambodia, we would need to set up our own non-government organisation (NGO). We all agreed that this would give us the ability to control the transparency, accountability and sustainability of our activities.

At the next extended family dinner, I shared with my parents and my brother and his family that we were considering registering an NGO in Cambodia. My mother, my biggest fan, let me down badly that night. She looked at me with utter disdain and said 'You're joking! Don't get involved, everyone is corrupt, you have no idea what you're getting in to, just leave it.'

I sat back in my chair, looked her in the eyes and said 'Ima,[2] I'm really disappointed in you. You, of all people. You know how impactful we can be, you know how many lives we can transform – and you know that when I set my mind to something, barriers don't exist. If the front door is closed, I'll try the window, if that's locked I'll try the roof, I'll lift the floorboards – if it can be done, I will do it, you know that, right?'

'You won't succeed – I don't often tell you that. But this is too big and you know nothing about it,' she replied.

'We'll see,' I told her.

## Building early foundations

A few weeks later, I was back in Cambodia and met with Linne, an educated, softly spoken young man who was the Registrar at Angkor University. While completing his degree a few years earlier, Linne studied a couple of semesters at Macquarie University in Sydney.

---

2   'Ima' is the Hebrew word for 'mum'.

We'd connected previously and I found his gentle and genuine nature to be a great sounding-board for ideas. I told Linne that we wanted to register an NGO for the purpose of providing quality education to Cambodian students from poor rural families. He was surprised.

'Really? You want to help so many Cambodians?' he asked with a big smile on his face.

'Yes, we do,' I replied with conviction. 'We want to help break the poverty cycle through education. Linne, those rural kids, they're smart, they're not stupid. Their parents are poor, and that means they have less opportunities – with quality education we can change that! We can sponsor students to study here in town, we'll send them to the best private high school, we'll open the doors of opportunity to their lives! And then they'll help their families and others in society – that's how social change is created, you know that, right?'

Linne had tears in his eyes. He cupped his hands and opened his mouth to speak, but the words didn't fall out. He was too choked up.

After a few moments, he said, 'This is an amazing gift for my country. You and your family are the most amazing people I have ever met. I want to help you – what can I do?'

Linne introduced me to the owner of Angkor University, who was also the Member of Parliament for Siem Reap, His Excellency Seang Nam. Seang Nam was a sixty-something chain-smoker, who held his meetings in the lobby of his City Angkor Hotel. A few years earlier, his son Lionel had graduated from Mentone Grammar in Melbourne and he was genuinely excited to help us. I asked Linne to advise Seang Nam that we would not be paying any bribes – our NGO had to be clean. His Excellency looked me in the eyes and said in Khmer, 'That is a very good decision. Leave it with me.'

Linne was too invested in his university career to accept the job of NGO Director (a local Khmer is required by law for this role), so I interviewed a few people I'd met on previous trips, and settled on Mr Kim Bona. Bona was about 30 years old and used to work for a French-funded NGO. Although he lacked charisma and charm, he had the right experience. He was fond of wearing long white pants, which were terribly impractical in Siem Reap's red-dust-filled streets. He was of medium height, and wore shoes that looked to be two to three inches too long, which made his feet look way too big for his body. He had short curly black hair, with a long curly fringe that annoyingly fluttered in the wind when we were sitting on the back of a tuktuk. He had pretty good English, having studied at the Australian Centre for Education (ACE) in Siem Reap.

Bona accepted the job as the local NGO Director and filled the rest of the required statutory roles with friends of his, to ensure the formal requirements were met. Two months later, in 2011, the Cambodia Rural School Trust NGO (CRST) was registered and we returned to Cambodia to recruit our first students (some years later we changed the name of the NGO to the Cambodia Rural Students Trust).

## Working within the system and showing respect

Being guests in Cambodia, we understood the importance of working within the system and showing respect to the local leaderships at all levels, from the national government in Phnom Penh to the provincial, district, commune and village level. Over the years, we have signed MOUs (memorandums of understanding) with the Ministry of Education, Youth and Sport, the Ministry of Environment and the Anti-Corruption Unit (ACU) of the Cambodian Government. In fact, when we approached the ACU to request an MOU, they asked why we wanted to do so – no other NGO in Cambodia had made that commitment previously. We advised them that it was important to us to teach our students that when you have a great vision, people should buy into your vision without you needing to pay them for it. In 2020 we became the first NGO in Cambodia to sign an MOU with the Anti-Corruption Unit of the Cambodian Government and enjoy the respect of being known as 'the clean NGO'.

## Finding our first students

I contacted Savong when I arrived and told him that our family had registered an NGO in Cambodia – of course he was surprised. I asked him if it would be okay to come to Savong School to let the students know we were offering scholarships to study at New York International School, one of the best private schools in Siem Reap. (A 30-minute drive from Savong School in Bakong Village, New York International School offers education from kindergarten to grade 12 in the national curriculum, as well as English and Chinese language programs.) He instantly replied, 'Of course!!'

By the time we arrived at Savong School the next day, word had already spread (from Savong) that we were coming to discuss possible scholarships for students who wanted to study in town. The students were eagerly waiting for us, and we went between the classes and announced that our family wanted to sponsor students to finish their high school studies in town, so they would get the best education possible. We would pay full tuition and a monthly living allowance to allow them to rent a room and live in town. Not all students were excited – some thought that town was too far from their village, and others thought they weren't good enough, or that their parents would not give permission. By the end of the week, however, the first 22 students had joined CRST and were ready to move to town. Among the 'first generation' students was Nak.

As the students settled in to their new school, they were very nervous – here were the 'country mice' coming to live in the city, going to school with students whose family-drivers were dropping them off and picking them up in fancy cars. This school was the real deal – not a rural high school with teachers who were your neighbours – and the teachers were more serious and less flexible.

I met with the school director and told him that these students were like my own kids and he should contact me personally by email should any issues arise. I told the students that Bona was our representative in Cambodia and would look after them like we would. We wanted to be sure they had all the support they needed to succeed – if they needed anything, they were to just let Bona know and we'd take care of it. The school tuition would be paid by us and Bona would pass their monthly allowances to them. If they had any concerns, they were to contact me by email at any time.

## Hitting our first hurdle

Bona lasted just a few months. His job was to ensure the students attended school, did well or got extra help when needed. He also had to make sure they got their monthly allowances, so they could live in a comfortable room, eat well and stay healthy. He incorrectly thought we'd throw a lot of money into an NGO with a fairly simple business model and relatively few 'moving parts'. When he realised we were not about to throw money at unnecessary assets and activities, he started short-changing the students' allowances – and being the shy Khmer country kids they were, they let it slide rather than find their voices and tell us. But of course, we found out pretty quickly, because I'm the sort of guy who likes to ask a lot of questions, even with a simple business model. Between replies from the school director and email replies from the students, we knew Bona was a goner.

I flew to Siem Reap and told Bona he was fired. He looked at me, smiled and said, 'You can't fire me, I'm the NGO Director.'

Of course he was right, so I switched to plan B to skin the cat another way. I met with the students and told them they needed to fire Bona – they were shocked.

'We're just students, we can't ask the director to leave!! What will happen to us? Do we need to go back to our hometowns?'

'Of course not!' I replied. 'You'll manage the NGO!'

'We don't know how to manage an NGO, we're high school students.' They must have thought I was either joking or mad.

I tried to reassure them that running an NGO wasn't that complicated, and was just like running a business, but without the need to make a profit. They responded that they had no idea how to run a business either.

'Okay,' I said, 'let's make it simple. Do you know who the Prime Minister of Cambodia is?' Of course they did, and they knew there were six Deputy Prime Ministers (six!) and a variety of Ministers.

'So our NGO is like the government, okay? Sathea, you will be the Prime Minister, and we're going to call you the NGO Manager and I'll give you a list of your responsibilities. Nak, you will be the Deputy Prime Minister; we'll call you the Assistant NGO Manager. Doeb, you'll be the Education Minister; we'll call you the Education Manager. I'll give you and Nak your list of responsibilities too, and we call that list a 'job description', okay? I will mentor you to manage the NGO, so you can learn new skills and become empowered with knowledge that very few other students in this school will ever have!' Now they were excited!

But first, we had to skin the cat. I told the students that we needed to get rid of Bona and the best people to negotiate that with him were them. To him I was just the money tree; to them he had the responsibility of an older brother, and he was much more likely to lose face in society as the person who crushed their dreams as he sought to enrich himself at the expense of their education. So they needed to meet with Bona and tell him that he and his friends had to resign so that the students could take over as the legal office bearers of the NGO. Bona got about $1000 of NGO assets, including our old tuktuk and some office furniture, but he could see the money tree wasn't going to continue to deliver, and he signed over his legal NGO responsibilities and walked off quietly into the sunset.

Sathea had some personal family issues and handed the reins to Nak, who became an exemplary NGO Manager, and to this day has stuck by the words he gave me back in 2009 at Savong School – 'I will not let you down.'

## Giving back

In 2023, Sathea returned to CSRT to lead a Business School class, sharing his knowledge and experience about leadership and management. He graduated with a bachelor degree in TESOL (Teaching English to Speakers of Other Languages), continued on to graduate from his MBA and was now a recognised and respected corporate trainer in Phnom Penh.

Jess wrote to Sathea to thank him for leading the class:

*WOW, thank you Sathea – how special of you to come back to Siem Reap and share your knowledge with so many generations of CRST students!! The gift of education does last a lifetime, and thank you for being generous with your time, knowledge and experience, and sharing that with so many people.*

*Did you ever think you would be in the position you are in now?! WOW ... I went back in time and found the photos from 2013. JUST 10 YEARS AGO!!!*

And he replied:

*My future was not that clear back then and I really had no idea. I was a rural boy navigating without a map. I'm so happy seeing the team grow and learn. And I hope the lessons I shared could help our CRST future leaders adjust their practices to be more effective leaders.*

## FOUNDATIONS OF LEADERSHIP TAKEAWAYS

- Own your past, live your present, plan your future.

- When you think you've dreamed big, dream bigger.

- If nothing was impossible, what could you achieve? Now plan how to achieve it.

- Gather an inner circle of supporters who can help you grow, not stroke your ego.

- Share your vision and walk the talk.

- Identify issues early and act on them gracefully.

- Be trusting, but not naive.

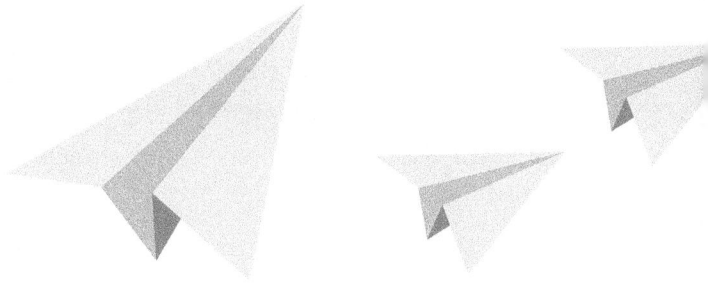

# Chapter 3

# Life begins at the edge of your comfort zone

When our first generation of 22 students relocated from their villages to Siem Reap, they experienced quite a culture shock. Most had been living in simple homes in the countryside, with little or no electricity, no running water and no toilets. In town, they had to learn to cook for themselves, wash their own clothes and generally be self-sufficient. And let's not forget they were 'just' high school students in their late teens.

Some years later, as part of our Ambassador Program, Veun wrote the following passage for his speech:

*When I joined CRST I had to move to live in town. It's only 20 kilometres from my home, but I had never been there before. I was very nervous and worried a lot about human trafficking. But I chose to take a risk to follow my dream to study. I spent many days riding my bike to see the lights, buildings and people because everything was very new to me. I grew up in a village and my family did not have electricity, or clean water or even a toilet.*

(I outline how our Ambassador Program came about in chapter 8.) Our role was to support them in this adjustment, but not take over. We also knew we wanted our students to continue improving their English.

## Finding the right English teacher

We started looking for a native-English-speaking teacher to help the students learn the correct pronunciation of so many words they found complex to their ears and mouths. For some reason the sound 's' was a particular challenge. They dropped it off when it was needed and sprinkled it in when it wasn't – 'house' became 'how' and 'ice' became 'eye'; conversely 'mother' became 'mothers' and 'fine' became 'fines'. Of course, an expatriate teacher also offered numerous other advantages – most critically, he or she would widen our students' perspectives beyond the English language and into a wider world view, discussing the news, views and opinions in an open-minded way.

Natasha was an Australian teacher from rural Victoria who had been living in Siem Reap for a few years – she had a few teaching jobs and had previously taught at ACE, the Australian Centre for Education. I asked her whether she would consider teaching our students English classes for an hour a day – she screwed-up her face and said, 'No, I don't think so.' I asked her why and she explained: 'Well, you see, I don't agree with what you're doing. You're not the first Westerner to come to Cambodia and think he can make the world a better place – only problem is, sooner or later you'll lose your drive, run out of money or get busy with your life back home. And then, these poor kids will be left to their own devices – only it will be much worse, because now you're opening their eyes and their brains and when you crash and burn, they'll be left with big dreams and no hope. So that's why not – I don't get involved with people who think they can make big changes that are not sustainable.'

That was quite a lecture. But if there's something I'm not, it's a quitter – and if there's something I am, it's a planner and doer. I told

Natasha that our NGO was unique – it didn't have some drop-out Western expatriate or corruption-prone person running it. Our NGO was led and managed by our students, mentored by us from Australia – we didn't need to live in Cambodia and, in fact, it was preferable that we didn't live in Cambodia, so our students would be less dependent on us and more empowered to be independent. Additionally, the NGO's expenses were only focused on education and the students' welfare – no fancy cars, no fancy offices. CRST was privately funded by our family and we had set aside sufficient funds to see our students through high school and university.

Natasha seemed to soften a little, so I offered her a deal – teach our kids for one month and, if you like what you see, stay; if you don't, just leave, no hard feelings. Natasha agreed – and she became our most beloved English teacher, forming close bonds with our students, watching them grow, mature and blossom, and teaching multiple CRST student generations over the following eight years. She took great pride in seeing her 'chickens' grow, and she's still a part of our wider NGO family to this day.

## Helping students help themselves

It took the first generation students about six months to settle in to their new surroundings in Siem Reap and settle in to the concept that even as high school students, they could take responsibility for themselves and for each other. Our family never considered moving to live in Cambodia and we never considered offering our students dormitory facilities. To this day, we believe that the best way to help people is to mentor them to help themselves.

If we had lived in Cambodia, the students would have been far too reliant on us and not sufficiently reliant on themselves. They'd be kids instead of young adults, just as every child plays their role in a family, while parents play theirs. Mentorship is not leadership and not management – we are mentors to future leaders, which means our students need to step up and do the leading and managing.

Enrolling our students to study at the private New York International School was daunting at first, but it allowed them to see that they were every bit as good as the students who came from wealthy families. Whether their family was rich or poor did not need to define their passion or ability to study and succeed at school. Our students were from poor families and wanted to succeed so they could get better jobs after graduating and help their families. Their new-found friends who were students from wealthy families may have wanted to succeed to receive recognition or rewards from their parents. All the students should have wanted to succeed because they were the beneficiaries of a gift as old as time, a gift that keeps on giving, a gift that lasts a lifetime and will shape your life if you let it – the gift of education.

The adage of not giving fish but instead teaching people how to fish doesn't even get off the ground floor at CRST. We set out to create an organisation that is a leadership-making machine – lead yourself, so you can lead others; we will infuse you with knowledge and skills, so you can create a far-reaching ripple effect in society. From our early days, we taught our students the 'CRST-speak' phrases they all still adore today – including 'there is no free lunch' and 'we have no passengers on our bus, everyone is a driver'.

Being teenagers in grades 11 or 12 and living alone in town was scary, daunting and challenging – but that was part of the attraction. Our family provided the safety net, but the trapeze act was up to our students – they had to learn how to fly. And fly they did – and still do. This gave rise to another of our CRST maxims: 'We'll give you the shoes, but the walking, running and flying is all you'.

Young adults, like older adults, learn to take responsibility and expand their comfort zones provided the ecosystem permits that to happen. Our NGO ecosystem didn't encourage responsibility – it was a given, a fact of life; you struggled for education, now you have the best education, we expect your best. From the early days, our students stepped up and took on roles and responsibilities beyond their years, and these roles and responsibilities are still woven into the DNA of CRST today.

## Focusing on overall wellbeing

In the first few months of our first generation students starting high school at New York International School, we noticed a high rate of absenteeism, and I emailed Nak to ask him what was going on. He replied that many of the students were frequently sick and had to miss school. We narrowed down the sickness to lack of good nutrition and arranged for all our students to eat lunch together every day at a small Khmer restaurant near their school – this allowed them all to catch up as a large family to communicate and exchange ideas and experiences, as well as eat as much healthy food as they wanted. Absenteeism went down sharply and grades went up.

Within a few months of starting CRST, we also created the role of Health Manager and offered the role to Samach, one of our grade 12 students. Samach was mature, responsible, motherly and no-nonsense – students could ring her when they were unwell and she would offer advice or take them to the pharmacy or the clinic. She mentored our students to eat well, exercise regularly and take time out to relax – if they were unwell after taking care of themselves, she was happy to help them; she dished out lessons to irresponsible students and received respect in return.

Soon enough she started keeping notes about frequent ailments and illnesses, researched causes and effects, and educated our students how to avoid these illnesses. We added Doeb, one of our mature grade 11 boys, to the Health Team, so we could facilitate gender-related health matters and avoid any embarrassment for our students. We then tasked Samach and Doeb to develop our NGO Sport Activity program, to ensure our students were keeping active and social, minimising many physical and mental health issues.

These days, the CRST high school students eat three meals a day at a local restaurant, ensuring they get the best nutrition – feed the body, feed the mind, reap the rewards. Over the years, the CRST Health Team has also developed monthly health presentations about common illnesses, common bites, personal hygiene – the list goes on and on. The basis of the education is that maintaining a healthy body just needs common sense – good nutrition, regular exercise and rest. Should the unexpected happen, such as a toothache, a dog bite, a motorbike accident or dengue fever, our Health Team and NGO are here to support our students. Our students look after themselves every day, and then we look after them when bigger health issues arise.

Samach and Doeb trained the next generation of health and sport managers, and they in turn trained the next generation – we mentor our students that a key responsibility of all leaders is to identify the next generation of leaders and mentor them. This enables knowledge-sharing, smooth transitions of roles and growth for everyone. Our two health and sport managers today, still one girl and one boy, continue to do outstanding jobs in leading our sport activities and health management. Any time that students feel unwell, day or night, they may contact our Health Team and request advice or assistance – and our Health Team has access to Samach and Doeb 24/7/365, even though Samach and Doeb are now married (to each other!), working, studying further degrees and raising their son, Thavut.

## Mental health and physical health

When something doesn't go to plan in business, it can have a severe impact on the company, dozens of jobs and hundreds of family members. As a business owner, I carry that responsibility each day and at times it can impact my mental health, causing stress and anxiety. Through the support of an amazing inner circle, I have learnt some ways of dealing with this.

At a recent Business School for our students in Cambodia, Jess and I spent several hours teaching that mental health is as important as physical health – take care of your mind and it will take care of you.

Jess and I shared how normal it was to carry unresolved past events and traumas, but when we do that, we become prisoners of life; 'putting down our baggage' or forgiving someone, even energetically, sets us free. We shared how normal it was to be anxious about the unknown future, and shared the need to trust the flow of life, that everything happens for a reason and that the universe is here to support us to be the best we can be.

We then distributed one-kilogram bags of rice to each student and asked them to carry the bag while sitting in class, doing class activities, taking a break and even going to the toilet.

'It's very inconvenient,' one of the students protested when we reconvened.

'It's holding me back from doing what I want. I couldn't even get a coffee in the break,' another contributed.

'Exactly!' Jess replied. 'Your baggage is holding you back from living your life to the fullest. So how would you like to learn how to put down your baggage and live a happier, more productive life?'

For the rest of the session, we taught how normal it is for humans all over the world to experience anxiety, symptoms of depression and other common mental health challenges. Through interactive activities, we taught numerous ways to manage mental health wellbeing, whether by taking a walk in the sunshine, talking to a friend, playing sport, listening to music, reading a book or meditating – the list went on. Stress is a part of life; recognising it as normal and managing it is also a part of life. We are not the victims if we have the strategies to manage what we experience.

Life in general and life in business can at times be a lonely, overwhelming and scary experience. A family and a team can make those moments more manageable. When life seems out of control, it's time to let others in and share the journey. The Business School students got to take their one-kilogram bags of rice home with them, as a reminder that a healthy body feeds a healthy mind and sharing makes it all the more enjoyable.

## Taking the next step

With the exception of two students, all our first generation students graduated from high school, and their parents put on their very best clothes as they came to town to witness their kids wear their graduation gowns and caps to receive their graduation certificates. In most cases, they were the first kids in their family to finish high school, some of only a handful in their villages.

After graduating from New York International School, we offered our students scholarships to university, and not surprisingly most took us up on the offer, while a handful felt obligated to return to their families to find work and generate much needed income. We first tried out Build Bright University (BBU), which was a collection of a few three-storey buildings, with a reputation of being affordable but not great. Over the first few months we found that professors often skipped classes (that's right – the *professors* skipped classes!) and non-CRST students who never attended classes still received high grades (with bribes being the rumoured reason).

I arranged a meeting with the Director of Pannasastra University of Cambodia (PUC), which was the best university in town. When I walked into his office, I knew I was in the right place – Keara had bookshelves lined with autobiographies of business leaders, including Jack Welch, Richard Branson and Donald Trump (well before his days in politics). Empowering and thought-provoking books by Robert Kawasaki, Stephen Covey, Edward de Bono and Dale Carnegie were also included.

I told Keara that we were looking to switch our students to PUC, but I needed to receive regular reports on attendance and grades, and above all I needed to be sure his university did not sell their grades. PUC was more than twice the cost of BBU and we were willing to pay, but only if our students were to receive knowledge, not just a meaningless certificate after four years of study. Keara assured me PUC was the real deal and after speaking with some of the professors, I reached the same conclusion.

Following my meeting with Keara I called a meeting with all our university students – I told them my family and I were very unhappy with the unprofessional and corrupt system at BBU. University should be about opening your mind, challenging you to look at subjects, concepts and events in an inquisitive, intelligent, critical way, so you can develop new skills that would serve you for the rest of your life. I told them that we were offering everyone the opportunity to switch to PUC, but they would need to stay at university for another one to one and a half years. (PUC's classes were all taught in English, and our students would first have to undertake a 6- to 12-month Intensive English for Academic Purposes program (IEAP) before restarting their bachelor degrees.) It was a big decision – graduate with a meaningless piece of paper 'degree' in two and a half to three years, or stay a little longer and graduate with a bachelor's degree from one of Cambodia's most respected universities. When your family is waiting for you to help them earn a living, that's a big decision – but a scholarship to PUC was like winning the lottery. You were guaranteed to be seen as one of the best, and highly employable on graduation.

I told the students they could think about it overnight and discuss it with their families, but they all said they could decide there and then – with the exception of two students, they were all ready to transfer to PUC. I told the remaining two students that actually there was no choice – all CRST students had to study at PUC because that was the best university and we wouldn't settle for anything but the best for our students. They then also agreed to switch and we've never looked back.

All CRST students still study their bachelor degrees at PUC in Siem Reap and many go on to study their MBAs at PUC or other high-quality universities in Phnom Penh.

## FOUNDATIONS OF LEADERSHIP TAKEAWAYS

- Start with the basics – good physical health, mental health and social health. Your physical health and your mental health are intertwined, and the wellbeing of both leads to a more meaningful and impactful life.

- People don't know what they don't know – be clear on the value you are adding; identify needs and provide solutions.

- When faced with rejection, offer to 'try before you buy' – collaborate for a minimal period, ensure mutual benefit or respectfully end the collaboration.

- Begin with the end in mind, figure out where you want to end up and make a plan to get there, with milestones along the way.

- You are the company you keep – roost with the turkeys or soar with the eagles.

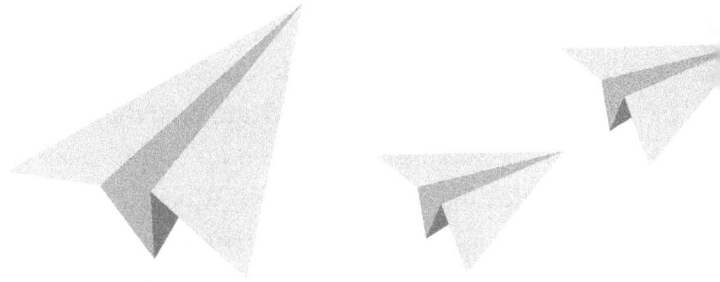

# Chapter 4

# Making a life by what we give, not what we get

At one of our early meetings with the CRST Leadership Team, I asked the students to explain to me their daily and weekly activities. This was back in 2012, while the students were still completing high school. Nak, our NGO Manager, and Doeb, our Education Manager and Health Team member, explained their daily schedules. Between studies, homework, assignments, revision, English class and some time to relax or play sport, their schedules seemed quite busy.

'What about the weekends? What do you do on the weekends?' I asked.

'We study on Saturday for half a day, and sometimes we go back to our hometowns to see our families on Saturday afternoon or Sunday,' Nak replied.

'I'm wondering,' I said, 'whether you think you may find some time to do some community service activities, to help other people in society. You see, you are the lucky ones – you have an NGO that supports you and gives you so much new knowledge and many new skills. Maybe you could think of ways you could share your good luck with others in society, so they too can have more hope for the future?'

I was expecting slumped shoulders and sighs, with rambling explanations of how busy and tired they were and complaints that they already had so little time off – and now we wanted to take even that little time away from them. What I received was the exact opposite – it was as if I'd ignited a spark to set off a firecracker.

'Oh, wow! You mean we will be able to help other poor people in the countryside? WOW! That is really such a GREAT idea! What should we do? Should we teach some of the younger kids in our villages, or offer help to some older people who don't have kids? What should we do?' Their excitement was palpable.

I told the team that it wasn't my job to tell them what to do – they could workshop some ideas, make a list in order of priority and then we could discuss it further. This is how our CRST social contribution programs began.

## Giving back

A few days later, I joined all our students at their NGO English class and at the end of the class, I was handed the list, written in Nak's neat handwriting.

*CRST community service activities:*

1. *build houses*
2. *paint schools*
3. *repair roads*
4. *plant trees*

This was the beginning of one of the most important departments in our NGO – the Community Service department, affection-ately known as CS. The dynamic duo of Nak and fellow-student Veun led our Community Service department with passion, heart and conviction.

The concept of the Community Service department was simple. Our students were blessed to be part of an NGO that was supporting them to become empowered – that empowerment was for their benefit, their families' benefit and for their communities' benefit. In CRST we call that 'the ripple effect' (also shown in the following figure). We teach our students that they are the pebbles being thrown into a lake, so they can create ripples that reach far and wide and touch as many people in society as possible. Over the years, our CS Managers and their teams have been tasked with seeking the most vulnerable and helpless people and families in rural communities and offering them hope, love and support.

THE RIPPLE EFFECT

Our CS activities are a core part of CRST – we teach our students that they are already empowered; they don't need to wait until they graduate, or get a job and earn money, or some other magical moment in time – they can already help someone today! In addition to showing our students that they are already making a difference in society, they become walking billboards for the power of education – villagers, young and old, come to admire them and chat with them about how they got to where they are, so young, but already making such an impact. Our message is always the same – send your kids to school, keep them going to school, and education will change your life too.

## Benefiting those most worthy

Nothing can describe the feeling of seeing an elderly woman cupping her hands in gratitude and shedding tears as she tells our students that she has nothing to give them except her blessings. Or the grandfather raising his granddaughter who is awestruck by our young scholars and promises to never let his granddaughter give up her education so she can become like them, and help others. Or the high school student who watched our students build her family a new home, and was then gifted a bicycle so she could ride to school, rather than walk for over an hour each way. Each recipient of one of our houses has their own unique story; they are all worthy, all special. I share two of those stories here.

### Grandma Loeurn

Grandma Loeurn lived in a 'chicken house' – a hut about 80 centimetres wide and 1.5 meters long, 60 centimetres off the ground. It was so small she could only lie in it when she was in a foetal position. She had no family and no land, and was simply worn out after surviving the Khmer Rouge, the civil war and a life of endless struggle as she walked around her village and nearby villages looking for any daily work she could do in exchange for some rice. We received permission from the village chief to build her a house on common land – she was so emotional as she cupped her hands and continually blessed our students. 'I have nothing to give you, thank you, thank you, thank you, thank you.' And she continued chanting blessings in Khmer. When I saw some of our students cry, I knew we did good.

### Grandma and Grandpa Mean

Grandma and Grandpa Mean lived in two huts next to each other – Grandma's hut was about 1 metre by 2 metres and it was raised about 50 centimetres off the ground, to avoid the inevitable flooding during the rainy season. Grandpa's hut was a similar size, but it was at ground level, so in the rainy season it got flooded. The couple were an average farming family when they were young and had one son; however, when he was in his 40s, Grandpa got sick and a visiting 'doctor' gave him some medicine, which left him paralysed from the hips down. They mortgaged their land to borrow money for treatment, but it was to no avail and Grandpa remained paralysed. When they couldn't repay the loan, they lost their land. To add to their woes, their son died in a car accident a few years later. So there they were, in their 60s, Grandma selling small snacks outside the local school to earn $1 to $2 a day, and Grandpa sitting on the ground all day, either inside his ground-level hut or on the side of the road. The local village chief had allowed them to build their huts on public land, literally 1 metre from the road; Grandpa didn't always make it out of his hut in time when he had to go to the toilet.

As the CRST Community Service activities became well known, we had local village chiefs and other NGOs contacting our team to suggest families we could assist. It was the local village chief who contacted Veun, our CS manager, and asked him if we could help Grandma and Grandpa Mean. He agreed to give them a little more land, still by the side of the road but over a ditch, so the house could be at street level for easy access, yet not flood in the rainy season. We built them a house with a small partitioned area where we installed a septic-tank toilet, so Grandpa wouldn't have to crawl out of the house each time he needed to go to the toilet. We also bought them a small TV (which we illegally connected to the nearby electricity pole – sorry) so that Grandpa could watch TV and have some 'company' when Grandma was out. We have a very touching photo of Pech, our CS assistant manager, showing them how to use the remote control – he asked me, 'How do I explain to them that what they're watching now is live? It's a ceremony that is happening right now in the Royal Palace in Phnom Penh.' I told him to tell them it was like good magic, and how wonderful that they could watch the ceremony in the Royal Palace in Phnom Penh from their own new palace.

## Honing our skills

As word spread about our students' CS activities and other organisations and village leaders sought our help, our processes became systemised and very efficient. From time to time we also have external volunteers joining our house-building community service activities; our guests are without exception blown away by the CRST students' work ethic, commitment and passion for helping rural families. We build our rural houses in just one day!

Everything from evaluating potential beneficiaries, sourcing the necessary permissions and required materials, and preparing workday plans and follow-up reporting are all handled by the CS team. One Sunday each month our students spent the day in the countryside, helping the communities they came from – rural communities where life is a struggle and there is rarely enough for everyone. The rural families who are the beneficiaries of new homes are also inspired by our students' empowerment, motivating them to keep sending their own children to school, so they too can make incredible social contributions.

To be sure, CS days are long and tiring – the cooking team starts at 4.30 am, preparing breakfast for 80 to 100 CRST students and their friends. The team and all the materials leave Siem Reap at about 6 am and arrive in the designated village by 7 am, with everyone gathering for breakfast and an introduction to the family for whom we will be building the new home. The students then work in teams as they set the concrete foundations for the new house, build the main structure using wooden poles that were pre-measured and pre-cut in town, and begin work to weave the palm-leaf walls. Lunch, at about 11 am, is also prepared by the cooking team, followed by a siesta often filled with singing, games, joking around and a quick nap.

The next steps are nailing down the bamboo floor and the metal roof, measuring, sawing and nailing the wooden stairs, fitting the walls, adding a door and one or two windows. The new home is generally ready by late afternoon, when the team gathers with the home owners to gift them a welcome-home care pack, which includes rice and basic food as well as some essential supplies. After the CS leaders thank our students and any additional volunteers, the home owners have the opportunity to express gratitude, and we take group photos with the family and a sign expressing gratitude to the home's sponsor. Our students head back to town – weary, yet fulfilled with the knowledge that they have helped change the course of someone else's life.

We've never taken longer than a day to build a house, but on one particularly challenging build, the team finished after 8 pm, using their phones for light in the pitch-black of the rural Cambodian night. That house was on the side of the road, over a steep ridge leading down to a pond – quite an engineering feat for a group of students. They were absolutely committed to having the family in their new home that night; after all, where else would they sleep?

## KHMER COUNTRYSIDE HOUSE

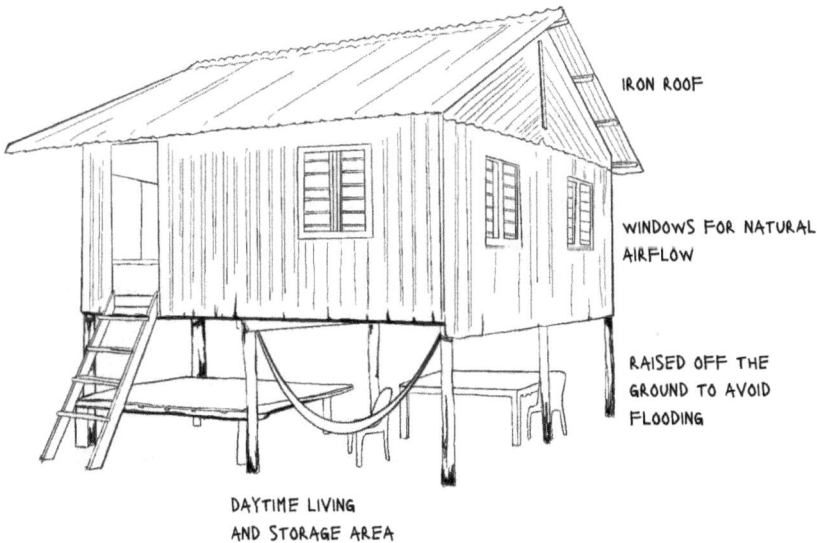

IRON ROOF

WINDOWS FOR NATURAL AIRFLOW

RAISED OFF THE GROUND TO AVOID FLOODING

DAYTIME LIVING AND STORAGE AREA

Each year our high school and university students share hope, love and humanity with those who live on the fringe of society. They know all about the hunger, the poverty, the helplessness, the loneliness, the darkness. In recent years, one Sunday each quarter, they become the spark that lights up someone else's life – someone they have never met, yet whose life they have just changed. Our students tightly embrace their roles of social-change leaders who are leading by example, leaving footprints for others to follow – the footprints of education, empowerment and inspiration.

To date, our students have built and repaired over 300 houses for destitute rural families, painted rural schools, repaired rural roads and planted thousands of trees to prevent erosion and improve the environment.

## Ongoing ripples

Fast-forward ten years to January 2022 and our CS activities came bursting back to life following the hiatus we had to take due to COVID-19 restrictions. Joining our 80 students in Siem Reap were our cohort of MBA students from Phnom Penh. The 100 CRST students were joined by volunteers who joined us from the Cambodian corporate sponsor of the new house we were about to build. Wow! A Cambodian corporate sponsor for our NGO's community service activity – how inspirational is that?! And it came about because of Nak, one of our first-generation NGO students.

After graduating with his bachelor degree from Pannasastra University of Cambodia in Siem Reap in 2019, Nak relocated to Phnom Penh to start his working life. His university graduation day was, of course, a major milestone in his family's life, as it was for us – he was our first university graduate! He soon settled into a career in real estate sales and, with CRST's support, continued to study his MBA.

Having grasped the fundamentals of management and leadership at CRST, Nak assembled a team and started training them with many of the lessons he had learned at our Business School classes. Always acknowledging his background and CRST's impact on him and his family, Nak led with conviction and empathy, and soon enough established his own real estate subagency selling off-the-plan residential units.

He contacted me very excitedly one day and told me about a new project he was pitching for – a rural residential land-development project. He put together a business plan which he asked me to review – and of course the format was very familiar, based as it was on the CRST Business Class teachings. I told Nak he had done an excellent job, gave him some feedback and wished him good luck for his pitch to the land owner.

'Actually, maybe I can ask you something, Aviv,' Nak replied sheepishly. (I could hear his shy smile over the phone.)

'Sure, Nak. You know you can ask me anything,' I replied.

'What would be really useful is if I could tell the land owner that my company has a big car, so we could bring potential buyers to see and buy the land. It's about a one-hour drive from Phnom Penh.'

'Yes, that's a good idea, Nak – have you got a big car?' I replied.

Nak told me that he didn't, but had found a suitable one for $18,000. The only problem was he only had $6000 – and no assets to take out a loan against, and no credit history either. 'You know, I'm only starting out and no-one knows who I am,' Nak said.

'I know who you are, Nak. I'll loan you the $12,000. What terms are you proposing?' I asked without hesitation.

'Really?? You'll loan me $12,000?' Nak asked incredulously.

'Absolutely! When do you need the money and what repayment terms will work for you? Check your cashflow budget and let me know,' I replied.

Nak came back to me the next day, and his proposal was simple:

1. Simple interest of 10% over two years.
2. 24 monthly repayments of $600, covering principal and interest.
3. Sponsor one CRST student.
4. Sponsor one house in the CRST Community Service program.

'I think I learned from you to give more than I receive,' he said.

Nak got the land deal, bought the car and sold all the lots within less than a year – well ahead of schedule. He then went on to be signed as the exclusive agent for a larger development. He was genuine, with a solid business ethic, and was developing a great reputation.

'I wouldn't have been able to do all this without you trusting me with the loan to buy that car,' he said to me after a year.

'You didn't get here because of the car, Nak', I replied. 'You got here because of who you are.'

By January 2022 Nak was employing 10 team members including fellow CRST MBA students Rith, Roeun and Vanndet. That month Nak was the corporate sponsor who brought his team to Siem Reap to build the house they were sponsoring!

## FOUNDATIONS OF LEADERSHIP TAKEAWAYS

- The greatest gift you can give is to help people help themselves.

- 'Busy' is a state of mind – make your own reality, make time, make it happen, and support others to make it happen.

- Give of yourself to others, so that they can give of themselves to others too.

- Always give more than you take.

- 'Victim' is a mindset, reframe it to 'empowered' – empowered to make a change, empowered to make a difference, empowered to learn, grow and succeed.

- Respect everyone and know that we are all the same – wealthy or poor, leaders or followers, we all put our pants or skirts on the same way, one leg at a time.

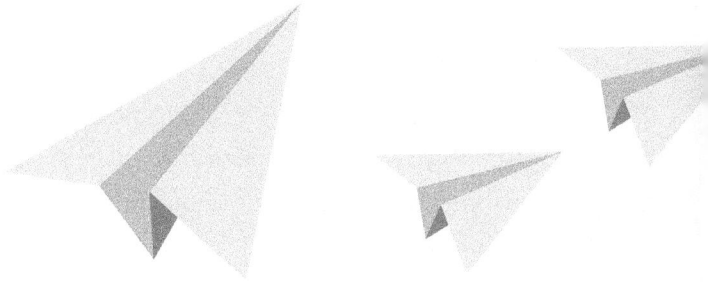

# Chapter 5

# Vision and commitment don't pay the bills

Any successful organisation (for profit or not for profit) needs three critical elements – vision, commitment and money.

The vision for CRST was easy – education opens minds, provides opportunities and creates a far-reaching, long-lasting ripple effect in society. Our commitment was the determination to stick it out no matter what the universe put in our path – and for this we also needed our students' commitment, not just our own. Our family provided funding for the first few years, but as we wanted to scale up, we had to start devoting time to marketing and sponsor relations.

## Sponsors, donors and grants

The CRST funding model has three income streams – private donors, corporate or organisational donors and grants. Jess and I have spent *countless* hours, days and weeks seeking funds for the NGO and individual projects (more on these in the coming chapters). If I was to estimate, I'd say we've spent *months* of 24 round-the-clock hours to seek new supporters, benefactors and grants. From small amounts like $50, which will pay for a bike for a rural student to get to school, to $3000 annual student sponsorships and tens of thousands of dollars to pay for key expenditure items such as our high school students' meals, the NGO's healthcare program or our project-specific contributions.

## Sponsors

We've been blessed to have some incredibly generous supporters – none more so than my own family. We started this NGO without the expectation of it growing to a point where outside funding would be needed – and we never advertised what we did, we just did it because it was right and because we could. As our annual financial contributions grew past a six figure sum, Roni, my brother asked, 'Where will it end? Is there a limit? I'm not sure I signed up for this.'

And he was right. As CRST continued to evolve and grow, we found many new opportunities for us to do more – and much more than we ever signed up for. Providing education, meals and healthcare were the basics we started with, but then we started our community service activities such as the house building mentioned in the previous chapter – at a cost of $1300 to build one house (or $2000 these days because we build a more robust metal-walled home), would we let an abandoned grandmother and her grandchildren live in a pig shed? Or for $60 a month, would we not provide food supplies to a differently abled mother and her differently abled daughter?

So, our family remained committed but we knew there would be limits – limits that kept us to 40 to 50 students per year, and limits to the community contributions we could make. In my mind, the limit was $150,000 per annum – $200,000 absolute maximum – but until the day I wrote this chapter, I didn't share this with anyone. We just did what we did and kept it to ourselves – I never sought to look like a hero. 'I'm not Mother Teresa', I remember telling MJ, who was our national sales manager and was keeping up with the happenings in Cambodia.

'Yes, but what you're doing is so *incredible*!' she said. 'I'm sure people will want to join in and contribute – you just need to tell them!'

She was quite adamant and started spreading the word among some Harvey Norman franchisees who were customers of our family's business. Some were more enthusiastic than others – some sponsored a student without a second thought, while others said they'd rather support a local Australian organisation – to which MJ replied, 'Does it matter which human on the planet you help?' Others said they would only support a tax-deductible charity, which at the time we were not, as if a tax deduction was the incentive they needed to help someone.

Let's be clear, a student sponsorship is $1000 per year – that's about $3, or less than one cup of coffee a day (a full scholarship is $3000 per year, but we break that down to three sponsorships of $1000 to make the funding more within donors' reach). If you could change someone's life for a cup of coffee a day, how many seconds would it take you to say, 'Yes! I'M IN!'?

MJ's efforts with our Harvey Norman franchisees is just one example of how sponsors of our students have come on board. Our private donor pool now includes an amazingly dedicated group of people who have visited Cambodia and found us, or have come to learn about our activities from friends or family. These sponsors generally sponsor one student and usually renew their sponsorship annually. They get the satisfaction of receiving monthly emails from their student so they can keep up to date with their studies and activities. Some sponsors write back, others don't. Most importantly, the students know their sponsors are people from other countries (and even some of our alumni!), who are supporting them. Imagine the feeling of a complete stranger coming to your aid, and helping put you through high school and university, so you are empowered enough to stand up on your own and support yourself and your family and contribute back to your society.

Of course, we have policies and guidelines for communication between students and sponsors, and all emails are copied to an NGO email address so integrity can be monitored. But other than that, we want the sponsors to have full access to communicate with their sponsored students, so they are not just a 'sponsorship cheque' at the end of the year. And should the sponsors visit Siem Reap, they will be welcomed as honoured guests and, of course, be able to meet their students. Such reunions are often very emotional – there's something incredibly humbling about meeting a complete stranger that is actually part of your life. While you have nothing in common, you have everything in common.

Our private donors have found the experience of exchanging the price of a daily cup of coffee for the opportunity to change someone's life (literally!) to be profound. And the ripple effect that flows on to our students' families and their communities has a multiplier effect. Every student sponsored helps to build and repair houses for destitute rural families every year, helps repair hundreds of bicycles for rural students to enable them to go to school, leads rural workshops that empower girls and promote gender equality, participates in environmental impact activities – the list goes on and on. In fact, the average CRST student participates in over 150 community volunteering activities every year! If that's not the best return you can get on the cost of a cup of coffee a day, I don't know what is.

One of the biggest issues with charities is transparency and account-ability – and, believe me, when contributing our own six-figure sum every year, we insisted on full transparency and accountability. To this day, every cent is accounted for by the Finance Team in Cambodia – receipts for even 10 cents are collected and our financial statements are prepared in Australia and then reviewed and audited by external auditors. Transparency and accountability were never an issue for us – CRST was built on that platform.

## Forming corporate partnerships

I talk more about our educational and social enterprise projects in chapters 6 and 7. Our first was 'Project Y – Frozen Yogurt', and of relevance here are our discussions about where we could get the $80,000 needed to fund it.

'What about Harvey Norman?' MJ, the national sales manager at our family company, asked. Harvey Norman were one of our national retail customers.

'I'm sure Gerry Harvey and Katie Paige haven't heard of us and would be highly unlikely to support an educational social enterprise over in Cambodia. They don't even have any stores in Cambodia. There would be nothing in it for them,' I replied.

'Yeah, I know, but what if we pitched this to Ben?' MJ persisted.

Ben was the general manager of Harvey Norman's computer division. He had a big personality, was warm and affable, and a natural leader whose team would willingly follow day in, day out onto the tough retail battlefield of computers, accessories and photo products. He was also 'big picture' and understood the value of lifetime relationships, both with suppliers and with consumers.

'What's in it for him?' I tested MJ.

'He'd love to help, I know he would. Many of the Harvey Norman franchisees already know what you're doing in Cambodia and we get asked all the time how can they get involved,' MJ replied.

A couple of weeks later MJ and I were in front of Ben in his office in Sydney, outlining the Project Y – Frozen Yogurt business plan. The social need was to upskill CRST university students in Cambodia to run a profitable business. We would teach them business fundamentals, and work with them to prepare job descriptions, reporting procedures, key performance indicators (KPIs), reviews and evaluations. Our plan was to divide the business into six common departments and have students spend six months in each department before rotating to the next. After three years, by the time they graduated from university, they would have rotated through all, or most, departments and will be 'real world' ready.

They would also have the opportunity of practising their English with countless tourists, sharing what we do as an NGO and explaining that all the profits from Project Y remained in the NGO to support more students' education. Our students would build their confidence, learn new skills and inspire others to join our journey.

Ben loved the idea and a couple of months later invited MJ and me to join the Harvey Norman Computers franchisee conference. I stood on the stage in front of the almost-200 retailers and outlined the business plans and store plans for our frozen yogurt educational and social enterprise store in Cambodia. Frosty Boy, the iconic Australian ice cream and frozen yogurt brand, assisted us in setting up a soft serve machine in the foyer of the venue and when the franchisees took their next break, they formed a long line to get their soft-serve ice cream in a cone.

Our family company heavily supported the promotion of the project with merchandise that the stores sold, and within six months we had reached the $80,000 we needed to fund the Project Y store.

Creativity, open minds, open hearts and a willingness to do whatever it takes won the day.

We invited some Harvey Norman franchisees to join us at the opening of Project Y– a handful said they would come, and two turned up. We treated them like the VIPs that they were, representing the rest of the franchisees who'd supported the project. Upstairs in the store, we hung framed photos of all the franchisees who contributed – we called it the 'Wall of Heroes'.

## Corporate donors and grants

Along with the help we've received from Harvey Norman, our corporate sponsors include family foundations and companies who aren't just talking about making a difference, but are also walking the talk. These corporate funds are normally used for specific purposes and projects, such as high school students' meals, students' health, house building, 'Project G – Empowering Girls', 'Project B – Bicycles for Education' and 'Project R – Refuse, Reduce, Reuse and Recycle Plastic Education Program'.

Grants are always a bit of a fishing expedition – applications take days and weeks of work and we often return empty handed. Still, if we don't put on our fishing gear and head out to sea, we will never have the opportunity of catching a grant that will create the sustainable outcomes we deliver. We were blessed to be selected for three grants from the Canadian Government's Canada Fund for Local Initiatives, enabling us to fund significant sustainable impact through Project G, Project R and 'Project W – WASH for Education Program'. (More on our projects in chapters 6 and 7.) Even large, well-intentioned organisations such as Rotary have convoluted grant processes that vary from country to country, region to region, and district to district – and the wording has to be exactly as the relevant selection-committee expects. One day we will have a specialist grant-writing volunteer, but for now it's a task that Jess and I do into the wee hours of the morning.

CRST does have a few advantages when it comes to attracting donors and grants – we are transparent, accountable, sustainable and all overheads are covered by our family, so every dollar donated is a dollar spent on education and community projects. These are critical factors to credibility.

Our family has always paid, and will continue to pay, for all non-educational or project-related expenses, so our sponsors know their money is hard at work. Of course, the rent for our campus in Siem Reap needs to be paid, as does the cost of the petrol for the tuktuks, and our electricity and water bills – but by our family paying for these, we allow sponsors to see that 100 per cent of their money is used for its designated purpose, not operational costs. Our financial statements are produced pro bono and, as mentioned, external auditors review and audit our financial statements, also pro bono.

I'm proud to say that for an organisation that delivers so much punch, we have a lean cost structure. Every dollar gets looked at before it's approved for spending – the departments' and projects' monthly budgets are reviewed down to the $0.50 notebooks, $0.75 breakfasts and the $1.50 petrol money for a motorbike for a student-educator to teach at a rural workshop. Transparency, accountability and sustainability are our hard currency.

## Our fundraising approach

We don't have a 'fundraising team' or a 'marketing team' for CRST – our students inspire new donors to join our journey as they tell the NGO story on their Ambassador Program travels; Jess and I do the rest. (For more on the development of our Ambassador Program, see chapter 8.)

Even with our sustainably low-cost delivery of outstanding education, mentored life experiences and inspirational community outreach programs, I find the fundraising aspect of our organisation the most personally challenging. I simply don't like asking people for money.

I'm confident of 'the product' and I can very easily describe 'the features and benefits'. A possible rejection doesn't scare me – whatever the reply may be, I know it won't be my baggage to carry. I've met with multimillionaires living in mansions and had wonderful dinner conversations that amounted to not even a bicycle donation. I've spoken with people who have just lost their jobs and asked them if they'd like to stop their sponsorships at this challenging time – without fail, they all continued to support their students.

We live in a world of plenty – there is absolutely enough for everyone, we just need a little 'wealth redistribution'. But that's not how many people are programmed – and that's what puts me off asking for money. I see a life of plenty, people who have houses with rooms they don't use, more cars than limbs, bottomless pit wardrobes, mega-fridges and butler's pantries that hold food for a village. I see people who have made it and will never go without – and I respect them for their success. I'm just left to wonder whether they think they will take it all with them when they die, or perhaps that their loved ones may ever go without; otherwise, what's the thinking behind not sharing their blessings when they clearly have more than they or their family will ever need?

As well as corporate sponsors from Australia, such as digiDirect, Australia's largest camera retailer, we've had Coca-Cola Cambodia as an early sponsor and Smart Axiata, Cambodia's largest telecommunications company, also come on board for specific projects. But I was particularly moved when a group of Australian teachers at a school our ambassadors spoke at pooled some money together to sponsor a student. Or when Lea, a work colleague, inspired her grandchildren to pool their Christmas money to sponsor a house for a poor rural family. Or when Mary, a pensioner from Ireland, sent $50 through PayPal, donating a bicycle for a rural student.

Those moments leave me inspired, knowing that we live in a world of plenty, we won't go without and wealth can so easily be redistributed. But I still don't like asking for money, I'd rather people offer. That's more noble.

## Tzedakah

The Jewish philosopher Maimonides (1138–1204), defined what he considered to be the eight-level hierarchy of 'tzedakah' – charity and moral obligation. The Hebrew word for 'charity' is 'tzedakah' – from the word 'tzedek', which means justice, fairness and decency. The concept of 'charity' originating from 'justice, fairness and decency' is pretty cool.

At the lowest level of Maimonides' charity giving is giving begrudgingly or unwillingly; at the highest level, the donor gives the recipient the ability and dignity to be self-supporting before he or she becomes impoverished.

The complete eight levels are as follows:

- *Level 8:* The donor is pained by the act of giving.
- *Level 7:* The donor gives less than they should but does so cheerfully.

- *Level 6:* The donor gives after being asked.
- *Level 5:* The donor gives without being asked.
- *Level 4:* The recipient knows the donor but the donor does not know the recipient.
- *Level 3:* The donor knows the recipient but the recipient does not know the donor.
- *Level 2:* Neither the donor nor the recipient know each other.
- *Level 1:* The donor gives the recipient the ability and dignity to become self-supporting.

My family and I have never sought to meet our students' families. We have met some on special occasions, but this was never a focus of ours. Sometimes, meeting a student's family was necessary if we thought it would benefit the student. I met Lita's grandmother and uncle, for example, when they decided to change their minds and not allow her to join the NGO. I invited them to Jaya House, my usual hotel in Siem Reap, for breakfast, knowing they would never in their lives have expected to be sitting in the magnificence of a room inspired by the Khmer Empire. I invited my friend Ms Aly, the Director of a free English school NGO, to translate. With love and respect, I explained that I normally don't meet our students' families, because it is our students who are the heroes, not me. It is our students' families who support Cambodia's future generations to bring much-needed social development and justice, while we merely provide the opportunities. Lita, I told them, was going to be the next Ms Aly, an educated woman, who would help thousands of others. 'Will you allow us to help you support Lita?' I asked them.

Ms Aly translated so wonderfully, with tact and warmth, and I could see Lita's grandmother, Som Lorn, had great love for Lita. She looked a little embarrassed that Aly and I had taken time to meet with them and explain to them that Lita's future would be so much brighter after we supported her to graduate from high school and university. Our NGO could empower her to help herself and help others, while taking good care of her – she was the future of Cambodia. Grandma wiped the tears from her eyes when she saw that we loved and respected Lita as much as she did – she turned to Lita's uncle and said she wanted Lita to have the best life possible and she could stay with CRST.

Lita's grandmother passed away the following year, just two months before Lita graduated from high school and started university. I told Lita that her grandmother would always be her greatest supporter as she continues to carry her in her heart.

**From: Aviv Palti**

To: Lita Seng

Subject: Our thoughts are with you Lita

Good morning Lita,

I was so saddened to hear that your grandmother passed away. I know that you had a very special bond with her – I could see that when I met Grandma at Jaya House last year.

I could feel how much you loved her and respected her, and that she loved you so much too, and admired you and your determination to study and make your life as powerful as possible. I still remember her wonderful smile and sparkling eyes – and she felt so special to be at Jaya House, sitting next to you and filling up with pride and joy that you are her granddaughter.

Grandma will live inside you forever, Lita – you are very special.

We love you – Aviv

In her first year at university, Lita became our CRST Campus Manager and later that year became an ambassador for the NGO and travelled to Australia to represent CRST and the Rotaract Club of Siem Reap.

We don't seek our students' gratitude, nor their families' gratitude. Their families don't need to see our faces to feel our love for their children. Our reward is our students' successes as they break their families' poverty cycles through their education, becoming self-supporting and restoring dignity to others through their acts of social justice. Tzedakah.

## Weeding out self-interest

Sometimes our sponsors don't fully understand the concept of giving with an open heart. As an example of this, a sponsor of two of our students emailed us to say they had some guests coming to Cambodia from Singapore. They wanted to distribute food packages to families in the countryside and visit a school in the floating village to distribute school materials to the students. I reminded the sponsor that we operate sustainably, responding to the needs of the community, not the needs of visiting tourists. We'd be happy to assist in the coordination if they had already identified the families and qualified the needs of the students in the floating village. They had done no such thing.

All too often, 'privileged' humans from developed countries come to developing countries to exude generosity and benevolence, leaving nothing sustainable when they leave. 'Photo opportunists!' I said to Jess. 'They simply want their friends back home to see how 'great' they are! Self-serving parasites feeding on the poor for their own vanity!'

Keeping our (strong) reservations in check, we weighed up the sponsor's request very carefully and sought feedback from the leadership team in Cambodia. The proposal had no ongoing impact, but distributing 100 sacks of rice was better than nothing. The students at the floating village may not need pencils and notebooks, but they could share them with others in their community or keep them for later.

Begrudgingly, we agreed to help the sponsor coordinate their group of 20 or so Singaporean guests who were coming to Cambodia and wanted to be seen as charitable. As often happens with missions that have alternate agendas, the results were embarrassing and undignified – the guests were uninterested and disconnected.

The guests refused our offer of a pre-visit briefing from our volunteer team. These briefings outline Khmer cultural norms, so the guests could be respectful and feel comfortable interacting with the Cambodians they met. 'My friends know how to behave', the sponsor told our team, and they advised their guests to skip the introduction session. Evidently, they didn't know how to behave.

Instead of engaging with our students as their hosts, they treated them as low-level ignoramuses. Instead of taking the time to learn about Khmer culture, the best way to show respect and maybe even two to three Khmer words, the guests disembarked their air-conditioned minibus and lacked humility as they gave their food packages to the rural families they visited. The photo opportunity trumped humanity.

At the school, the guests patted students on their heads – a massive faux pas in a Buddhist country that considers children's heads as sacred, only to be touched by parents and monks. They tossed the school supplies to students, in a culture that shows deep respect when receiving a gift personally, and allows the recipient to express gratitude with the gift cupped in their hands whenever possible.

Reminiscent of characters in the movie *Crazy Rich Asians*, they were dressed inappropriately, spoke inappropriately and behaved inappropriately. The gentle Cambodians were left traumatised – our students didn't even know where to start their feedback report – they had no words.

We let the matter settle for a couple of weeks and then our leadership team sent the sponsor our hosting feedback report – and the sponsor was not happy. The guests came to show benevolence, how dare the beneficiaries provide feedback on what could be done better next time? As respectful as the report was, laying no blame but seeking lessons and improvement, the sponsor was not swayed – we were ungrateful. He didn't renew his sponsorships of the two CRST students; to their credit, both students continued to write to their now ex-sponsor, sharing their success in life and expressing gratitude for supporting part of their journey. We arranged alternate sponsors for them and both went on to graduate from their bachelor and master's degrees.

As a postscript to this experience, you can imagine my surprise when a few months later another sponsor, related to the first sponsor, contacted me asking us to host another Singaporean group. Again, the group seemed to want to drive a full-size, five-star tourist bus on the narrow roads and tracks leading up to a bamboo and palm-leaf hut, stop out the front, get out, give some rice, take some photos, get back on the bus and drive off in a puff of dirt. We offered more respectful alternatives – such as meeting in a community hall, pagoda or local school, where the guests and beneficiaries could interact in a meaningful and mutually respectful way – but each suggestion was rejected.

We ended up declining to host this group. After this decision, the second sponsor, who sponsored three of our students, also chose not to renew their sponsorships. The experience only strengthened our resolve that our students, their families and their rural communities were not for sale. Every person is entitled to respect and dignity. Our students bring too much to the table to be treated like disposable napkins.

Vision, commitment and money – the three critical ingredients needed for any organisation to get started. Then comes the rest ...

## Scaling up

'How will you scale this up?' he asked me.

'We can't scale it up, David. Our family has committed to seeing all students to the end of their bachelor degrees – we're going to stay at 40 to 50 students,' I replied.

'But what if money wasn't an issue? What could you do?' he persisted.

'Well, we'd probably grow to 100 students and set up more projects to address social-need issues – but right now we know our limitations,' I told him.

David was an advisor to our family company's board – with a background in accounting and finance, he often saw boundaries as territories worth exploring.

'Why 100 students?' David asked.

I replied that I'd read several leading psychology articles and books that spoke of the ideal community size of 80 to 120 people. Once you exceed 120 people, relationships and communication start to degrade, and people feel they've become less significant and valuable, and so are less bound to the group. Larger groups often fracture into individual sub-groups, often becoming less productive and effective.

We are frequently asked about our focus on *quality* education – why do we spend our money on the best high school and the best university, rather than educate our students at significantly cheaper schools, allowing us to reach many more students for the same amount of money. Our reply is always the same – you are the company you keep, and to be the best you can be, you need to study with the best so you can create the most impactful outcomes. 1000 students graduating high school and earning $200 per month was not going to be as impactful in the long term when compared to 100 students graduating with a BA, going on to manage or own a business, and helping bring in the tide of prosperity for the whole of society.

David was satisfied with the logic of 100 students.

'Why don't you register as a tax-deductible charity and raise more money?' he asked disarmingly with a grin on his face.

'That's a *massive* learning curve, David – and a long road with a stack of documentation, and no guarantee of success.'

'The sooner you get started, the sooner you'll get there,' he said, again with a big grin.

In December 2016, the Cambodia Rural Students Foundation received Australian government accreditation as a tax-deductible charity. Our board included an accounting industry veteran, a partner in a law firm, a marketing executive and three CEOs. We were ready to increase our sponsors and donors, and scale up sponsorships and projects. In 2017, we had 55 students, and 66 students in 2018. By 2020, we reached our target, with 103 students sponsored.

## FOUNDATIONS OF LEADERSHIP TAKEAWAYS

- Vision is not enough; you must be a clear and effective communicator. Communicate with yourself and then communicate with others.

- Always have your elevator pitch ready – in 10 seconds be able to tell people what you do, while still leaving them inspired and wanting to know more. Here's ours: 'We founded an organisation in Cambodia that empowers rural students out of poverty and into middle class in just eight years.'

- Know your USP (unique selling proposition) – why are you different? 'Our organisation in Cambodia is entirely managed by our students, who receive extensive mentoring and hands-on experiences, empowering them to become future leaders in society.'

- Know the value you are adding. 'Our students receive formal and life-skills education that lifts them and their families out of poverty, creating sustainable impact for generations to come.'

- Be generous with your time, and be generous with your being.

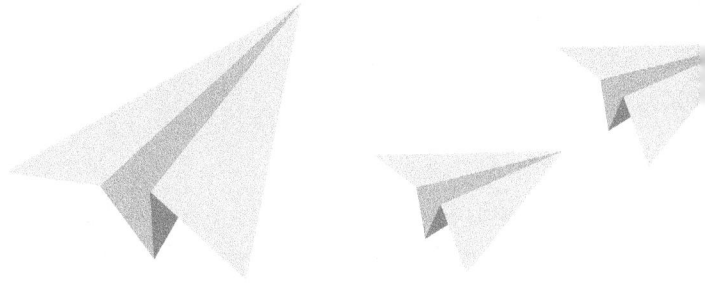

# Chapter 6

# 'Luck' is being ready when life comes your way

She parked her scooter at the curb and took off her baby-pink helmet. She looked around to make sure her scooter was steady and then walked towards us. I was sitting outside the Blue Pumpkin Cafe with Nak, Doeb and Sreng (students sponsored by CRST) and stood up – 'You must be Sompeas[3],' I said with a big smile and cupped my hands in greeting. A grin came across her serious face and she cupped her hands in return, as she politely said, 'So nice to meet you.'

The five of us chatted for about half an hour. Sompeas already knew a lot about CRST – a few days earlier, Sreng had asked me if he could recommend a student to join the NGO. 'Of course', I said.

He smiled and said nervously, 'She's my sister', not knowing how I'd react.

'Great! If she's anything like you, we'll have another star!'

'I think she's better than me,' he replied sheepishly.

'That's almost impossible, but let's see,' I said with a big smile on my face.

---

3    Despite the complicated spelling, the pronunciation of Sompeas is 'Sumpo'.

## Early recruitment

In the early days of CRST, we didn't have a formal application process – the first 22 students, 'Generation 1', were all from Savong School; the next few generations were introduced by these original students. Michelle and I met with these potential students each time we came to Siem Reap and assessed whether we thought they were committed enough to their education and the NGO's community service activities.

Such was the case for Heang and Pech, who rode their bicycles for two hours from their villages near Dom Dek to meet with us. They arrived half an hour late, but that wasn't unusual in Cambodia – in fact, running somewhat late is almost normal (many call it 'Khmer time'). Heang and Pech were wearing dusty black shoes, long pants and long-sleeve collared shirts – their commitment to look their best was reflective of their respect for the upcoming meeting, sweaty shirts and faces notwithstanding.

We met at a cafe not far from our guest house in Siem Reap and as I stood up to meet them, I noticed Pech's bike had no seat – just the stem for the seat. I greeted them and asked, 'Where's your bike seat?'

Pech seemed embarrassed as he laughed and looked away, wiping the sweat from his face. 'Did you already put it in your backpack?' I asked with good intention, knowing that in Western countries some bike riders remove the seat and carry it with them to make their bikes less attractive to thieves. Heang came to Pech's aid and said, 'Oh, it's broken, there is no seat.'

My eyes opened wide and I asked incredulously 'You rode here for two hours with no seat? You were standing on the pedals the whole time??'

Pech kept laughing nervously, his eyes darting away, looking everywhere but us. He was clearly so embarrassed. I made light of the situation by telling him that I could see his commitment to meeting with us – and that's exactly the sort of students we were looking to support. He relaxed a little and we ordered some cold drinks for them as they sat. At the end of the chat, Michelle and I nodded to each other and we told both Heang and Pech that we would love to welcome them to CRST. If that was okay with them, Nak and the team would help make the arrangements.

Heang had tears in his eyes as he said, 'Oh my god. Really?? Oh my god!!' I don't think he expected us to fall in love with him so quickly, but he and Pech became some of our best and most productive students. Before they left, I asked Pech how much a new bike seat would cost. 'About $2,' he said shyly.

I gave him $5 and said, 'Please buy a new seat in town before you go home – and use the rest of the money to stop on the way and buy a snack and a drink for you and Heang, okay?'

'Oh, no, no, no, no,' he said, so politely, while smiling broadly. I told him that when he joined CRST, he would quickly learn that he is the most important person in the world – he must take good care of himself so he can be helpful to others. I put the $5 in his hand and he cupped it between his hands as he said goodbye and bowed his head in respect.

## Finding a star ...

Within the first five minutes of meeting Sompeas, I knew she was an absolute rock star. She was super-polite and respectful and owned who she was, without the arrogance that often comes with self-confidence. She told me a little about herself, what she studied, what she had been doing and why she would like to continue her studies. She seemed happy to share, but at the same time seemed a little guarded, as if she'd been hurt before and her trust would need to be earned over time. Her English was very good – and she wanted to be a lawyer, so she could be the voice to represent people in society who were voiceless, uneducated, oppressed and couldn't defend themselves. Wow!

Sompeas asked a little about our family, and why we were helping Cambodian people – she seemed genuinely touched that despite not being Cambodian and not living in Cambodia, we followed life's path and were helping complete strangers. I told her that we were seeking to invest in students to be the best they could be, with the understanding that their responsibility was ultimately to help others by sharing their knowledge and experience. We weren't just providing scholarships; we were breaking the poverty cycle through education and educating future leaders.

At the end of our chat, Sompeas thanked me for my time, stood up and cupped her hands. She returned to her scooter, popped on the pink helmet, walked the scooter backwards into the street and drove off.

Sreng looked at me with a nervous smile. 'What do you think?' he asked.

'She's in!' I replied simply.

Nak and Doeb looked at each other with wide grins. 'You mean she can join the NGO?' Nak asked.

'100 per cent yes! She's an absolute winner! A leader in the making – a STAR!' I said.

Sreng breathed a sigh of relief – he had taken a risk suggesting his younger sister meet with me. I told him he could ring her to tell her the news, and he said he would wait until he got home, so he could tell Sompeas in front of their mum.

Sompeas started her bachelor degree at Pannasastra University of Cambodia, but had to settle for a Bachelor of Business Management as they didn't have a Law Faculty. Her mature, no-nonsense manner was calming and inspirational to many of our students, and she became a role model for our girls. The boys respected her because she was smart, respectful and had worthy opinions; the girls loved her because she was much of what they aspired to become.

## ... And a trailblazer

Sompeas was the first girl in our NGO to join the football (soccer) team and, because she was the only girl, she didn't mind playing with the boys. Soon enough, more girls wanted to play football and we had enough girls to start a girls' football team. In time, we found other girls' football teams in Siem Reap so they could play matches – and our boys were a great cheer squad!

During her time in CRST, Sompeas was a member of our Senior Leadership Team and held roles as our marketing manager and the manager of 'Project V – The Volunteer Experience', hosting overseas volunteers. She also held a variety of roles in our educational social enterprise, 'Project Y – Frozen Yogurt' (more on this later in this chapter and in chapter 7), where she spent six-monthly rotations, managing each of the marketing, finance, production, sales and human resources departments.

She approached me at Project Y one night and asked whether she could wear dark pants instead of the dark skirt that was a part of the store's uniform. I looked at her quizzingly and asked, 'Why not?' She explained that in Cambodian culture, girls and women never wore pants.

'Oh, I see. Well, you're a new generation, Sompeas. From my perspective, you can wear whatever makes you feel comfortable and proud to be who you are,' I replied.

'Are you sure?' she asked politely.

'100 per cent. I'll announce to the team that all the girls may wear pants or skirts, that's our new uniform policy – would that be helpful?'

'Very,' she replied with a wide smile. I expected she would have already raised this with the Project Y leadership team and probably didn't get everyone's support.

From the next evening, Sompeas wore pants whenever she felt like it – and more of our girls followed her lead. Our boys loved it too – we were breaking social barriers, creating new social norms, leading by example, respecting the past, living today and creating the future.

*October 2017*

*Sompeas was selected to travel to San Francisco, Philadelphia and Melbourne to represent CRST, speaking at schools, community and business gatherings as part of our Ambassador Program. This is her ambassador presentation:*

Hello, my name is Sompeas and I am so happy to share with you today about the life of women in Cambodia.

20 per cent of girls in Cambodia do not finish primary school.

In the society I come from, women are not valued as much as men and we are supposed to do what we are told. We are stereotyped as weak and powerless. We are not encouraged to pursue education because we will become housewives, but men should get an education because they will be leaders.

I have never believed in these nonsense things and I have struggled to do what I think is right and what I believe in. I grew up in a family where everyone values education and my uneducated mother has worked so hard as a single parent just to put her children in school. So, I tell myself I should be tough and fight for her.

I am here today to share how we have overcome these gender challenges with the support of CRST. I want girls to believe that social norms should not be a barrier for them – so this is the story that shaped the way I am today.

When I was three, my father died after a long illness. I was separated from my family and sent to live with my grandmother about 300 kilometres away.

Even though I stayed close to my grandmother, I didn't feel included. She could not share her love easily and I lived with many cousins. During that time, I really needed someone to lift me up and give me some encouragement, but I could never find anyone to do that, so I had to stay strong on my own.

I remember when I started school, I was eight years old. I went to school alone on my first day and I felt so jealous to see other children with their parents. But I was fine and I loved school – it was the only place I could go so I did not feel lonely. Whenever I was at school, I felt it was a lot better than home.

When I was 12, my grandmother started to get very sick, and I was the one who took care of her because everybody else was busy. Together she and I went to a hospital in Phnom Penh. I was responsible for my grandmother's health and I felt overwhelmed by the city and medical information. I was so afraid that we would get lost. Two months later, my grandmother died and I could not stop crying – I had nobody left even though there were so many people around.

A week after my grandmother's funeral, I was asked whether I wanted to live with my aunt or move back to my family. Even though I was young, I knew that nobody would be as good as family, so I decided to go back to live with my mum and siblings.

I was very nervous to see them again. I hadn't seen my mother in almost 10 years and I did not recognise her – I thought she was just my neighbour. Learning she was my mother, I could not open my mouth to say the word 'mother', the only word that I dreamed to say. I was criticised for not calling her mother. Slowly that changed and today we are close. After moving back to my home, I felt I was loved and included in my family. Until that time, that was the most happiness I had felt in life.

But life was not always happy. After my father died, all we had left was one old bicycle. Our land and belongings had been sold to treat my father's illness. That was not enough, so we borrowed money and we were left in debt.

When I came back 10 years later, the financial problems had not changed. My mother still bought and sold recycled items, which is considered a low, dirty job and earned $5 a day. Because of her job, she was looked down on. I used to ask her why she would pretend not to see me whenever we met on the street. She said, 'I do not want you to be embarrassed having me as your mother.' I told her 'You have nothing to be ashamed of. You work so hard just for us, so why would I be ashamed of having you as my mother?' I could not forget what my uncle said about me to my mother: 'She will not know how to read and write and she will end up just like you.' I was not afraid to tell people about my family and I sometimes helped my mother buy recycled items when I was free after school.

Later, when I was 14, I decided to do something for my family financially. Once a week, I helped a neighbour to sell lotus flowers that people give as an offering to Buddha. I normally got $2.50. That $2.50 was enough to buy a whole meal for a whole family. So, I gave some of my money to my mother and sisters and kept the rest for my school stationery.

It was not enough, so I got a job as a waitress when I was about 15 and I earned $60 a month. I had to work between 8 and 10 hours a day, 29 days a month. It was so exhausting. I left work at midnight, and I had to wake up at 6.30 am for school. In class, I was sleepy and I could not concentrate.

I spent four years working in restaurants with the same amount of pay. I struggled through it and finished high school in 2014. But I failed the grade 12 exams. More than 70 per cent of students failed that year because the government cracked down on the cheating system. The students usually paid money to pass the exams rather than using their own ability. It was common in schools. Because so many students failed, we were given the chance to retake the exams and I told myself that I could not fail twice.

So, I quit my job and prepared myself for the exams. One month later, I retook them and passed. First, I thought I was lucky to have a second chance, but then I realised it was me who did all the study hours, so that was not luck.

Despite passing my grade 12 exam, I could not think of furthering my education at university – the only dream that I had at that time – because my family could not afford it. I thought I would go back to work as a waitress and earn that little money to help my family.

In late 2015, I was offered to apply for a scholarship at CRST. I felt the future had opened up again for me. I was given a lot of support from my family, especially my brother. Incredibly, I was chosen. Suddenly, I was able to go to university, my one dream. It was a miracle to me.

I became a member of Cambodia Rural Students Trust, CRST, the non-government organisation founded by Aviv Palti and his family with the mission of 'Breaking the poverty cycle through education'. It offers life-changing opportunities, programs and activities. The NGO gives an equal chance to boys and girls to access quality education. It educates students and encourages them to give back to the community.

Being a part of CRST really has made my life more meaningful and has taken me out of my comfort zone. The NGO supports my belief that I can achieve my dream of becoming a lawyer. I was so inspired by my brother who is now the NGO Manager and has achieved so much in a short time and I thought it was impossible for me to be like him.

I always wondered how could I help others because I thought I needed money, but I was wrong. I regularly volunteer and join community service, one of my favourite activities in the NGO. We help the most needy families in rural areas. We often build houses, paint schools, plant trees or clean up around town. Through these activities, I learned that to help somebody, I don't need to wait until I have a lot of money. As long as I can help, I need to help.

Through building houses, we also make sure to promote gender equality. Main structure building, like digging or heavy work, are for boys and wall frame building, like attaching palm leaves to bamboo, and cooking are for girls. That is common. I remembered someone introduced the idea of girls working in the main structures team and boys cooking. Everyone laughed, but I can tell you that boys cook very good food. And girls enjoy working with heavy work.

In Cambodia, not many girls are given the chance to work in leadership roles. But in our NGO, our girls are powerful leaders. We manage departments at CRST and Project Y, which is our educational social enterprise.

I still remember when I worked in the Project Y marketing department, the first day I went to a hotel I felt so shy and embarrassed. I thought they would not treat us with respect because we were girls and so young with no experience. But – it was fine! Now meeting new people does not bother me at all.

A friend of mine who was assigned to work in the finance department at Project Y had never done any kind of job, but she did very well. She learnt to understand all the working processes and led her team very effectively.

I think it's great that female students in CRST are changing our society. We want them to have more freedom and choice and to live their dreams. Our NGO supports some families in rural villages and our female students travel long distances to bring them food supplies. We are independent and empowered.

All the students attend workshops to discuss relationships between men and women. We also look at the importance of respecting other's decision-making and gender equality. Our female students are encouraged to take part in social activities and speak up about things they are not happy about.

You are a sport loving nation; you might find it surprising that our society tells women not to play sport because women are supposed to act gracefully. Well, I do not think it is right. In our NGO, we have a boys' football team and a girls' football team. I joined the girls' team and I love it. Some people will say, 'She plays sport because she just wants to get the attention', but I don't care. I don't need the attention – I play sport because I like it, it's great for my health and a fun team atmosphere.

I have also become a 'bong srey' – a big sister. I talk to new students who have just moved from their home to live in the city. They often feel lonely and scared. I remember talking to one young girl who had just moved to live in town. She seemed sad whenever I met her and she just wanted to hug me. After sharing my experiences with her, she has settled down and she is happy. And she is a good footballer!

Because of so many things I have gone through, my mother is so proud of me and she always pushes me to continue my dream and do what I think is right and what I believe in.

I believe that girls have to get education because we need to have a voice. CRST is playing a very important role in making these changes. We are making sure female students stay in school and giving them the chance to prove to themselves and society that we are not weak and vulnerable like people say.

Girls, themselves, are stepping up and people are starting to respect us. It's very important for me to see women treated equally because everyone deserves the same rights and to be truly valued. Women are not just weak and vulnerable like some people say.

I invite you to join us on our journey in empowering girls to get an education that will enable them to follow their dreams and have amazing careers and be greater contributors to society.

## The sky's the limit

Sompeas was an active member of the NGO, and never afraid to take on new challenges and leadership roles. Sitting in class one day at one of our Business School programs, she struck up a conversation with Liz, the wife of our friend Steve, who was one of the visiting mentors at the week-long program.

The Business School program was developed to offer our students an immersive learning experience with business professionals from around the world. Supplementing the theoretical studies at university and the experiential learning from leading and managing the NGO and our projects, Business School was a week-long opportunity to learn from overseas mentors who shared their professional knowledge and experience. We held classes at one of the local universities during the day, enabling our students to still take their regular university subjects at night. No doubt this was a heavy workload, but it was also incredibly impactful.

Steve was one of our first Business School mentors, sharing his professional knowledge and experience in business and finance. His ability to simplify and explain accounting principles and recordkeeping was inspirational. His experience as a businessman and Finance Professor at Temple University in Philadelphia enabled him to weave business accounting into practical terms, easily comprehended by our students. I also appreciated his humility as he asked me to interrupt him at any time I felt our students needed him to slow down or rephrase his teachings. He empowered many of our students to see that financial literacy was a life skill, not just a profession – and he inspired many of our students to take up finance as a career.

At this Business School, Liz was particularly impressed with Sompeas. Liz said to me in the break, 'She's determined and smart and polite and has excellent English.'

'She's one of our stars,' I replied. 'Sompeas is considerate, yet happy to push boundaries if she feels something could be done differently. She's an incredible role model for our girls. She's often their voice and the boys respect her because she's passionate and logical in her views.'

'You know she wants to be a lawyer, right?' Liz asked.

I replied that I knew that and asked Liz, 'Did she tell you why?'

Liz's eyes welled up as she was clearly moved by Sompeas's vision and purpose for wanting to be a lawyer.

'She wants to be "the voice of the voiceless"! She wants to represent those in society who are being taken advantage of because they are illiterate or poor or disadvantaged. That's incredible!' Liz replied.

'I know,' I said. 'Isn't that amazing? She doesn't want to be a lawyer for prestige or wealth or connections – she wants to represent the voice of the thousands of poor, illiterate Cambodians who are often taken advantage of by others in society. It doesn't get much better than that, Liz – Sompeas is the real deal, she's already balancing the gender scales in the NGO.'

The next morning at Business School, Liz walked up to me before Steve started his class. 'Steve and I want a quick word with you – have you got a moment?' she asked.

We stepped out to the open corridor and walked to the end of the building for some privacy. Liz looked at Steve, clearly wanting him to start the conversation.

'Aviv, Liz and I are really big fans of Sompeas. She's just so wonderful. And she has such an incredible future ahead of her! Liz and I discussed this last night and we have a proposal for you. We know that CRST students have to stay in Siem Reap while studying their undergrad degrees, so they can get great life skills and business skills as they lead the NGO and the activities. That's a really impressive organisational model and we love it.

'But we're wondering if you could make an exception for a student who is exceptionally bright and determined, but doesn't have the major she'd prefer available to study here in Siem Reap.' Steve was painting an excellent case as Liz looked on with a mix of admiration and resolve.

'We know that Sompeas is an incredible contributor and leader in CRST, but for her benefit and for the benefit of Cambodia, we're wondering whether you would consider allowing us to sponsor her to study law. We'd sponsor her undergraduate law degree at the American University in Phnom Penh and then sponsor her to study her postgraduate at any university she chose in the United States. It means she would need to relocate to Phnom Penh, and we would support that too, including her rent and living expenses. It's an incredible opportunity for her and we're hoping you'll support it,' Steve concluded.

No doubt, this was an amazing opportunity for Sompeas – it's not often that someone offers to sponsor you to study your Bachelor of Laws, followed by a Master of Laws at any university you choose.

'So you'd support her to study at any law school?' I asked incredulously.

'Anywhere she chose and was admitted to, Aviv,' Liz replied.

I knew they were serious.

Jess and I discussed this almost never-in-a-lifetime opportunity as Steve was taking the Business School class. Our conclusion was obvious – we would never stand in any of our students' paths to get the best education possible, even if it meant that they would become remote members of CRST, unable to contribute to the daily leadership and management of the NGO.

At the morning class break, I told Sompeas that Steve and Liz would like to have a chat with her. As the three of them stood at the end of the open corridor, I could see Liz getting a little emotional and

Sompeas cupping her hands, incredulously, in sincere gratitude. They stood there chatting for a while longer and as they returned to class, Sompeas cupped her hands in front of me.

'Thank you, Aviv, this is so unbelievable. Thank you for allowing me this opportunity. None of this would be possible without you and your family.'

'It's all you, Sompeas,' I replied. 'You're very special, a real diamond. We really love you and want to see you succeed in your life, and we know you could make a lot of impact in Cambodian society.'

Sompeas left Siem Reap at the end of that semester and moved to Phnom Penh. Four years later, she graduated with her Bachelor of Arts in Law degree from the American University of Phnom Penh. True to their word, Liz and Steve sponsored Sompeas to study her Juris Doctor degree in the United States, at the University of Arizona in Tucson.

### December 2022

*Sompeas is studying her Juris Doctor degree at the University of Arizona in the United States. This is her end-of-year reflection email to Liz and Steve, her generous sponsors, and us.*

Hello Steve, Liz, Aviv and Michelle,

I trust you are doing well.

The fall semester is finally over. I finished all my exams yesterday. Today and tomorrow will be packing days since I have an early flight back to Cambodia on Monday. I'm looking forward to seeing everyone at home for a month.

By far, this semester has been the highlight of law school here. I wrapped up this semester with a lot of good memories.

One of the things that I enjoyed the most this semester was working at the Veteran Advocacy Law Clinic. As I shared earlier this semester, I had the opportunity to represent veterans and active military members in the Tucson City Court. I worked directly with my clients and advocated on their behalf in front of the presiding judge. In addition,

I represented clients outside the courtroom on the benefits and discharge upgrades cases. I had an incredible experience in this clinic because I have incredible professors, whom I also consider my mentors.

The class is hybrid – in addition to classes, we represent clients in a typical firm setting. I was assigned to represent a veteran on a Purple Heart case after she was injured while deployed to Iraq. I was hands on with everything – from conducting legal research to organizing the meeting, meeting the client, drafting the mini-brief, and putting together the application. During the course of my representation, I exchanged ideas with my professors and the team. The feedback and the conversations I had with the professors were invaluable.

If you are interested to learn about my professor, her name is Kristine A Huskey. She was involved a lot in human rights cases before she became a professor. One of the major cases she took was when she volunteered to help defend Guantanamo detainees. I am so incredibly honored to have worked with her and learned so much from her.

In addition, I also had memorable experiences representing veteran defendants in the City Court. My first day on the court was nerve-racking. I worried that the judge would not be able to understand my accent. However, the judge, the prosecutor and everyone in the courtroom were so positive and supportive toward the new clinic's students.

After a few times appearing in front of the judge, I became confident, and I was able to competently advocate on behalf of my clients in front of the judge. On my last day, the judge handed me the Certificate of Appreciation for my professionalism. I am so honored to have had the opportunity to represent people who have fought and sacrificed for this country.

Aside from these experiences, everything went well this semester. A week before the final exam, Vatey's father's friend invited us to spend Thanksgiving with them in Chandler. They picked us up from Tucson and took us to Mount Lemmon before we left for Chandler. It was great to meet some Cambodian people there and eat food that we missed so much. I felt at home. We planned to do some fun activities; however, something came up and we did not end up doing much.

They also drove us back to Tucson, so we had a relaxing week before the final. When I came back and prepared for the final, my wisdom teeth hurt so badly. I had it [the pain] for about two years and thought I did not need to remove it, but it became worse in the last few weeks that I had to take Advil. So I plan to have it removed when I am in Cambodia. I wanted to have it removed here but the insurance does not cover it, so I thought it would be cheaper to wait until I go back to Cambodia.

As you are aware, next semester is my last semester in law school. I only have three classes, one of which is the Criminal Defense Clinic. I am most excited about this clinic because I will get to serve and represent indigent clients in the Pima County Public Defense Services at Pima County Superior Court. I talked to one of my friends who did this clinic a while back, and he said he had incredible experiences. He had a chance to do a trial at the Superior Court. I hope to also get the same experiences. I try to do different clinics hoping to explore different areas of law and get a sense of what I enjoy. I did enjoy my experiences with the Veteran Advocacy Law Clinic; however, I want to do something more challenging. I think this clinic will allow me to do so.

Because it is getting closer to my graduation, which will be May 13, 2023, I have been looking for jobs. I had a few interviews but did not make any of them. I am not losing any hope and will continue to apply. My plan is to work here on my F-1 visa for one year. I also wish to continue to stay if I get a sponsorship. Vatey decided to go back to Cambodia after the bar exam because her parents wanted her to go back. I have not decided where I want to settle after my graduation. I will decide when I land my job.

Unlike last time, I have some photos for you!! I am sorry I usually do not take a lot of photos. I got featured in the Law School Newsletter and a subscription newsletter for lawyers from my summer experiences. I'm also sharing these with you.

Finally, I am so thankful to Steve and Liz for allowing me to experience all of these incredible things.

Best,

Sompeas

## May 2023

*Sompeas graduated from her Juris Doctor degree at the University of Arizona in the United States. This is her email to us ahead of taking her Bar Exam.*

Hello Aviv and Michelle,

I trust you are doing well.

I am finally done with law school. Yeahhhhh!!!!!!! I wrapped up my last semester yesterday. Now I only have to worry about the bar exam, which is scheduled for July.

I keep saying this, but it feels like yesterday when I first came to the US. I was so worried about everything, the living, and the school. I think the mass shootings in the US last year were the most stressful time I ever felt living in the US. I became stressed and lost all my focus and desires. I made a decision at the time that I would not live in the US because I was scared. I thought about whether I would make it to the end. Thinking back, I think I almost made it. I have created good memories and made good friends here. There were times when I did feel the loss of the immediate support, acceptance, and presence of friends and family I have in Cambodia. As time passes and I settle into life in a new country, I find that friends step in to fill the gap. They help me adjust and adapt to new realities.

Besides all that, I am graduating this May 13. I am sure you are busy and will not be able to join. However, Steve and Liz are coming so that is all I am asking for. I am half excited just to be done with school and half worried about the bar exam. I have about two and a half months to treat it as a full-time job. After that, I am just excited to finally practice law.

Now my next goal is to pass the bar exam because all these job offers are on the condition of passing the bar exam.

My friends and I took some photos last week with our graduation gowns. I attached them below. I will send you more on the actual graduation so I can share this achievement with you.

Sending you lots of love,

Sompeas

*Sompeas passed her Bar Exam in Arizona in April 2024.*

## FOUNDATIONS OF LEADERSHIP TAKEAWAYS

- A primary function of leadership is to identify future leaders, support them and develop them.

- Provide the stepping stones, not the barriers.

- Set the rules, but remember that flexibility is a strength, not a weakness.

- Respect is not negotiable; give respect to earn respect.

- Develop your team by identifying what they need and supporting their development.

- Everyone has a dream; as you help others achieve their dream, they'll often help you achieve yours.

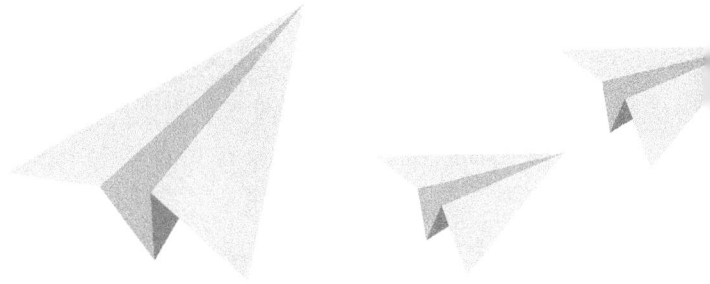

# Chapter 7

# The impact of an educational social enterprise

New ideas and projects were often discussed at our extended family Friday night dinners – when we sit down to eat, someone will often look in my direction and say, 'What new project are we going to hear about today?'

'Well,' I said on this occasion, 'we're thinking of starting up an educational social enterprise in Cambodia.'

'A what??' came back the reply.

'A small business, to teach our students how to run a business with all the profits remaining in the NGO, to fund more students. So current students will learn how to lead and manage a profitable business, and at the same time reinvest the profits in new students to grow the NGO.'

My brother Roni looked at me and said, 'And I suppose you already have some business in mind?'

'We're thinking of a self-serve frozen yogurt store – there are plenty of tourists, the weather is warm, and the business has relatively few "moving parts", so it will be easy to teach and manage,' I said.

'Do you know anything about self-serve frozen yogurt?' one of my nephews asked.

'Nope, but we're about to find out', I replied.

## Establishing contacts and setting up the basics

I mention David at the end of chapter 5. He was a board advisor to our family company, with a background in accounting and finance, and was well respected. He also had an enviable list of contacts. 'A yogurt shop? What do you want to open up a yogurt shop for??' he asked on the phone when I rang to pick his brain.

After a few moments hearing me out, he said, 'That's a bloody good idea – you need to speak with David W from Colombo Frozen Yogurt, he'll tell you all about yogurt. Here's his number and I'll call him to let him know to expect your call.'

A few days later, I met with David W and, sure enough, he knew all there was to know about frozen yogurt – and he opened all the doors we needed. Within a few weeks, I was in Brisbane to meet with Dirk, the CEO of Frosty Boy, the renowned Australian ice-cream brand that also made frozen yogurt powder. They were also a family-owned business, and Dirk *loved* what we were doing in Cambodia. He offered to sell us all our frozen yogurt powder and flavours at cost, as well as introduce us to their distributor in Cambodia, so they could assist with shipping and warehousing. He also introduced me to Allan, who was the founder and chairman of hospitality and catering equipment leasing company Silver Chef. Allan also loved what we were doing and offered us the four self-serve ice-cream machines we needed for the price of one.

We still needed to learn how to manage a frozen yogurt store, so we connected with Tim at Yozen, a self-serve frozen yogurt store not far from our home. He agreed to meet with us and, after hearing our plans, offered to teach us all we needed to know. Steph offered to volunteer at Yozen for three months to learn the business from store opening to store closing, and everything that happens in between – she ended up being such a valuable team member that Tim offered her a job, which she politely declined. She was off to Cambodia to train our team.

Jess and her husband Aaron worked on the concept store plans, looking at everything from traffic flow to colour scheme, lighting, fit-out, uniforms, signage and the name. We brainstormed some names and finally Jess said, 'Why don't we call it Project Y for now and then come back to the name later?'

Well, the name stuck and 'Project Y – Frozen Yogurt' was our first educational social enterprise.

## Getting our students involved

On my next visit to Cambodia I attended English class, as I did quite often when I was in town. I asked our teacher, Natasha, to finish a little earlier, so I could make an announcement. Our classes were held at Green School, a collection of open rooms, all at ground level, with exposed brick walls separating the classes, a whiteboard at the front and an open back, facing the students' motorcycle carpark. The rooms were covered with a tin roof and had rudimentary steel and wood desks – if we paid a little extra, we got electricity for the fluorescent lights and rickety small ceiling fans.

Our students loved Green School – it reminded them of their villages and it was the one hour in the day when the high school students and university students all got together. They also loved Natasha, who always made the classes fun by sometimes reading and learning from newspapers and at other times reading, learning and working through a story, in addition to following the pre-agreed curriculum.

At the end of the class, I stood in front of our students and said, 'I have some very exciting news for you, everyone! We're planning to open a small business here in Siem Reap, so we can mentor you to lead and manage a profitable business, and provide you with hands-on practical business experience!'

The class exploded into cheers and claps, which had the students in the neighbouring classes leaning in to see what the commotion was about. Of course, our students all wanted to know what the business was going to be.

'Your homework for tonight is to think of a good business for Siem Reap – if you had the opportunity to open your own business, what business would it be? Now, keep in mind that you have no business experience, so don't make it too complicated, right? Keep it simple, so you can learn and have fun, and inspire others. I'll see you all tomorrow and you can share your ideas with me.'

They all streamed out of the class chirping about this amazing opportunity and how they would come up with the best idea, so their idea would be chosen.

The next day the whole English class was dedicated to our new project. I started by explaining what an educational social enterprise was, how it might work, and who would benefit and how. I then asked the students to share their homework, 'Okay, so what ideas have you come up with for our potential business?'

That was a little like asking rural Cambodian students what they would like to be when they grow up – almost everyone would say they'd like to be a teacher, policeman or doctor, because these were the only steady professions they knew. No-one ever said they'd like to be an engineer, a physiotherapist or a computer programmer – most likely, they have never even heard of those job opportunities.

The ideas our students shared were the ones they knew – Khmer restaurant, vegetarian restaurant, Western restaurant, pizza restaurant, guest house, foot-massage shop, tour company, market stall.

I then asked them if they've heard of a frozen yogurt store. 'It's a little bit like ice cream from a machine, but frozen yogurt is a little healthier,' I explained.

I then showed everyone photos of self-serve frozen yogurt stores in the United States and Australia, as well as the concept drawings and marketing material Jess and Aaron had prepared. Everyone clamoured around the A3 sheets and the excitement was palpable.

When everyone calmed down a little, I asked them to open their notebooks and the real lesson began.

'If we're going to have a business, a shop which sells self-serve frozen yogurt, what will we need?' I asked.

Silence.

'Nak, what will you need when you open your business?' I asked.

'Well, Aviv, I will need a shop,' Nak replied.

'Great,' I said and wrote 'shop' on the whiteboard. 'What else?' I asked.

'Oh, we will need the yogurt to sell, and the people to sell it,' Nak replied.

'Yes!' I said, adding these two points to the list on the whiteboard.

'We will need money, so we can operate,' Sreng added.

'And we will need marketing to tell people that we are an NGO shop,' Doeb contributed.

By the end of the class, we had an outline of the basics:

- A soft-serve frozen yogurt store has the potential of being highly profitable because the raw material costs were low and the margins were high.
- The product was easy to make and easy to sell by providing free samples.
- The business model was simple and could be managed through six business departments – sales, marketing, production, operations, finance and human resources.
- Each member of the team would have a job description, job processes, reporting procedures, key performance indicators (KPIs) and regular reviews so they can correct and continue.
- The organisational structure would have a general manager, an assistant general manager, department managers and team members.
- CRST university students would have the opportunity of joining the Project Y team, being trained for a specific role, working in

the role for six months, training the next team, and then rotating to another role in another department. This would enable everyone to learn and experience sales, marketing, production, operations, finance and human resources, in preparation for getting a job after graduation.

- We would 'sell the sizzle, *and* the steak' – promote that Project Y is an educational social enterprise, with the store's profits remaining in the NGO to sponsor more students' education, while also allowing our guests to enjoy world-class frozen yogurt from Australia.

'Now we need to work out who our competitors are and where to store our raw materials. Does anyone know a self-serve frozen yogurt store in Siem Reap?' I asked.

Of course no-one did, because the two frozen yogurt stores in Siem Reap were new and unremarkable.

'I've done some research and I know Phnom Penh has a few frozen yogurt stores. If we go to Phnom Penh, we can also meet with a company that has a large food warehouse where we can store our materials, and another company that may help us to fit out the store,' I said.

Everyone moved back to excitement-mode – none of our students had ever been to Cambodia's capital, Phnom Penh. It was about seven hours by bus or an hour's flight away, yet it felt to them like a whole other world.

'I'm going to suggest that two of you fly with me to Phnom Penh to evaluate our potential competitors and have the business meetings,' I said, as the students started clapping and screaming with excitement.

'The opportunity will be open to all of you. We're going to have a little competition – your homework for tonight is optional. If you'd like to have the opportunity of flying with me to Phnom Penh, you'll need to write a compelling business case for the owner of the food distribution warehouse, explaining why we would like him to allow us to store our materials in his warehouse for free. You just need to tell him who we are, what we are doing, why we would like his assistance and what social benefits he will be helping us achieve,' I said.

The students wrote their homework in their notebooks and filed excitedly out of the class.

The next day some students eagerly handed in their homework and we spent the class reviewing their work.

By the end of the class, I asked Doeb, Nak and Sreng to come forward. 'I think these are the three finalists, does everyone agree?' I asked. Everyone clapped excitedly.

I turned to the three students and said, 'I have a proposition for you, and you can think about it and let me know tomorrow. As I said yesterday, two of you will have the opportunity to fly with me to Phnom Penh to evaluate our potential competitors and have our business meetings. But now there are three of you. So you can decide between yourselves – would you like me to select two to travel with me and one of you will miss out; or would you prefer that the three of you take the bus to Phnom Penh and then all three of you will fly back from Phnom Penh with me?'

Without hesitation they all said, almost in unison, 'The three of us.'

## Research and meetings in the big city

I walked into the Eric Kayser Patisserie at the White Mansion Hotel in Phnom Penh, and there they were – Doeb, Nak and Sreng, wearing their best shirts and pants, clean black shoes, perfect hair and big smiles.

'Good morning team,' I beamed.

They stood up to greet me and we exchanged pleasantries. They were so excited that they hadn't slept very much on the night bus from Siem Reap. They arrived early in the morning and checked into their guest house, took a shower and came to meet me for breakfast.

The White Mansion Hotel is the former residence of the US Ambassador in Phnom Penh. It's an imposing French colonial mansion with tall ceilings and elegant public areas that was turned into a boutique hotel. At the front of the building was an excellent French patisserie that was very popular with young Khmer professionals. I knew our students would love seeing this new generation enjoy the benefits of a good income and a good environment.

'I love this place,' Nak said as he looked around. 'We don't have anything like this in Siem Reap'.

'Well, if it's in Phnom Penh, I'm sure it will come to Siem Reap when the time is right. The important thing is that you can see the new Cambodia – a Cambodia you haven't seen before. These couple of days will open your minds to what's already available in Cambodia and what's possible,' I replied.

I explained that the economies of Siem Reap and Phnom Penh were very different. Siem Reap was a large country town servicing the nearby countryside and the Angkor Wat tourism trade. Phnom Penh, on the other hand, was the commercial and government centre of Cambodia – its businesses were supported by steady commerce and government jobs, not low-income farmers and unpredictable tourism. That's why more wealth was in Phnom Penh, along with more people, more jobs, more opportunities – more of everything.

After breakfast, we hopped in a tuktuk and drove to Phnom Penh's riverfront, the three students in awe of the dense urbanisation, intense traffic and tall buildings. Everywhere they looked were people, motorbikes, tuktuks, cars – so many cars, and fancy cars at that. Oh, they knew their fancy cars – 'There's a Rolls Royce, no it's a Bentley', 'There's a Porsche and a Lamborghini'. Yeah, a lot of money was in Phnom Penh.

We strolled along the riverfront and I explained the variety of ways to research the market, from the internet to referrals and by simply asking around. I explained that when entering a store, any store, we had to engage our senses – what did we see, smell, hear, taste and touch? The best retailers in the world understand they need to engage all your senses – providing what's called 'the retail experience'. If your eyes are happy with what they see, your nose is happy with the scent, your ears with the sound, your mouth with the taste and your hands with the products or surfaces you can touch, I explained, you were more likely to stay longer, spend more and return more frequently. You were also more likely to share your experience with your family and friends. That meant more business, more customers and more profits.

I gave an example of a store that used natural wood panelling, slim black tables and trendy white chairs, all really appealing to the eye, calm and inviting. Or a store that baked bread and brewed coffee, so the scent could circulate in the store, a store that played trendy music loud enough so you could hear it but soft enough so you could talk with your friends, or a store that had really tasty pastries that were flaky in your hands and melted in your mouth.

'Do you know any store like that?' I asked.

They all giggled and said no store was like that in Siem Reap.

'Right,' I confirmed. 'And now think back to how much you enjoyed having breakfast at the Eric Kayser Patisserie this morning. What was special about it?'

The penny dropped.

The Eric Kayser chain had nailed the art of engaging the five senses – and that was one reason they were very successful in attracting and retaining customers.

'Now start to imagine how we will engage the five senses in our Project Y store, and as we visit other frozen yogurt stores, pay attention to what they do well and what they don't,' I said.

We visited four frozen yogurt stores in Phnom Penh and none of them left a lasting impression on us. They looked drab, had uncomfortable seating, dull signage, unhappy-looking team members and, above all, not very flavoursome frozen yogurt. One store advertised six flavours but, although they all had different colours, they all tasted the same.

Our meeting with CY and Dickson at the food distribution warehouse we wanted to use went really well and they agreed to allow us to store the yogurt powder at their warehouse for free – we would only need to pay the freight to Siem Reap. CY also introduced me to Dan, who agreed to assist us in renovating our store when we found the right location.

We had time to visit several shopping malls, go up and down the malls' escalators several times ('What an incredible invention!') and visit countless stores as we learned the basics of successful business models. 'Good business people make money, ordinary business people make a living, and bad business people make debts,' I told them. 'We must be good business people.'

After two busy days, it was time to head to the airport – that mysterious place our students had only ever seen from outside the front of the terminal. They were very nervous and very excited as we walked up to the check-in counter with our carry-on bags and handed over our ID cards.

'Hi, we're flying to Siem Reap today,' I said to the agent. She instantly understood this was the students' first flight and chatted to them in Khmer as they replied shyly, giggling. They ended up being happy to check in their carry-on bags – they wanted the full experience. The agent put the luggage tag on the first bag, pushed the button and the bag moved down the conveyor belt and out of sight.

'Where are they taking my bag?' Doeb asked me with sincere concern in his voice. I explained that the bag will meet him in Siem Reap.

'How will they know where to take my bag? How do they know I'm going to Siem Reap?' he asked anxiously as I explained the mechanics of the airport baggage system.

'Are you sure?' he asked me.

We received our boarding passes and the luggage receipts and proceeded up the escalator to the departure level.

Next was the security checkpoint, and an explanation of why it was needed, what the equipment was and how we made our way through it. And, finally, was the boarding process. We made sure we were the first on the plane, so Doeb, Nak and Sreng could experience it for as long as possible. I explained about the seat numbering system, seatbelts, the tray table and the safety card. After take-off each student visited the toilet to see how that works, as well as the galley. They had lots of questions, I took some photos and before we knew it, we'd landed in Siem Reap.

'That was so quick!' Sreng said.

'Much quicker than the bus,' I replied. 'This was your first flight, but I'm sure it won't be your last!'

We walked down the stairs from the plane at Siem Reap's little airport, took some more photos in front of the plane, and then proceeded to the terminal building. We all watched through the large windows as their bags came down the conveyor belt from the plane, on to the baggage trolleys to be towed to the terminal building, and then on to the luggage carousel.

'Wow, that's a great system!' Sreng exclaimed with a broad smile.

## Securing a location

A couple of days later Nak, Sreng and I had dinner with Keara, our students' university Director, to discuss our students' progress and provide some feedback. By now we had over 20 students at the university and had developed a mutually beneficial relationship to ensure our students were able to respectfully express grievances and concerns and be assured they would be addressed.

Keara loved the fluffy bread rolls at Tell Steakhouse, so that was our usual dinner venue when we caught up.

'Thank you for giving permission for the students to skip two days of university and join me in Phnom Penh,' I said.

'I'm sure they learned a lot from you,' Keara responded as Nak and Sreng nodded their heads in agreement.

We discussed our plans for the frozen yogurt educational social enterprise and Keara loved them. He was thrilled about the concept of the store and the prospect of his students getting hands-on business mentoring and experience.

'When will you do this, Aviv? Is it soon?' Keara asked.

'As soon as we find the right location,' I replied. 'Ideally, we want to be in the Night Market, because that's where the tourists go.'

'You're right, Aviv, that's the right area. After dinner, let's go for a walk and take a look, okay?' Keara said excitedly.

We left the restaurant and turned right towards the Night Market, which was just 100 metres down the road. Scores of tourists were milling around looking at the plethora of stores and stalls, interspersed with foot-massage businesses, open-air shops and food stalls. Music from a variety of sources and the scents from the numerous food stalls filled the senses. The atmosphere was happy and relaxed as Western tourists haggled over pairs of $5 Ray-Bans, $6 fisherman pants and $4 T-shirts.

We walked up to a shuttered store with a small black and white sign on the metal shutters.

'This store is for rent!' Keara exclaimed. 'Let me take a photo of the phone number and I'll ring the owner for you tomorrow.'

'No, we can't take this store,' Sreng said. 'Look.' He pointed to the store next door. Just our luck, it was a Snow Yogurt frozen yogurt store, just like one of the stores we'd visited in Phnom Penh.

'Oh, that's interesting,' I said with a smile on my face. 'Should we try some?'

The yogurt tasted just as bad as at the Phnom Penh store.

'So why do you think we can't take that store?' I asked Sreng.

'Well, a competitor is here already. We'll need to find somewhere else,' he replied.

'No, I don't think so, Sreng. With a competitor next door, we just need to be better. Our store has to look better and smell better; we need to have great music, a vibrant team and the best-tasting yogurt. Simple, right?' I replied. He still looked sceptical.

The location in the Night Market was great – close to the main road most pedestrians used to enter and leave. The store had a wide frontage and a second floor for possible seating; the building looked run-down, but nothing some paint couldn't fix. We walked up and down the street a few times and were convinced this could be the home of our first educational social enterprise.

Keara was true to his word and the next day arranged to meet with the owner at the coffee shop of the Hotel de la Paix, one of the fanciest hotels in town. Nak, Sreng and I were sitting outside the coffee shop as Keara waited for the owner to arrive. An elegant Khmer woman entered shortly after, and we could hear Keara's jolly voice and laughter as they conversed.

About 15 minutes later he came out to see us. He had a big smile on his face as he explained that the store's owners were the parents of one of his students at the university. He asked us to join them and within 10 minutes we had the heads-of agreement on a multi-year lease!

It was a whirlwind trip with a great outcome. I sat in the tuktuk on the way to the airport to fly back home, with Doeb, Nak and Sreng accompanying me to the airport.

'Sreng, how would you like to be the first general manager of Project Y?' I asked. He was shocked.

'Me?' he asked as he laughed nervously. 'Noooo, I have no experience, I don't know what to do.'

'No-one has experience, Sreng, we'll teach you what to do. That's why this is an *educational* social enterprise, right?' I replied.

'You can do it, Sreng,' Nak pitched in. He was a true leader and wanted the best for everyone. 'I didn't know anything about managing an NGO and Aviv taught me what to do. We'll all help you – you'll be a great Project Y GM!!'

By the time we arrived at the airport, Sreng had accepted the role and was ready for the adventure that would help shape his life.

## Getting everything ready

Jess and Aaron completed the store plan, and our friend Tony advised us on how to plan the small kitchen to be able to maximise its use. Dan (who was assisting us with the renovation) came from Phnom Penh to Siem Reap to see the store and estimate costs. Over the next few months, we gutted and rebuilt the store with four street-facing self-serve yogurt machines, each with two heads, so we could serve eight flavours.

When the store was fully renovated, we flew some of our Australian team members to Siem Reap to train our Cambodian Project Y team. Damian, our CFO at Lifestyle Brands, and Aaron ran workshops on the point-of-sale system we used, handling cash, banking, reporting and human-resource management including rostering and payroll. MJ, our national sales manager, ran workshops on how to approach people, 'break the ice', make connections, and 'sell the sizzle *and* the steak'.

The second floor of the store became our classroom, with a wall-sized whiteboard, colourful inspirational quotes along another wall and colourful cafe chairs. It was a fresh, young and dynamic space we could use for group lessons during the day and our customers could use as a social space to eat their frozen yogurt at night.

Steph trained the team on yogurt production and store operations, while Michelle and Jess led sessions about our products, marketing and public image. We arranged colourful polo shirts for our team, tuktuk signs promoting 'Project Y – Frozen Yogurt' and, of course, our colourful and distinctive storefront stood out in the Night Market like a beacon of light.

Our two weeks of training were intensive, with the students attending our workshops and their university studies during the day, and the store's 'soft opening' in the evenings. (A soft opening is where you open your business to allow the team to gain hands-on experience while being trained, prior to an official opening.) All students were on hand as we practised what we learned with Damian, MJ, Steph, Michelle, Jess, Aaron and me leading by example and backing up the team as they gained confidence and took on the management of the store.

## Taking time to celebrate

I often think that we don't celebrate enough of our successes; we're too busy looking through the front windscreen for better ways to add value, instead of the rear-view mirror to see what we have accomplished. I always acknowledge the birthdays of our team members at work and didn't want CRST and Project Y to be any different. Amid the intense two-week training before we opened fully, we took time out to celebrate.

'Are you ready?' I yelled out to MJ from downstairs. 'Yes, we are!' she yelled back. I walked up the stairs with the birthday cake, candles flickering as I did my best to move slowly enough to ensure they didn't blow out.

'Happy birthday to you, happy birthday to you, happy birthday dear Veun, happy birthday to you!!' we sang as I reached the top of the stairs. 'Hip hip hooray, hip hip hooray, hip hip hooray!!' Everyone was laughing and clapping – 'Happy birthday Veun!!' I said, handing him his birthday cake. Veun's eyes welled up, 'I've never had a birthday cake, Aviv,' he told me.

'Well, let this be the first of many more for the rest of your life, Veun,' I replied. 'You are the most important person in the world, Veun, and the day of your birth is an important day to celebrate! We *love* birthdays in our family and now that you are a member of our NGO family, we love to celebrate you!!'

MJ told Veun that he could make a special wish as he blew out the candles on his cake, and he closed his eyes tight as he blew out the candles on the first birthday cake of his 22 years of life. Everyone yelled out in delight and Veun proceeded to cut the cake and distribute it to everyone. 'Where's your piece?' MJ asked him when he was done.

'Oh, there isn't any left – I shared it to everyone,' he replied. And that sums up the special young adult we have all grown to love and respect so much – Veun gave away every piece of his own birthday cake, his first-ever birthday cake. It was my turn to well up as I couldn't even begin to pretend to comprehend his selfless act of generosity and open-heartedness.

'No, no, no, that's not what you do!' MJ retorted as she laughed. 'You take the FIRST piece, the BIGGEST piece – it's YOUR birthday!!' she continued, before asking the students who had the biggest piece. Well, by that stage, all the students had left was the thick layer of icing, and Veun was delighted to taste the icing on his first-ever birthday cake.

## Opening day – with a very special guest

Our two weeks of training and soft openings flew by and it was soon time for the official opening of our Project Y store. Keara introduced me to the Governor of Siem Reap Province and we invited him to join our official opening, along with other dignitaries and the traditional blessings by the monks. It was a pretty significant event and the whole street in front of the store was closed for a few hours, with police redirecting traffic as we hosted about 200 guests, including all our students and some of their families.

'No, she won't come, Aviv. I've asked her many times over the past few weeks,' Sreng replied to me when I asked him whether his mum would be coming to our official opening.

'I've tried too, Aviv,' Sompeas added. 'She said she won't join and I couldn't convince her.' Sreng and Sompeas (who I talk about in chapter 6) were two of our bright stars, siblings who had a separated upbringing for much of their childhood.

'Why not?' I asked. 'Is she unwell?'

'She said she doesn't want to leave home,' Sreng replied.

'That's ridiculous, Sreng – your mum isn't housebound,' I replied.

'No, she's too afraid to come here, with so many important people. And she's afraid to meet you – you know, you are so important to my family,' Sreng said.

'Well, tell your mum that I'm as normal as she is and I'm not at all important – it's important she will be here so she can see how incredible her kids are!' I replied.

Sompeas laughed. 'She won't come, Aviv. She's really not comfortable with being so close to the Governor and all the other officials who will be here.'

'Well, they are people just like her, just like you and me, right? Those people shouldn't stop a mother's pride in seeing her kids shine. *Nothing* should come in the way of rewarding a mother's love and her hard labour over many years – she *needs* to see your success; *that* is her reward,' I said emphatically. Sreng and Sompeas remained silent. I knew they had done their best, but respect prevented them from trying to convince their mum, countering her perspective.

'I'll make it easy for you,' I said. 'Tell your mum that Michelle and I will be at your home tomorrow morning at 8 am with a tuktuk to pick her up to join us for the Grand Opening. She will sit in the front row with us, she will be a member of our family and we will honour her and respect her. We won't leave her alone; she will be with us all the time.'

Sreng and Sompeas didn't know what to say. 'You don't have to give me an answer. Michelle and I will be at your home at 8 am tomorrow,' I told them, leaving no room for discussion.

After they walked away, Michelle approached me. 'You were a little rough on them, don't you think?' she asked.

'No, I certainly wasn't,' I replied. 'Their mum *needs* to be here. She *deserves* to be here. It's our job to *lead and support*, not capitulate to irrational fear. This Grand Opening is as much her celebration as it is ours. We will be there to collect her tomorrow morning and we will *not* deny her the opportunity of seeing what incredible kids she has raised!'

Michelle seemed satisfied with that, but we didn't have to collect Mrs Sokh the next morning. Sreng contacted us that night to say that after Sompeas and he told their mum that Michelle and I would come to collect her in the morning, she agreed to join. She would arrive with them, so no need for us to collect her.

The next morning Mrs Sokh sat in the front row, in awe of Sompeas and Sreng who led our Grand Opening ceremony. She was very emotional as she watched her kids welcome the Deputy Governor of Siem Reap Province, who represented the Governor, and other government officials, and deliver speeches in Khmer and

English. We asked her to come to the stage to receive a gift from us, as a representative of all our students' parents, expressing our gratitude for always supporting their children to receive the education that was changing their lives, their society and their country.

Mrs Sokh was grateful and humbled, and deeply moved at seeing Sompeas and Sreng being given the respect and appreciation they deserved. That day, she experienced the empowerment of education and the opportunities it provided. She was finally rewarded for her many years of determined struggle, fighting economic hardship and social stigmas as she took on jobs from fisherwoman to market seller and recycled-rubbish collector, all just to keep putting food on the table and support her children's education.

## Building on success

Over the next few years, Project Y became the heart of our NGO in so many ways. Our students met thousands of people from all over the world, sharing the inspiration of an NGO that is entirely led and managed by the students themselves. We invited scores of disadvantaged students from other NGOs to join us for free frozen yogurt parties, adding rays of sunshine to their lives. We celebrated Khmer New Year, International Women's Day, football World Cup finals, movie nights, Christmas, New Year's Eve countdowns and countless other occasions.

The Project Y educational social enterprise laid the foundation for so many of our students' future careers as they received hands-on opportunities to gain practical knowledge and discover their strengths and passions. Supplementing their theoretical university studies, they had the opportunities to practise leadership, management, effective communication, finance, operations, sales and marketing during their university years. Project Y became the incubator for many of our students, who went on to incredible new opportunities when they graduated from university:

- Yeat, our best sales person at Project Y, graduated with an MBA from the National University of Management and led a team of ten sales professionals, making thousands of dollars a month in real-estate sales.

- Samach, our first finance manager at Project Y, graduated with her master's degree in banking and finance and has a high-powered, high-paying job in a large private company.
- Doeb, our first assistant general manager, is about to commence his master of laws degree and is the CRST mentor-in-residence and Executive Director in Siem Reap.
- Nak, our second general manager at Project Y, graduated with an MBA from PUC and runs his own real-estate sales company in Phnom Penh.
- Sompeas passed the Bar Exam in Arizona after graduating with her Juris Doctor law degree from the University of Arizona.
- Sreng, our first Project Y general manager (accepting the role on that fateful tuktuk ride to the airport), graduated with an MBA from the American University of Phnom Penh and was poached by the Ministry of Economy and Finance, after working at KPMG Cambodia as a senior IT auditor.

Keara continued to be one of our biggest fans, teaching about Project Y in his entrepreneurship classes at university and leading regular class field trips to teach what we did, how and why.

Project Y was followed by more projects, each designed to address a social need by providing education and sustainable solutions. Fortunately the English alphabet has 26 letters for us to move through! Here's what we're up to so far:

- Project G – Empowering Girls (2018)
- Project V – The Volunteer Experience (2018)
- Project B – Bicycles for Education (2018)
- Project R – Refuse, Reduce, Reuse and Recycle Plastic Education Program (2019)
- Project W – WASH for Education (2020)
- Project L – Light for Education (2022)
- Project T – Trees for Life (2023)

To date, we have reached over 80,000 rural Cambodians through our projects.

In April 2020, almost five years after its opening, Project Y became a casualty of COVID-19. As 'isolation', 'social distancing' and 'lockdowns' entered our daily vocabularies, the tourism industry in Cambodia came to a complete standstill. With no tourists and no sales, we shuttered the store and ultimately vacated our incredible incubator, ending an era of experiential learning that produced some of the finest students we've ever had.

When the tourists return and the time is right, we plan to restart the engine of our entrepreneurial educational social enterprise. It may not be a frozen yogurt store, but we are determined that it will be just as empowering and impactful.

## FOUNDATIONS OF LEADERSHIP TAKEAWAYS

- No-one knows everything – get an education and don't be afraid to ask questions.

- Share your vision, don't sell your dream – sharing your vision is much more empowering for the team.

- Lead the team to reach conclusions; don't conclude for them.

- Stretch the team and play to each team member's strengths.

- The competition is here to make you better than they are.

- Identify or create a need for your product or service, and then work on your uniqueness.

- Be memorable – sell the sizzle and the steak.

# Chapter 8

# Don't let others hijack all you can become

Every now and then we lose a student before they graduate from their bachelor degree – they leave the embrace of our NGO family and rejoin the big wide world to chase whatever they think they're missing out on. 'The grass is greener on the other side' syndrome is universal. Sometimes it's freedom, other times it's money, a relationship or the allure of a great opportunity, which inevitably crashes and burns.

Our leavers have all survived, but few have thrived.

We make it clear to our students that CRST is a one-way door – if you leave, you can't return, so think very carefully and ask for help before you lock yourself out of the house.

Sokey and Visith, for example, left to get work – they became unqualified teachers and earned about $80 a month. While that was more than the $60 NGO monthly allowance offered at the time, they gained no new knowledge through participation in NGO leadership roles. They, of course, continued to live happy and fulfilling lives. As Visith said some years later, even though he left CRST early, the learnings he received with the NGO have made him stronger and more successful. Kakada and Tok also left to get jobs – they were already further in to their bachelor degrees, however, and had some experience at Project Y, so they had more knowledge and experience and were able to earn $250 a month working in tourism and retail. They also understood the power of education and continued to fund their studies themselves to graduate with their bachelor degrees a few years later.

## Understanding the return on education

We teach our students that their real value is only going to become apparent when they graduate from the NGO and university. At the bottom of the earning pyramid are the masses – the farmers and labourers who earn the least because there are so many of them and they require minimal skills. The next level in the earning pyramid are the high school dropouts, who have a little more knowledge so they can do a little more. Then come the high school graduates, followed by the university bachelor degree graduates from the low-level universities, the bachelor degree graduates from high-level universities, the quality university graduates with experience, the master's degree students and the master's degree graduates with experience.

As farmers and labourers, our students' parents earn $150 to $200 per month, while their siblings who graduated from high school can earn $200 to $250 per month. When graduating from Pannasastra University of Cambodia (PUC), and after a few years' experience leading and managing the NGO and our projects, our students enter the job market at $450 to $600 per month. Within two to three years, while working and studying for their master's degrees or second degrees, they earn $600 to $1200 per month. (This is also shown in the following figure.) And that is the essence of CRST – educating future leaders means investing up-front, for a reward that will last the rest of our students' lives.

TOP MANAGEMENT

MANAGEMENT

CRST GRADUATES' AVERAGE MONTHLY INCOME AFTER 2 YEARS $916 [OVER 4X THEIR FAMILY'S INCOME!!]

ADMINISTRATION

CRST GRADUATES' AVERAGE MONTHLY INCOME $651 [OVER 3X THEIR FAMILY'S INCOME!!]

HOSPITALITY

MINIMUM WAGE
FARMING

CRST STUDENTS' FAMILIES' AVERAGE MONTHLY INCOME $200

$150  $200  $300  $500  $1,000  $1,500

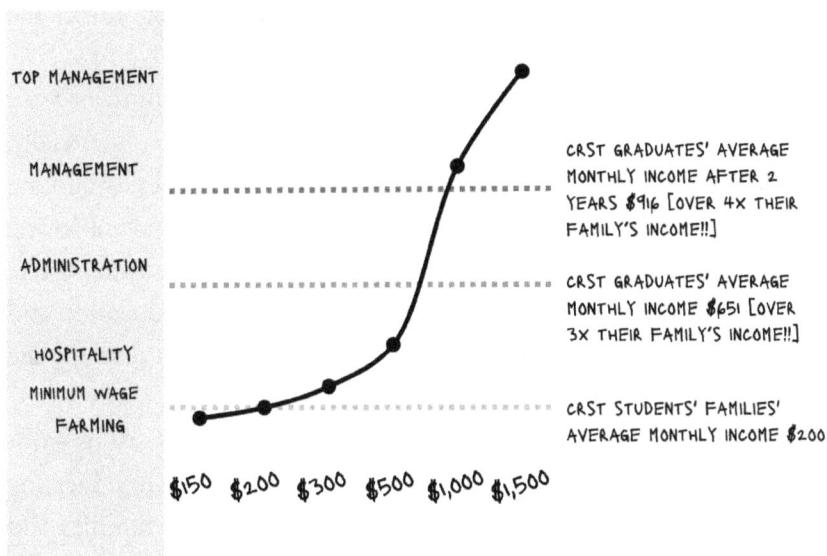

The lifetime value of our NGO's work is a social game-changer. Earning $200 a month over a span of 30 years, without inflationary adjustments, our students' farmer parents can earn about $72,000. At the base of the employment pyramid, supply outstrips demand and wages will always remain low. We estimate that over a 30-year career, scaling the employment pyramid with just a 10 per cent annual pay increase on a starting monthly salary of $600, a CRST graduate will earn $1,184,357 over their lifetime!

When we change a family's earnings by over 16 times, the social ripple effect is far and wide. Society evolves and develops, creating opportunities that lead to evolution, development and more opportunities. All that's needed is vision, commitment, passion – and trust. (Okay, and money, as I noted in chapter 5.) When you're an 18- or 22-year-old CRST student and we tell you that you will change your family's life through your education, you need to trust us. Our students currently earn a $120 NGO base allowance. They have plenty to eat, clean water on tap, share a comfortable room in town with a toilet and a shower, and study in air-conditioned classrooms. How do you reconcile that with your parents living in a hut, showering out of a bucket with a ladle, defecating in a field, working all day under the scorching sun just to earn enough so they could eat?

And then you see your cousin earning $200 per month or your friends earning $300 – they're helping their parents financially, have money in their pockets, have girlfriends or boyfriends and are planning to get married and start a family. But you have a loving NGO family teaching you that you're not missing out on life, you're just on a different track. First, enrich yourself through education and empowerment, and then enrich your life and those you love for the rest of your life!

I can't describe the humility I feel when our students trust us – nor the responsibility we carry to deliver on that trust. We're educating 100 of Cambodia's future leaders – our students, their families and their communities all depend on us delivering on our commitment to educate and empower them, teaching them the values of quality education and social leadership.

## Providing some extra help

Despite our dedication to our NGO family, every now and then a student succumbs to financial or social pressures and leaves our embrace. Such was the case with Veun.

Veun was a first generation student who moved from Savong School to study in Siem Reap. After graduating from New York International School, he started at Build Bright University and switched to PUC. He was doing well in the NGO too, holding the important role of our community service manager – he was loved, admired and respected by everyone who met him. However, his easy-going nature, warm smile and empathy made him easy prey – and his education also made him a good catch. She was the cashier at some establishment, they struck a conversation, they met a couple more times – and the fish was hooked. That's all it takes in Cambodia – even if you just have a healthy boyfriend–girlfriend relationship, you are expected to marry that person. It was difficult for us to understand that 'you touch, you buy' cultural expectation, but a few years later we developed CRST's Healthy Relationship policy, to protect our students. NGO students now have clear guidelines – see everyone in the NGO as your brothers and sisters and no boyfriend–girlfriend relationships at all are permitted until the second year of your bachelor's degree; these requirements may sound draconian, but they are loved by our students because they remove social and peer pressure.

Back to Veun, who advised us that he needed to leave the NGO. 'Of course I don't want to leave – everyone is my family – but I have no choice,' he said almost in tears. He had to leave because he needed to marry the girl, so he needed to get a job. He was crushed – the life force seemed drained out of his eyes.

I asked him if we could help with anything – could we speak with her or her family and explain how important his education was to him, to his family, and to his future? Veun was so mature as he explained to me that he didn't love her, but he had to own the relationship – he hardly even knew her, but now her parents demanded he marry her. Their honour and her honour were paramount – his life was collateral damage. He had no choice but to leave the NGO partway through his bachelor degree.

We kept in touch regularly with Veun through the other first generation students, who were all his friends. A year or so later, I heard that things weren't going so well for Veun and the woman he was saving money to marry. He had a job, but needed to borrow $3000 more, just for the wedding. I met him on my next trip to Siem Reap – and I instantly remembered why we loved him so much. He was stressed, but still his warm, genuine and loving self. I asked him how things were going.

'I don't see her very much – she moved back to live with her parents and I work seven days a week and sleep either in my hometown, or with some of our students here in town. I give her almost all my salary, but she's still not happy – she wants more money and she wants to marry now. I told her we need to save more,' he said shamefaced.

My heart went out to him – in Australia few 23 year olds would have to go through this futile anxiety just because they followed their natural instincts, which were welcomed and encouraged by a consenting partner. They hardly knew each other, were not in love and had very little in common. But this was not Australia and my position was not to provide cultural advice – I was here to support, not agitate.

'Veun, if there is anything at all we can do to help you, please let me know. I'm not judging you, or your relationship or your culture – tell me if there is something we can do to help.'

Surprisingly, he didn't just say no – he actually started thinking of something, but he wasn't sure he could say it.

'You can tell me anything, Veun – I love you. I'll walk this journey with you as much as you'll let me,' I said.

He told me that he told her that he doesn't love her and he knows she liked him because she thought he would make a good husband and, based on his education, he would earn a lot of money. But that wasn't enough for him and if she forced him to marry her, he would divorce her and leave as soon as he could. She was extremely angry and didn't speak with him often, while her parents kept pushing him for a wedding date. Finally, the two of them decided to see a senior monk, who found a way for the two of them to separate while preserving her honour – she wasn't happy about it and her parents were furious. Veun saw this as his opportunity for an exit – if the monk said it was acceptable, that was the answer to violating the cultural norm. He told her that's what they would do and she reluctantly agreed, if he gave her more money.

I asked him what he thought he might do next and he said, 'I'd love to come back to CRST after I made such a big mistake, but I know I can't do that. I know we have a one-way door policy and I'm out. I'll continue working, pay her the money she asked for and after that I will register at a lower university and finish my degree.'

'No, Veun,' I said. 'You won't do that. You'll come back to CRST and our NGO family will welcome you as a returning brother – you will resume your studies at PUC and we will increase your allowance so you can have enough money to pay that woman what you promised. In return, you will study well, continue to be a leader in the NGO and teach others to learn from your mistake.' For Veun, in these circumstances, we were willing to make an exception to our strict policy.

His eyes welled up.

'Really? You will let me come back home??' And he stood-up and gave me a warm hug.

His return to the NGO was triumphant – he settled back in to his studies and exuded maturity beyond his years. His combination of heart and head enabled him to become a beloved and impactful mentor to many of our students.

## Letting our students do the talking

Before heading to Cambodia on one of our trips, Michelle, Jess, Steph and I were discussing how humbling it was that our sponsor base was growing – people who heard about what we're doing wanted to know more, and would often end up sponsoring a student or helping to build a house for a poor rural family. I said to the girls that while we could tell the NGO story pretty well, it would be even more powerful if our students could share their perspectives – where they've come from, where they are today, and what their aspirations were.

'That's a great idea, but they're in Cambodia and we need to tell our story in Australia.' Jess expressed what they were all thinking.

'So we'll bring them to Australia!' I said.

That was the beginning of our Ambassador Program, which has upskilled many of our students to experience life outside Cambodia, as they share their life stories and inspire more supporters to join our journey.

## Finding our first ambassadors

A few weeks later, we gathered eight students, including Veun, at the Gloria Jeans Café in Siem Reap. The students had never been to this 'fancy' coffee shop and felt very special and excited. Everyone stood at the counter gazing at the overhead drinks menu – and when we said they could also select a cake or a biscuit from the display, they politely declined. We ordered some to share anyway.

We gathered some armchairs around a coffee table and I asked the students what they thought of the decoration of the Gloria Jeans Café, which had a raw concrete floor, industrial-urban furniture and trendy light fixtures. They thought it was cool and modern and they liked it; it was different from what they were used to.

'Well, we're glad you like it, because some of you may see more stores like this when you come to Australia,' I said.

They looked at each other as if they had misunderstood what I'd said.

'You heard me right,' I said with a big smile on my face. 'We brought you to a Western coffee shop to let you know that we've decided to launch a new NGO program. We're calling it the Ambassador Program and we hand-picked the eight of you as the possible first CRST Ambassadors to travel overseas and share your story and the work we do in the NGO. And when you do your job well and connect with people, we're sure many more people will want to sponsor more students and more community project activities, so we can help many others break their families' poverty cycles through education. What do you think?'

They were very hyped, of course, and I explained that while we would mentor them in the art of writing a speech and public speaking, this was going to be a competition – they may not all get the chance to travel. Only the best of the best would get that opportunity. That seemed to excite them even more! They said that learning new public speaking skills was just so powerful, and if they got to travel, that would be a bonus.

The program was quite simple – we'd already selected the eight students who spoke English well and were mature; we looked for leaders within the NGO, who other students would look up to and aspire to be. We'd now have each of the students write down their life story, how their lives had changed since joining the NGO and what impact they were leaving in society. These essays would then be edited to an inspirational and empowering 10-minute speech, which the students would be mentored to deliver in front of English speaking audiences, including high school students, community groups and business gatherings.

Of course, every simple idea has a million details leading to its successful implementation, so we still had some work to do.

## Getting stuck in

First, we needed two Siem Reap-based mentors for our students, to teach them to write, edit and practice their presentations, so we approached Natasha, our English teacher, and Simone, who was a freelance photographer and journalist taking some professional photos and writing some press releases for us. We suggested to them that in exchange for volunteering their time to mentor four ambassadors each, we would fly them to Australia to watch the ambassadors present, and of course they would have time to see their own families and friends as well. They both loved the idea and got to work.

We wanted to ensure that our students' presentations were empowering and supporting their ability to learn and become all they could be. It's easy to get distracted and emotional about past life-traumas, but we were not after sensational 'poverty porn'. We encouraged our students to include any of their past life challenges they felt comfortable to share, but from a perspective of self-development and empowerment, not a victim's mindset.

Whether it was the loss of a parent at an early age, or not ever meeting your parents; whether it was hunger or having to drop out of school to get a low-paying job just to be able to buy a little food, our students wrote their life stories. They covered not only where they had come from, but also where they were today and where they were heading. They also shared what they loved about CRST and their ability to contribute to society despite still being students, without an income; they could already understand their value and ability to help others, creating impact in their communities.

Numerous ambassador presentations over several years are shared throughout this book. We left them largely in their original vocabulary and format, to reflect their authenticity and emotions. Sharing your life with complete strangers can be confronting, scary and overwhelming. While each ambassador received extensive training, public speaking is by its very nature experiential and needs to be lived in order to be owned.

While we did edit to get the scripts tight and powerful, we never changed our students' styles or concepts – we kept their voices. From time to time, we had to work extensively on pronunciation, or even change words, to ensure their words were clearly understood. While I mentored our students on public speaking fundamentals, Western eating etiquette and the skills needed to hold a conversation while eating or drinking at a cocktail party (a little more on this later in this chapter), Jess did extensive work on passport applications, visa applications and scheduling the trips and presentation opportunities.

'Self-confidence starts with you, so what gives you confidence?' I asked the ambassador students in one of our mentorship sessions.

'I need to feel good', 'I should feel like I belong' and 'More experience' were some of the replies. I explained that experience can't be bought and is just a matter of time, but feeling good and belonging was absolutely achievable. So we started with personal grooming and dressing for confidence, including clipped and clean nails, no little facial hairs popping out of noses, brushed and well-presented hair, clean shoes, socks above the ankles, professional pants or skirts, clean shirts – and a smile. A constant smile – remember, I told the students, you are here to enjoy, you should not look like you are suffering.

## Keeping focused on the positive result

Overall, Natasha and Simone did an excellent job with the ambassadors and we were sincerely grateful. The ambassadors practised their presentations with us several times in Siem Reap, and they also had the opportunity to present in front of visiting overseas guests. Liz and Steve (who I introduced in chapter 6) were visiting from the United States, and one afternoon generously arranged a meeting room and finger-food catering at their hotel, so the ambassadors could practise presenting at a cocktail party environment. The team at the Belmond La Residence d'Angkor Hotel made us all feel like VIPs coming to hear the CRST Ambassadors present. We had about 25 guests and the ambassadors were super-nervous.

They did pretty well, although Veun crashed and burned – he jumbled-up his lines, lost his confidence and kept glancing at Simone, his mentor, who sat confounded in the back row. I interrupted him and suggested he take a couple of deep breaths, drink some water and smile at his supporters in the audience who by now were all clapping and cheering. He recomposed slightly and concluded his presentation. A lot was riding on this – only two of the eight ambassadors would be selected to travel to Australia to represent CRST at multiple events, and I'm sure that in his mind, his disastrous presentation was the end of the chance to travel outside of Cambodia – ever.

At the end of the presentations, I thanked our eight ambassador students for putting their whole being into this program – from sharing dark moments of their pasts, to their empowered lives as members of the NGO. They had left us, the audience, inspired with a call to action to join the NGO as supporters. I also thanked Natasha and Simone for the hours of mentoring they have dedicated to the program and their commitment to our students. We were euphoric that in a few days we would announce the two Australian ambassadors; Veun, on the other hand, seemed resigned to the idea that he'd miss out, and Simone was just angry he performed so badly.

A couple of days later, we arranged a celebratory dinner at Malis Restaurant, a fancy Khmer restaurant on the riverfront, and invited our eight ambassadors and two mentors. Everyone put on their most beautiful clothes and we had a wonderful night. Our ambassadors in particular loved the night because they could practise the Western socialising, drinking and eating protocols we'd been practising for months. They ordered their non-alcoholic drinks at the bar and held them in their left hands while leaving their right hands free for handshakes. They smiled, chatted and mingled, and at the table they placed their crisp white napkins on their laps and felt confident in handling the multiple sets of forks, knives and spoons. Other restaurant guests would have had no idea that only a few months earlier, our students were oblivious to Western culinary manners and etiquette. In Cambodia, as in much of the developing world, food is merely fuel to be consumed to gain energy. Families would often sit on the floor to eat, food would be shared from a common bowl and the only cutlery used were spoons.

## A crash course in Western culture

In the preceding months, I'd held countless classes at Jaya House teaching our students the etiquette of polite Western socialising, drinking and eating.

For the cocktail meet-and-greets that would be part of our ambassador schedule, we taught them the art of excusing themselves from a conversation, so they could mingle, and to look out for each other. As well as teaching them to hold glasses in their left hand, leaving the right hand free for handshakes, we advised them to avoid all food at cocktail parties – everyone would want to talk to them, so they should keep their mouth free for that. And smile, all the time.

We ate Western breakfasts, lunches and dinners together, so they could learn what common foods were and which ones they liked. We ordered breakfast eggs in all their possible variations, and ordered appetisers, salads, mains and desserts so they could note their likes and dislikes. We even ordered various coffee options, and preferences were written down to be committed to memory.

We all set the table using three sets of cutlery and learned to use them from the outside in towards the plate. We learned what different plates and glasses were used for and how they were arranged. We also learned about the 'geography of the table' – who would sit where and why. What noises are not acceptable at the table or in public, and how to cough, blow your nose, order food politely, ask someone to pass something to you, offer the last piece on a shared plate to others first, and excuse yourself when going to the bathroom.

We also covered grooming. I kept reminding the students that people love to judge others – and they would first judge you by the way you look, so look professional! Then they would judge you by the way you speak and interact – so be thoughtful! They would also judge you by the way you eat – show them you're worldly!

'You are representing Cambodia, ambassadors!' I told them. 'Do your country proud, do your families proud, do our NGO proud, and be proud of who you are, where you've come from and where you are going!'

So here were our ambassadors, at Malis, Siem Reap's fanciest restaurant, eating with wealthy families, celebrities and politicians. A moment to behold.

## Not getting hijacked

Thinking back on the dinner, I began to wonder whether Simone was a bit too interested in Veun and his performance. Okay – I was *made* to wonder by MJ, Mich, Steph and Jess. I'd been oblivious. The ladies had noticed some signs, exchanged glances, nodded, and looked knowingly at each other. To them, Simone was on the prowl.

Over the next few days, after I was told the cues to look for, it seemed clear that Simone had Veun in her crosshairs. She hung around him at every opportunity, told anyone who would listen how wonderful he was and what a wonderful family he came from, and posted on Facebook how happy she was to spend time with him on the back of his motorbike travelling to CRST activities to take photos. She also made it known that Veun was much better when he presented to her and we should let him audition again for the Australian ambassador trip.

I caught up with Veun to take his temperature on the 'relationship' – he was as oblivious as I was before I was re-educated by MJ, Mich, Steph and Jess. He said that Simone was his mentor and he appreciated that she was helping him – in fact, she'd asked him to come to her apartment a few times over the next few days, so he could practise his presentation some more. Okay, I may be naive, but that was a red flag.

'You mean she will have a few friends there, and you will present to them and they will give you feedback?' I asked as if not understanding.

'No, I don't think so, Aviv. Just her and me,' he replied innocently and as soon as the words fell out of his mouth, his eyes widened and he cupped his open mouth. 'No, no, no, she's just my mentor – nothing is happening, really, nothing!!' he said worriedly. 'I'm not looking for any relationships, no, no no!!'

I just kept looking at him.

'Oh my god!!' His eyes widened even more. 'You think she *likes* me like *that*?? She's my mentor, that's *impossible*!! Oh my god!!' he exclaimed with a quiver. 'What do I do??'

I explained to Veun that I'm not a relationship expert, and that Western women have much better honing instincts when it comes to spotting the subtleties of 'moves'. But we may be wrong, so let's keep an open mind and he should now be more aware and not put himself in any compromising situations. For sure it was strictly against the NGO's policy for Simone to invite Veun to her apartment without an accompanying student – she was walking dangerously close to the red line that must never be crossed.

We kept observing and Veun always ensured he was not alone with Simone, even in public spaces. He's so gentle, he didn't want to hurt her feelings.

## Making our big announcement

Mich, Steph, Jess, Aaron, MJ and I had a meeting – we had to decide which two students we'd choose as the ambassadors to travel to Australia. It was going to be a tough choice, because all eight had poured their hearts and souls in to the program. A trip to Australia was a once-in-a-lifetime opportunity, even if the schedule would be gruelling, with early morning flights and two to three presentations on some days. It's *Australia*, after all!

'You're going to choose more than two, aren't you?' MJ asked with a smirk. 'You can't choose just two – they're all so good!'

'What if …' I started as Jess cut me off.

'Here we go.' She started to laugh.

'Well, what if we have more ambassador trips? What if we choose two ambassadors to come to Australia, and then two to go to New Zealand, and four to the US?' I asked.

'You're kidding, right?' Mich asked, but she knew I wasn't. She'd heard the eight presentations countless times as the students practised in front of us – she knew their life stories and struggles, and their commitment to get educated, change their lives, help their communities and be the generation that help develop Cambodia. How could we, the ones who put this program together, hold them back, wake them up from their dreams?

On Sunday the students arranged for us to visit Chanrong's family who lived on the edge of town – her parents were insistent that they wanted to thank us. We piled into the tuktuks and 20 minutes later arrived at Chanrong's house to find her parents waiting for us, along with all our CRST students dressed in party clothes, colourful flags hung from trees and music blaring!

'What's going on?' I asked with a big smile on my face.

'Happy birthday!!' Everyone yelled.

'But it's not anyone's birthday,' Michelle started explaining.

'We know, we know,' Veun replied excitedly, 'but your birthdays are in the next two months and you're both here now, so we're having a big birthday party for both of you today!'

Everyone clapped and the party continued with blaring music, dancing, some games and food the students had prepared. Mich and I were very touched – the students had obviously gone to so much trouble planning, preparing and organising this event for us to feel valued, special and loved. We sang and we danced, Tok did an Apsara dance (a Khmer classical dance) in full regalia, Sineang was the MC and some students spoke of their gratitude. Mich and I shed some tears, humbled by our students' thoughtfulness, gratitude and warmth.

We then had an opportunity to thank everyone for our surprise birthday party and express appreciation to the organisers and everyone who joined.

'While we have you all here, would you like us to announce the two ambassadors who will be travelling to Australia later this year?' I asked.

The students' excitement level was at fever pitch at that point!

We asked all eight ambassador students to come to the front – they were as nervous as the day they joined the NGO. Smiling, laughing nervously, telling the others that they were better and should get selected ahead of themselves, and that they themselves loved the mentorship and so many new lessons, but accepted that they weren't good enough.

'So today we're going to announce the two ambassadors who will be travelling to Australia!!' They again erupted into shouts and claps – and the other sixty-odd students were just *so* ecstatic for our ambassadors!

'Michelle, can you please announce which ambassadors will represent CRST on a trip to Australia?' I asked.

'Sure – the two ambassadors who we would like to invite to come to Australia are ... Sompeas ...' and the students went into a frenzy! Sompeas was the only girl in the first Ambassador Program group, simply because we knew she was the only girl who could take the pressure, be a shining star and leave stardust for the other girls to follow. Selecting a girl was such a powerful message for us to send but we had to ensure she had all it took to succeed. Our students so loved that we selected the only girl in the program to be an Australian ambassador!! Sompeas ran over to Michelle and gave her a big hug, and then to Jess, Steph, and MJ – I got a respectful cupping of the hands in front of her face as she expressed sincere gratitude and respect to me. Sompeas was not comfortable hugging men, and of course that was absolutely fine with me.

When the group settled, I asked Mich to announce the second ambassador.

'And our second ambassador for Australia is … Mr Veun!!' The students went berserk! Absolutely nuts!! There was screaming, clapping and running to the front of the group to congratulate Sompeas and Veun. Veun was another popular choice; we knew he still needed to work on his presentation skills and we chose him because he'd touched the lives of many of our students with his warm manner and advice. We knew that Sompeas and Veun would shine bright and leave inspirational footprints for others to follow, as well as connect well with our Australian audience.

## Stopping the hijacking once and for all

A couple of days after the announcement, Veun asked to meet with me because he still felt uncomfortable with the Simone situation. She'd asked him to rehearse with her and meet for mentoring sessions at her apartment and maybe meet for drinks one night, just as friends – and now she was going to travel with him to Australia and spend ten days with him.

'Aviv, what do we do?' he asked me seriously.

'I thought you were going to take steps so she would back off,' I said. He just looked at me.

'Veun, you're a legal adult,' I continued, 'but in developed countries there is a thick red line that teachers and mentors don't cross.

They know that a relationship between a teacher or a mentor and a student is completely unacceptable – it may be legal, but ethically it's wrong. That's because the teacher has the power and the student may feel compelled to be placed in an unwanted situation. So, in Australia, if Simone wanted a relationship with you, she couldn't be your mentor – she could not have any association with CRST. Do you understand?' He nodded.

I told Veun that I could speak with Simone and tell her we had observed an unhealthy relationship with Veun and we held her accountable. Based on her feedback, I told Veun, I might need to advise Simone that she could no longer mentor him or do any work for the NGO, and she would not be joining the trip to Australia.

Veun felt awful about it, but I advised him that he must not carry the guilt for someone else's actions. He was so concerned that Simone would be hurt, or lash out in anger. I assured him I would ask questions and be tactful, but for sure if she had crossed the line, she couldn't continue to interact with anyone in our NGO, that was not negotiable. Our highest priority, above all else that we do, was our students' safety and welfare – we owed that to our students and their families.

I asked Simone to meet me at Jaya House for breakfast the next day. We made some small talk, and I got to the point – we noticed some unusual interaction from her towards Veun. She instantly stiffened in her chair. As our conversation continued, she tried to defend herself, telling me her actions had nothing to do with me, and Veun was an adult who could make his own decisions.

'Well, you're wrong, Simone,' I told her. 'It's got everything to do with me. Veun is gentle and polite, he doesn't want to hurt anyone's feelings, but he's still recovering from his ill-fated last entrapment – he's not looking for a new one. As the NGO founder, my first and foremost responsibility and obligation is our students' safety and wellbeing. No teacher, no mentor, will *ever* sway that. If you were in Australia right now, you would never dare to have a relationship with your student, so what makes you think it's okay to do that in Cambodia??'

'We're both adults', she replied.

I knew she understood, and I knew she didn't want to cause issues for Veun. She wasn't a bad person, she was just after what we all want – someone to love, and someone to love us. But the thick red line was crossed.

I reached across the table and gave Simone an envelope with $1200 – I told her this was the money I calculated we owed her for the hours she had spent mentoring our ambassador students. I told her that we genuinely appreciated that she was volunteering her time in exchange for a trip to Australia, but under the circumstances, she would not be able to join the trip and the money was to compensate her for her time.

She pushed the envelope back towards me and said she wouldn't take it – she still really wanted to come to Australia. I told her that was just not possible – and the money was hers. She again said she wouldn't take it, so I suggested that I give it to the Jaya House General Manager, who had just entered the breakfast room, and she could collect it from him the following day. She looked in Christian's direction, took the envelope, put it in her bag, stood up and walked away.

Christian came over and said, 'Is everything alright?'

'Sure,' I said, 'everything is as it should be.'

## Another big announcement

Later that week, at the end of one of our Business School classes at PUC, I asked the eight ambassador students to come to the front of the class. They all came up nervously and I told everyone that we were ready to announce two more ambassador trips – one to New Zealand and one to the United States!

The students once again went crazy yelling and clapping – we thought some of the other professors were going to come in from neighbouring classes to see what we were up to.

After a few moments, the class settled again and Jess announced that Roeun and Rith would travel with her and me to represent the NGO in New Zealand. We then announced that Nak, Sreng and Sompeas would travel with Mich, Jess, Aaron and me to attend a business conference and make presentations in San Francisco. We had originally planned for Doeb and Yeat to be our ambassadors on a trip to Singapore, but unfortunately we couldn't make that happen and it left them without a trip. I assured them in front of the class that they were winners too – we just needed to find the right opportunity for them to travel; a year later they joined two of our girls as ambassadors to Philadelphia. (See chapter 12 for more on that trip.)

## FOUNDATIONS OF LEADERSHIP TAKEAWAYS

- Trust is the currency used between leaders and followers; never lose it.

- Know your value and worth. If you undervalue yourself, others will undervalue you too.

- Leaders hold the door open for others first and walk in last.

- Always carry your moral compass.

- Walk the talk, don't talk the talk – actions speak louder than words.

- Be the voice of the voiceless.

- Trust your gut, follow your intuition – it has no ulterior motives.

- Respect yourself first, and then respect others.

- Setting boundaries is an empowered way to respect yourself and others.

- People who don't respect you also don't respect themselves.

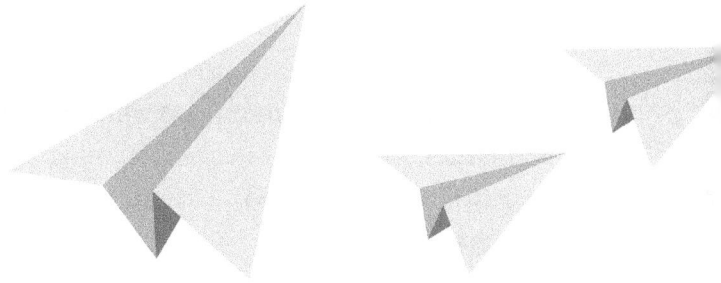

# Chapter 9

# Chance encounters are signposts from the universe

'I think I'd like to do a detox for my 50th birthday, so I can recharge my energy. What do you think?' I asked Michelle.

'Sounds great – enjoy!' she said with a feigned smile.

'Maybe we'll go to Thailand to one of those retreats and detox there,' I said.

'*We?* No, I don't think so – you should go and I'm sure you'll enjoy it, but it's not for me,' she replied.

So, there I was, south of Phuket, in a detox 'resort', paying a fortune to get starved, drink cleansers and pop probiotic pills. A few other Aussies were also guests, and we enjoyed conversations over dinner plates sparsely populated with raw vegetables. Marisa was a school principal from Sydney and I told her that our family had founded an NGO in Cambodia. 'It would be great to have some Australian high school students come and volunteer with our Cambodian students – that would be a real win–win,' I said.

Marisa went on to explain that her school, Campbell House, wasn't a mainstream school – it was a school for students who needed additional support and possibly alternate study streams. The school also had a high teacher-to-student ratio, and used trauma-informed practices to support their students who came from challenging life circumstances. Engagement in social learning and conflict management were used to provide a positive education experience while supporting their students' wellbeing.

*Wow!* I thought to myself. *This IS special!*

'Well, perhaps we could sponsor some students and support teachers to come to Cambodia,' I replied.

Marisa looked at me trying to read my face and then she smiled. 'Really? You think you could do that?' she asked.

'Why not?' I replied. I went on to explain that even the worst-off Australian students could learn to appreciate all they have when they came to Cambodia. We live in an entitled society, with the expectation of government and social services support – we complain while standing in lines for support services and whinge that we never receive enough.

'I'm sure your students will come back with a different outlook on life, Marisa,' I said. 'When they see someone sleeping in a hut, with no food and no-one to care for them, they'll understand how blessed we all are. They may have challenging lives, but they can already help someone – how empowering is that?'

We discussed that we could work on a 10-day program that would include building a house in the countryside, volunteering with our students to teach English at another NGO, a sport activity, some sightseeing and enough time for daily debriefs.

Marisa was genuinely appreciative of the offer, but still had reservations.

'I love it, Aviv,' she said. 'And I know this would really have such a wonderful impact on some of our students. But, honestly, I'm not sure we could do it. I would never get the budget from the Department (of Education) and our students' families couldn't afford it,' Marisa replied.

'Marisa, when I said we'd sponsor some of you, I meant it. How many of your students do you think could make this trip and how many teachers would you need?'

'Maybe five students?' she asked me, trying to read my face for my reaction.

'Okay. And how many teachers?' I replied.

'Oh, we'd need a one-to-one ratio,' Marisa said, almost apologetically.

'Okay, five students and five teachers – sounds good. We'll take care of the flights, accommodation and on-the-ground costs. Your students and teachers can pay for their own meals, so you'll all have some skin in the game. But that won't be much – you can budget on $10 to $15 per day, $20 including spending money. Would that work?' I asked.

Marisa just looked at me, processing.

'What's next?' I asked.

'It would take us a year to get permission from the Department – there would be so many questions and so much paperwork to complete, I'm not even sure it will be possible.'

'Marisa, I'm a patient guy', I lied. 'Let's give it a go.'

## Australian students in Cambodia

Literally one year later, we got the green light from the Department of Education. During that year, MJ and I had visited the students at Campbell House (CH) a few times to share information about CRST, covering what we do and why. We also worked with the CH team on what to expect – from weather, to accommodation, food and activities. We spoke about the Khmer empire, the Khmer Rouge, Khmer culture and common customs.

The CH students had never been on a plane before, let alone travelled overseas. The teachers assisted the students' parents and guardians to apply for passports and we applied for their Cambodian visas. At follow-up meetings, we reviewed the lesson plans the students had prepared for their classes and we reviewed each day's activities, so they could start to picture themselves in Cambodia.

While MJ and I were working with the CH students and teachers in Australia, the CRST Hospitality team in Cambodia (later to become the 'Project V – The Volunteer Experience' team) were busy planning the 'ground-content' of the trip. Foresight and logistics are critical when hosting and every small detail needs to be accounted for. Tuktuks were needed to meet the guests at the airport, as well as daily tuktuk transportation, lunches, dinners, briefings, debriefings, activities, volunteering, socialising and planning for the unexpected, in case it happened.[4]

## Diving in

When the five CH students and five teachers arrived, 40 or so CRST students and I were at Siem Reap's airport to meet them – holding a large poster that Kakada had painted, welcoming them to Cambodia.

We had dinner at The Red Piano, a Siem Reap icon, on the open balcony overlooking Pub Street, so that the guests and the CRST students could meet each other. The CH students were well and truly out of their comfort zone – first time on a plane, first time overseas, dealing with the tropical weather, a strange country and new people. It was all pretty overwhelming. I made a brief welcome speech and introduced each of the guests. I told the CH students that our CRST students had given them the nickname 'AV', Australian volunteers. I also reminded the AV that this week would change their lives – I'm sure they wanted to believe me, but they had to experience it for themselves.

During dinner I sat next to Marisa who was patting one of the students on her back as the student placed her head between her crossed arms and bent forward on the table.

---

4    On an unrelated Project V program a few years later, all the Australian teachers had to tend to sick students and couldn't leave their guest house. The Project V team led and managed the remaining Australian high school students without any Australian teachers. Less than ideal, but the CRST team exuded care and responsibility that allowed for an impactful and inspirational day. The contingency plan even allowed for some of the CRST students to accompany the unwell students and their teachers to the local clinic.

'Is everything okay?' I asked.

'I think Lauren is a bit tired and maybe a little unwell,' she smiled at me as she continued to pat Lauren's shoulders.

'Well, why don't we take a walk, get some fresh air? That should make you feel better, Lauren. Come on, Marisa will come too.' I said.

We went down the stairs and into Pub Street, which after dark becomes a lively pedestrian-only mall with brightly coloured lanterns hanging over the street. Hundreds of people were milling around, walking, talking, lingering, all in a relaxed and almost festive atmosphere. It was a typical Cambodian warm night, with aromas from the many different restaurants converging in the street – Khmer, Indian, Italian, Thai, Vietnamese.

Music blared from different venues, creating a kaleidoscope of sounds. Across the road a band of landmine victims sat on the ground playing traditional Khmer music on traditional Khmer instruments. Tuktuk drivers walked up and down the crowded street – 'Tuktuk, tuktuk, do you want a tuktuk?' they asked anyone who made eye contact with them.

Pub Street sent every sense into overdrive.

'I think I'm going to be sick,' Lauren said.

And sure enough, she was – right in the middle of Pub Street. I asked Marisa and Lauren to stay where they were for a moment and dashed back to The Red Piano. I returned with two large bottles of water and a bag of sand. One bottle was for Lauren to rinse her mouth and splash her face, and the other bottle and the sand were to use on the street.

## Jumping into classes

The next morning, we arrived to pick up the CH crew at 6.30 am – but they weren't there. We hung around their guest house lobby and all 10 of them came down the stairs at about 6.50 am.

'Good morning, everyone!!' I said chirpily. 'Did you all sleep well?'

The students were keen to get going and I asked the students and the teachers to gather in a circle with our CRST students.

'I'm glad this is happening on the first day,' I said 'because I don't expect I'll have to say it again for the rest of the time we are hosting you. When we say we will meet you at 6.30 am, that means 6.30 am. Not 6.50, not 6.40, not 6.31 – it means 6.30. If you find that a challenge, we will make arrangements to start earlier – would you prefer that?'

Lots of head shaking and exclamations of 'No way' and 'No, no, no, no, no.'

'Good, because these CRST students had to get up at 5.30 am to make sure they are here on time – and you sure don't see them running late, do you?' I asked. 'Let's be clear: if you're late, you'll be left behind – and that includes your teachers.'

Everyone cracked out laughing, taking some of the sting out of the bite. They were never late again.

We arrived at the free English school NGO we were teaching at and everyone was super-nervous. We made our introductions to the school Director and the teachers and headed for the class we were going to teach. The Cambodian students were already inside chattering among themselves – they seemed an age mix of 8 to 15 years old and at an intermediate English level. I invited the CH students to the front of the class while their teachers stood or sat at the back. The students followed me to the front and sat at some empty desks. I quietly reminded them that teachers stood in front of the class; they didn't sit in the front row.

One by one they stood up, joining me in front of the class – except for Lauren. She sat at her desk, grabbing it with both hands and was adamant she would not stand up. Marisa approached me and suggested that Lauren might sit out this class – I told her that Lauren was in the right place and in good hands, and gave her a nod and a wink. To her credit, she smiled gently and returned to the back of the class.

I touched Lauren on the forearm and said, 'Lauren, please trust me. You can just stand here with your friends. You don't have to say a word or do anything, just stand here with us. Would that be okay?'

Lauren got up and stood next to the other four CH students, and I asked the Cambodian students to stand up. As they rose to their feet they said 'Gooood mooooorning, teeaaacher,' and broke out in laughter. The AV laughed along with them, and everyone breathed a sigh of relief.

'Now you have to say "Good morning, students and ask them to sit down",' I whispered to the CH students loudly enough so that the Cambodian students giggled. The five CH students greeted their class and the students sat down.

I wrote the five volunteers' names on the whiteboard in large blue letters and we played a name game. The volunteers faced the class while I dashed behind them hovering the palm of my hand over their heads as the class yelled out the volunteer's name. Everyone had a good laugh, the ice was broken, and the lesson could begin.

The CH students taught classes all week – and by Friday, Lauren was taking the class all on her own, as the CH teachers sat at the back of the class, some shaking their heads in disbelief, others tearing-up.

## Seeing living conditions first-hand

It was an incredible week of breakthroughs and achievements for the CH students and their teachers. Early in the week, we went to visit the family of one of our students, who lived in the countryside about half an hour from town. Sokey's dad lived on his own – her mother died when she was young and her siblings had moved away. As we arrived, Sokey's father came to meet us. He looked like he was in his sixties, and was cupping his hands in greeting and gratitude, with a broad smile on his face and emotion in his eyes.

Sokey went up to her father and cupped her hands as she greeted him. They exchanged some words and she turned back to us and said, 'Everyone, this is my dad. He said he's sorry to be emotional, but he never thought his daughter would ever bring foreigners to his home. This is such a happy day for him.' Now we had tears in our eyes too.

'He told me that he only had $2 but yesterday he went to buy a new shirt, so he can welcome you all and I would be proud of him.' Sokey started to cry.

I went up to her and gave her a hug.

'I'm sorry, this is a special day for us,' she said.

'It's a special day for us too, Sokey,' I replied.

Sokey recomposed herself, flashed her beautiful smile and said, 'I'm okay now,' wiping her face with her hands.

We stood outside Sokey's humble home, made of wood, palm leaves and bamboo. She explained that we were very welcome to take a look inside, but perhaps we could just stand at the top of the wooden stairs to look, because the floor of the raised hut was made of bamboo and might not be stable. In reality, the floors of traditional Khmer homes are made for lightweight people.

One by one our guests ascended the stairs and peeked into the dark room, about 3 metres by 3 metres, devoid of furniture, with a few articles of clothing hanging on nails in the palm-leaf walls.

As we walked around the home, Sokey showed us the outside kitchen, which included a fire pit, a pot, two or three bowls and some spoons. On the other side of the house was a large ceramic vat that looked like an outdoor planter full of water. 'We use this ladle to take a bath,' Sokey explained as she scooped up water from the vat and poured it back in. 'We pour it over our head and it comes down our body as we wash,' she said.

'Where does the water come from?' asked one of the Australian students.

'Oh, the well is over there.' Sokey took us around another side of her house and showed us how they pumped the water and then carried it in a bucket to the kitchen or the water vat.

The CH students and teachers were wide-eyed and aghast. They'd never come face to face with developing-world poverty – real poverty.

'And where does your dad go to the toilet?' Marisa asked.

'Anywhere in the forest over there,' Sokey replied, pointing beyond the house.

Silence. Long silence.

'As you can see,' I said to our guests, 'this is how rural Cambodians live, but they are still happy and proud people. Sokey's dad uses a car battery to power the one light bulb he has inside his house. And when that battery is flat, he takes it to the market and replaces it with a charged car battery. People in developing countries have so much less than we do in our developed countries, yet they are grateful for what they have. Their government doesn't give them social-security benefits or health care – they look after each other and help each other.

'When someone is poor in a country like Cambodia, they have very little. They don't have a wardrobe; they just have two or three shirts, maybe two pairs of pants and one pair of sandals. They don't have a fridge, or a pantry with food, or cupboards with utensils – they just have all they need for day-to-day living.

'They eat a cup of rice three times a day and supplement that with a few vegetables or morning glory leaves and maybe a little fish or chicken, all boiled in a broth. They buy their vegetables and maybe protein every day – not only because they have no fridge, but often also because they have no money. They live day to day.

'One important lesson our family learned when we came to Cambodia was not to judge, not to compare,' I said. 'We have so much and waste so much, yet we still search for purpose and happiness. Our Cambodian students and their families have so little, but they are so grateful for the little they have and they are genuinely happy to have opportunities to do better.'

It was a lot for the Australian students and teachers to take in.

'What does your dad do for work?' asked another Australian student.

'He's old now,' Sokey said. 'He just does some jobs around the village and gets a little money so he can live.' There was no judgement or sadness in her voice; this was life and it was normal.

We continued chatting a little longer and expressed our gratitude to Sokey's father for hosting us. He cupped his hands and smiled broadly, a little shy, as he spoke to Sokey in Khmer.

'My dad wants to thank you, Aviv, for giving me a scholarship. He really wants to thank you for taking care of me and he is very grateful.'

I asked Sokey to translate that we were so proud of her and that she was a great student and a wonderful social contributor. And I thanked her dad for supporting her to study, so she could have the best life possible and always look after him. I cupped my hands and said, 'Awkun chran.' (Also spelt 'Orkun chroeun', this means 'Thank you very much' in Khmer.)

We all said our goodbyes and hopped back on our tuktuks for the ride back to town. The CH teachers had a long debrief with their students that night.

The trauma of coming face to face with poverty makes you realise how blessed we all are. As hard done by as we may feel from time to time in the West, we all live a life of relative plenty. We often judge success by our achievements and possessions, instead of by our relationships, joy and contentment. We live in a competitive society where accumulation of possessions too often leads to hoarding instead of sharing. We have more than we need, yet we still accumulate and hoard.

In our developed countries, we also feel entitled. We feel the government owes us – they owe us social services, unemployment benefits, a pension, health care, quality education, safety, security, good roads, electricity, water, sewerage, you name it, we're entitled to it. Society owes us, schools owe us, businesses owe us – we're entitled to receive a lot.

In developing countries, no-one owes you anything – if you want to survive, you need to work. If you're sick, you better look after yourself. If you want help, you better help others.

## Giving back

For the rest of the week, the CH volunteers carefully juggled experiences with debriefing sessions, so the students and teachers could carefully process and learn to appreciate their enriching experiences.

We went to the countryside on Sunday and built a home for a poor rural family – in just one day. We changed that family's life.

We joined a Khmer wedding, and had a night of karaoke. The Australian volunteers joined our NGO's English classes and ran their own classes for our NGO students, making tie-dye t-shirts, painting, baking muffins and singing songs.

There were tears at the airport as the CH students and teachers said their goodbyes. Our Cambodian students and the Australian volunteers shared life experiences that will remain with them for years to come. They felt connected, and they felt humanity in action.

Marisa contacted me a few weeks after they returned to Australia to let me know the CH students had changed so much as a result of their trip. They were all still talking about this life-changing experience. She also told me that Campbell House School would like to sponsor one of our students, and they continued their sponsorship for the next nine years, supporting Kakada and then Ney.

## The ripple effect continues

Towards the end of that year, MJ and I received an invitation to the Campbell House School Graduation Dinner. We were honoured to be invited.

We knew this would be a humble and dignified event, resembling a large supportive family celebrating a milestone that few of them ever thought they'd reach. The CH teachers were passionate educators, bringing a mix of mentorship, counselling, parenting and a lot of heart. A lot of heart. Each of the teachers were hand-picked, they were not your 'garden variety' teachers.

The students and their families were working-class, down-to-earth people, toiling through life's ups and downs, not having too much, hoping never to have too little. They were proud, and what you saw was what you got, there were no pretences. For this special occasion, they all dressed simply and beautifully, and many of the ladies had their hair made up in some special way – everyone made the effort to look their best.

It was wonderful to see 'our' students again, a few months since they had returned from Cambodia; they seemed more mature, more confident, more self-assured, yet humble and grateful. The students introduced us to their families, who were so thankful to us for sponsoring the life-changing trip that enabled their kids to open new doors to their lives. MJ and I felt incredibly touched to be embraced by their warm words and genuine gratitude.

The dinner was at a local community club and everyone was allocated a seat at one of the 15 or so round tables. I was invited to sit next to Marisa and MJ sat with some of the students who came with us to Cambodia. The speeches were limited to a couple of teachers and the graduating class of five students, three of whom had joined the Cambodia trip.

Josh spoke about how much he loved building a home for the impoverished family in rural Cambodia. It was a long day under the hot sun, yet it was fulfilling to work alongside his Cambodian brothers and sisters from CRST. He spoke of the family's emotional gratitude at the end of the day, when we stood in a semicircle around them and they thanked us for building them a new home, so they could be protected from the sun and the rain. He spoke of the poverty and the dignity and the kinship he experienced in Cambodia. And he thanked his dad for allowing him to travel to Cambodia, for all he's ever given him, and for all he's always taken for granted.

Bella spoke about how much she loved teaching the CRST students how to bake and the unique experience of joining a Khmer wedding. She also spoke of the care our CRST students had shown and how she felt so accepted and embraced by our students.

Next was Lauren, who confidently walked up to the lectern in her flowing lavender dress, clutching cue cards in one hand. She stood there for a moment, looked down at her notes, took a breath – and we had lift-off. Lauren spoke passionately about Cambodia, her anxieties and her fears, and her sickness on her first night. This was her first time away from her loving family, in a foreign country; she said she just wanted to cry. But there was kindness and love and acceptance, and she felt embraced and supported to be all she could be, no more, no less. She went on to describe some highlights of her trip, making jokes, pausing for the laughter to die down before she continued. I looked over at Marisa, tears streaming down her face.

Lauren got a standing ovation. Looking around the room, there were not many dry eyes.

## Even more ripples

A couple of weeks later, I opened an email from Cheryl, which said that she and her husband wanted to sponsor a couple of students in Cambodia. It was a great surprise and I emailed Cheryl to thank her for her generosity and ask how they found out about CRST. She wrote back saying that she knew all about CRST – she was Lauren's mum.

I rang Cheryl to thank her personally.

'Do you remember meeting us the other night?' she asked politely.

'Of course I do, Cheryl, I remember meeting you and Ken – it was such a wonderful night, wasn't it?'

We made some small talk and I told Cheryl that while we sincerely appreciated the offer to sponsor two of our Cambodian students, there was really no need for this generous gesture. I knew that Cheryl and Ken were getting by, but didn't need this added financial burden.

Cheryl explained that they had gone through the family's finances and worked out how to do it. This was something they really wanted to do – it meant a lot to them.

'You know, Aviv, that night at the graduation, that was the first time Ken and I met our Lauren.' She burst out crying.

For a moment, my heart sank.

'We've never seen her so happy. So confident, so talkative, so funny,' she continued through the tears. 'That was the first time we met our Lauren, thanks to you. How ever can we thank you for bringing us our daughter?'

Now it was my turn to tear up.

Cheryl went on to share with me that Lauren had mild autism, and that she was sometimes withdrawn, often evading eye contact, always avoiding the unknown, shutting down.

On graduation night, speaking in front of 150 people, they saw the daughter they'd never met. 'I was crying so much throughout her speech,' Cheryl said, 'I didn't even get to see her speak!'

Marisa invited Cheryl and Ken to Campbell House the following week to hear Lauren deliver her speech again, this time in front of the entire school – they got to see her speak, and they got the recompense that every parent craves.

Cheryl and Ken continued sponsoring Pech and Sompeas for a number of years, changing their lives too.

---

### FOUNDATIONS OF LEADERSHIP TAKEAWAYS

- The most important person in the world is you; if you don't take care of yourself, you won't be able to take care of others.

- How good you're going to be depends on how good you want to be.

- How do you climb a tall mountain? One step at a time. How do you create a great team? One member at a time. How do you make a better world? One person at a time. Start today.

- On the other side of fear is empowerment; on the other side of empowerment are opportunities.

- Leadership means flexibility to lead from the front, from within and from behind.

- Be an authentic leader, because people easily spot fakes; when you're authentic, you know your leadership is not about you.

- Leaders empower others to empower others.

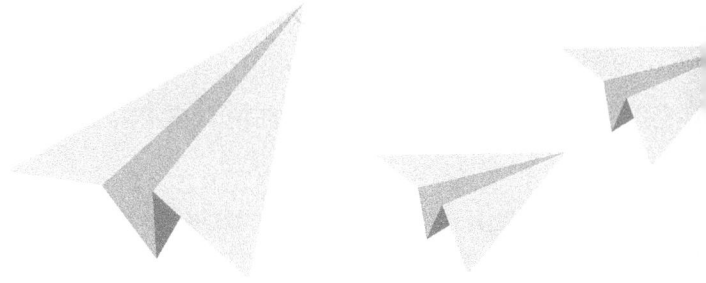

# Chapter 10

# Finding diamonds in a rhinestone world

The NGO's recruiting processes evolved from one year to the next – we've always known, however, that we needed processes and procedures to ensure efficiency, transparency and fairness. Selecting the right students is critical – we're seeking bright students from poor rural families, ones who already understand that education is their ticket out of poverty. Ones who are self-motivated, because we aren't going to be there at 6 am to wake them up to go to school six days a week. Ones who are committed to their studies, and show that through their grades and lack of absenteeism. In Cambodia students are graded each month and ranked by each teacher. We are only looking for students who are regularly in the top 10 in the class, but preferably the top three.

We also seek out students who take on extracurricular activities, because they know they can already help others and, by doing that, they themselves reap the rewards of self-satisfaction and inspiration. Some students are class monitors, others organise school clean-up days, or assist the teachers with organising special celebrations or events – in other words, they already understand the concepts of working as a team, delegation and responsibility for outcomes.

## Finding the diamonds

Attracting applicants for CRST isn't the issue – the key is finding the right ones; we are looking for rough diamonds. We focus on students who can join us from grade 10 onwards – so grade 9 graduates join us in grade 10, while grade 12 graduates join us at university level. Starting the students in grade 10 has two distinct advantages – firstly, they are more mature, almost always older than 16 years old, so they are more independent; secondly, if they stick it out to reach grade 10, they are really committed to their education.

In Cambodia many NGOs work with primary-age students – they're very cute, loving and appreciative. Of course, it's easy to form a relationship with a child who has few worries and loves attention. The problem in rural Cambodia is that many primary students start secondary school and then drop out – the older they get, the greater the pressure they face from their families to stop that school 'nonsense' and get a job to help the family make ends meet.

Another issue for rural students is that rural high school teachers may be compensated less than their urban counterparts, which leads to two dire consequences. Firstly, it may lead to less motivated and passionate teachers taking the rural jobs; although we have met some absolutely remarkable rural teachers. Secondly, to make ends meet, the underpaid rural teachers often run 'extra classes' with more teaching and additional work, for which they charge each student about $5 per subject per month. So if you're a grade 10 student and you need to take 'extra classes' in the five key subjects, your poor farmer-parents have to give you $25 per month. On a family income of $200 a month, that's a lot of money. And if you have two or three siblings, it's absolutely impossible for your parents to fund the $60 to $75 for the 'extra classes'. The trouble is, without these classes, you're possibly going to fail – and when you fail, you drop out of school, get a low-paying job and struggle for the rest of your life. That's called a poverty cycle.

Education does not immediately put food on the table, and any non-working family member is costing money and weighing down the whole family. Working in the rice fields or as a labourer helps pay for the family's daily living expenses – and when local work isn't available, many go to Thailand as illegal workers. Few ever come back with money – the traffickers and 'employers' make sure of that.

## November 2017

*Roeun represented CRST as our ambassador to New Zealand. This is his ambassador presentation:*

I went to school for two weeks when I was seven – but I hated it. I could not see how it could help me. I felt so bored. I didn't go back until I was 15.

Just eight years later I am in my first year of university! I can't believe how much my life has changed and the opportunities that are open to me. I would like to share my story with you – and how just a small amount of encouragement and support can change a person's life.

Until I was five years old, my family all lived happily together. Then my father passed away after a long illness. We did not have money for proper medical treatment. But I remember seeing the villagers put my father's body into the coffin. I did not understand what was happening. Then, two years later my grandmother died. At that time, my family was so upset and we felt lonely.

Three years later, my mum married again and had a daughter. Often in Cambodia a new husband does not want to take care of another man's children, and my mum focused on her new husband – and forgot her children.

When I was 12 years old, a neighbour asked me to live with his family and look after the buffaloes. I really did not want to go but my mum made me. If I worked seven days a week for three years I would get one buffalo. I lived there for only one and a half years. One day I went out with the buffaloes at ten in the morning and brought them back at six at night. I was so hungry, and exhausted. I looked for dinner but they said, 'Everybody has eaten, there is no food left.' I was so angry and ran home – I never went back.

A month later I had a chance to go to school. I was 13 and thought I was too old. But I realised education was the only way for us to change our lives. Our hope was my younger brother. He also lived with a family looking after buffaloes so I did my brother's job so he could study. Even though it was so hard, I committed to meet the contract to get a buffalo.

No-one in my family monitored my younger brother's studies, so after one month he dropped out of school. I told him again and again not to.

I was so disappointed and angry. Now he is a construction worker and often drinks too much. Anyway, I finished the three-year contract and I brought a baby buffalo home with me. I worked over three years in total for one buffalo.

By that time, I was 15 and my older brother who was a monk took me to live in the pagoda to get an education. He knew not having an education was very complicated and living conditions would be very poor. My family could not even afford food. At the pagoda, poor, young, Khmer boys and men can get free education and food. Sometimes I was lonely, and missed my family and friends.

At the pagoda, I started to learn the Khmer alphabet with the small pagoda boys. You might think that I would be embarrassed to be in a class with small children when I was 15 but I was just so happy to have started my education. I wanted to learn as much as I could. I practised again and again. It only took six months and I could read Khmer writing very well. Have you seen Khmer writing? Have a look! It is so complicated.

One day I looked at the sky and I realised how much my world had expanded because I could read and write. And I said to myself if I can do this in six months, I can do so much more. People had told me I would never go to school and put me down. But I started to trust myself and believe I could do it. I was so happy and proud of myself.

I asked one of the monks to enrol me at public school. I was 16 and I was put into grade five. By grade six I was top of the class.

When I went to grade 10, I moved to town. Everything in town was more expensive. I did not have money and I got a job as a waiter but it was from 3 pm to midnight. I worked six days a week and earned $60 per month. My school results were poor because I never reviewed the lessons. I came to school late all the time. Often, I fell asleep in class. Before I started working, I was about number five in the class. But after getting a job, I fell to below 30. I failed nearly all the exams because I never did homework. I wanted to drop out of school but I was the person who told my youngest sister and friends never to give up on education. I had to take my own advice.

Before I went to grade 12, I got a job as a security guard working six days weeks, and I earned $50 per month but I had more time to read lessons and do homework. It was difficult for me but I loved learning and I knew its value.

I was so thin because I only had money to support my education. In the morning, I only drank a glass of water and I could afford only 50 cents for lunch and dinner. That is not enough for a healthy meal. I did this every day until finishing high school. I was always hungry.

But I never asked for money from my mum. She had nothing to give and I knew I had to stand on my own.

During grade 12, I never imagined going to university. But one day I heard about the Cambodia Rural Students Trust NGO and their scholarships for students from poor rural families. I allowed myself to hope for the first time. Amazingly, I was chosen. My dreams might be possible after all. It pushed me to really focus on my exams so I would not lose this opportunity.

When I passed the grade 12 final exam, I was so proud of myself and I said, 'I did it!!' It was a big step on my journey.

My university is Pannasastra University of Cambodia – all the curriculum is in English, which makes learning harder but will be great for us in the end. Teachers care about us and there is no corruption – if students fail, they need to repeat. Corruption is a problem in Cambodia's education system.

The NGO provides me a lot of education outside university such as how to be a good leader, how to take care of my health, business classes, workshops, and how to use computers. I think I learn something new every day. With each thing I learn, my world expands more.

In 2015 our NGO opened the 'Project Y – Frozen Yogurt' store. Our students are mentored in running a profitable business, have the chance to improve their English and all profits remain in the NGO so we can sponsor more students. I am working there every Saturday and I love it so much. I have learnt team work, and I improve my English by speaking and making conversation with customers.

Today I am more confident about following my dream of having my own business. My major is business administration and the NGO provides additional business mentoring for our students. This has made my passion stronger to have a business of my own one day.

When I joined CRST, I started volunteering in social projects like all our students. Then I was promoted to Volunteer Manager, Community Service Manager, Project Manager and now I am the CRST NGO Manager!!

The students in our NGO are so active in learning, helping each other, and helping society through volunteer and community service projects. We build houses for poor rural families, plant trees, paint schools and repair washed away rural roads.

I love CRST so much because it helps poor people in rural areas. I had never imagined I would be able to help people in my community.

The vision of CRST is to help break the poverty cycle through education. Education has changed my family's ideas – my sister is 16 and still at school and my mother encourages her. They know that living without education is really miserable.

Everything has changed for me. I went from looking after buffaloes all day and having no hope to being a university student with so many possibilities.

When I was 15 years old, I started learning the alphabet – today, I'm 23 and studying my bachelor degree!! To sponsor a student in CRST for one year costs only $1000, but Aviv believes in me and encourages me – he knows that education has a value higher than diamonds.

Education is changing my life – it's changing my family, my village and changing the world.

Thank you for joining us on our journey in breaking the poverty through education!!

*Roeun also represented CRST as an ambassador to Australia in 2018. He was one of our most beloved NGO managers and after graduating with his bachelor's degree he went on to graduate from his MBA. He's now working in real estate in Phnom Penh with Nak, our first NGO Manager.*

## Fine-tuning our recruitment processes

Initially, our Senior Leadership Team (SLT) took on the task of finding and selecting new students to join the NGO – they approached the provincial Department of Education and received permission to visit rural high schools in the province to announce that we were offering scholarships. With the appropriately signed documents, they visited 10 rural high schools and met with the school directors to introduce our NGO and scholarship program.

We were offering more than just tuition at a private high school or university in town – we also offered a monthly living allowance, three meals a day for high school students and extracurricular activities that taught and promoted empowerment and community contribution. It was quite a package and all the school directors welcomed our team with open arms, eager to see some of their students selected for such an opportunity.

As our NGO grew, we formed the New Student Selection (NSS) team – they were tasked with preparing a business plan for selecting new students and integrating them into the NGO. Selecting the students involves three stages – a written test in both Khmer and English, an interview with some of our team members, and a family visit to the potential new students' homes. The school directors allow our NSS students to present at their school's morning assemblies, when all the high school students stand in neat rows in front of the Cambodian flag in the school yard.

One or two of our team members stand on the elevated mound under the flag and share with the students that they are from CRST and that we are offering scholarships to study in Siem Reap for the next academic year. If we have CRST students who previously attended that high school or came from that district, they are the ones to speak. How incredibly powerful to see someone who you went to school with, or was from your neighbouring village, stand up in front of you and share how they became empowered! Looking sharp and wearing their NGO T-shirt, speaking eloquently and telling you that if you join this NGO, it will change your life too – and no matter what, never give up your education. Their former teachers often stand at the sidelines of the assemblies and look on with great pride and admiration.

Following the assembly, the rural students come up to chat with the NSS team and pick up the CRST application forms. A week or so later, our students return to the school to answer any questions and collect the completed forms.

In our first year of the new recruiting process, 350 students applied to join CRST; the following year as word spread, we received 600 applications, then 1100. Even during COVID-19, with schools closed, we received 550 applications as rural students followed us on Facebook and returned application forms that had been left at their closed schools – some students came to town especially to drop off their application forms at our humble NGO office.

No matter the number of applications, all of them then have to go through our three-phase recruitment process.

## Phase 1

Each year, except during COVID-19, we invite all students who have completed the CRST application form to take an entrance test on a designated Sunday morning in June. The test includes Khmer general knowledge questions, as well as basic English grammar and concepts. We arrange with four or five high schools in the province to allow us to use their classrooms and the hundreds of applicants attend their nearest designated school.

As the potential new students sit one to a desk in the classrooms, the CRST students – who themselves may have been sitting at a desk taking this test just a year ago – distribute the test papers and supervise. At the end of the 90-minute test, the team collect the tests and bring them all to our campus for checking. After an NGO-family lunch, the team split the papers between them and spread out across the campus – at desks, on the floor, in the yard. Each test is marked by two CRST students who grade the paper individually – if the discrepancy between the two grades is more than 10 points, a senior student reviews the test and grades it.

## Phase 2

Applicants are graded according to their academic levels, so a pass grade for grade 9 is 50 per cent, for grade 10 it's 55 per cent, 60 per cent for grade 11 and 65 per cent for grade 12. All students who pass are invited back to the rural high school for an interview within three to four weeks. No doubt this is daunting – one applicant sits in front of three or four CRST NSS team members who do their best to casually chat with the applicant about their life, family, school, education and community contribution. Of course, applicants are super-nervous – some break down and our team reassures them; others are very serious because they want to appear professional.

Each of the interviewers takes notes and grades each interview, and at the end they share their perspectives and agree on a score for the applicant. With as many as 200 interviews, this is a time-consuming process that can't be rushed and the whole process can take a month to conclude, with team members fanned across a few schools. The interview is a critical phase – we need to assess the applicant's personality, commitment and passion. We don't mind how old they are, what they look like, or whether they're quiet or loud. The potential new students need to be from a poor rural family and committed to their education; if they already undertake some community service work, even better.

## Phase 3

By the end of the month, the pool of applicants is narrowed down to between 60 and 80 students and the NSS team schedule the last phase of our recruiting process – family visits. We visit each of the students' families to assess firsthand the family's living circumstances and support for their child's education. Our team introduce themselves and the NGO, and in a subtle and sociable way ask questions about the family's situation, family members and the applicant. Each NSS team member takes their own notes in their notebooks – these are vital for the next stage of the selection process. After meeting the family, the team walk around the village, speaking to neighbours and the village chief, again asking questions about the family and the applicant – all in a convivial, low-key spirit; more notes are taken.

The family visit phase also takes three to four weeks because the applicants' families are spread across Siem Reap province and beyond. We often have final-phase applicants who have left their faraway villages in search of better schools and education, so we hire a driver and a van for a few days and visit families in provinces right across Cambodia. Applicants from faraway provinces usually join our NSS team in the van, taking the opportunity to hitch a ride to see their families, who they don't see very often after moving away.

At the end of an exhaustive four- to five-month process, the debates within CRST begin. During the student and family interviews, the NSS team members take notes about every encounter. By now every team member has formed an opinion on who may be their top choices for the 5 to 20 applicants we will invite to join the NGO. You read that right – we only accept 5 to 20 students in to the NGO every year to keep our total at around 100 students. We go through our exhaustive selection process to find just a few rough diamonds, the best of the best. Despite extensive mentoring, CRST is a student-led and student-managed NGO – our student numbers are capped at around 100 students to ensure we don't lose our culture, the DNA that binds this unique cohort of young adults. Each student receives personal attention, support and mentoring – no-one is ever a faceless number. Every student receives a private high school and private university education, a monthly living allowance, full health care and the high school students receive three nutritious meals a day. All university students receive laptop computers and everyone is taught management and leadership skills, everyone is valued and everyone contributes. We monitor and evaluate everything from school attendance and grades, to the number of monthly volunteer activities, number of positions in the NGO and skills that need to be developed. And we offer enrichment programs – from developing public speaking skills to business classes with successful local and overseas mentors, and classes in Word, Excel, PowerPoint and Photoshop. This is all in addition to daily English classes and optional Chinese and Thai classes, football and Taekwondo. Many of our extracurricular classes are led by the CRST students.

As already mentioned in previous chapters, we develop new projects to address social needs, and our young leaders inspire countless other rural students with the empowerment of education. All these activities are led and managed by young adults, all at high school and university – there is no middle-aged NGO Director telling them what to do. Our student numbers are capped at around 100 to allow our leadership teams to be effective, productive, aspirational and inspirational.

The debates between the NSS members on which students should be offered a sponsorship can take two to three weeks as each member of the team advocates for their top students to make this year's cut. Normally the top 5 to 10 are agreed to by all; it's the remaining openings that are hotly contested. Students are ultimately ranked by the team in order of priority and preference, and our family receives biographies and photos for about 30 to 40 students. On a weekend afternoon in October, Michelle, Jess, Aaron, Steph and I sit around our family room and review each of the bios, making notations on each – yes, no or maybe. We don't get up until we are all in agreement about the 5 to 20 lives we are about to change – at times we've had to settle on more students than originally planned, so we could bring the discussions to an end after a few hours.

When starting with 500 to 1000 applicants, we know many spirits will be crushed and we can only hope that the students who didn't get accepted will not give up and will try again next year. Many of our current NGO leadership team students failed to join the NGO on their first attempt, but they persisted and tried again when they had improved their English by the following year. Srey Leab, our first female NGO Manager, got in on her second attempt; Ang failed twice and succeeded on his third attempt – he was a member of the senior leadership team and for a time was our New Student Selection manager.

### October 2020

*Ang represented CRST numerous times in Siem Reap, hosting guests and volunteers from around the world. This is his ambassador presentation:*

I remember the worst situation when I faced so many defeats. I was rejected many times before I became who I am today. I asked for jobs but got rejected. I applied for scholarships but failed. Oliver Goldsmith, an Irish novelist, said 'Life is a journey that must be travelled no matter how bad the roads and accommodations.' If I fail, I keep going; if I succeed, I still keep going. That's why I can stand here today. In 2019, I successfully joined Cambodia Rural Students Trust (CRST), a non-government organisation. CRST supports me in so many things. Without being supported by CRST, I might be working part-time living day to day and hand to mouth.

Hello everyone, my name is Ang Bun. I am 25 years old. I am a second year student of business administration at Pannasastra University of Cambodia, Siem Reap.

I lived without my parents since I was six years old. I was born in a poor family in the countryside of Cambodia. My parents were uneducated.

When I was six years old, they broke up because my mother was addicted to gambling. After their break-up, they went to live in other provinces, and they left me to stay with my grandmother. Since they left me, they never visited me. I grew up, survived, and was inspired by my grandmother. My grandmother was very poor and also uneducated; however, she always encouraged me to go to school. I love her so much. During my time with my grandmother, I usually asked her, 'Grandma, when will my parents come back?' She replied, 'If you want to meet your parents, go to school.'

Some years later, on the saddest day of my life, my grandmother passed away. I felt nothing and hopeless. It was the darkest day in my life ever.

Besides my grandmother, I had nobody to support me, so I decided to become a monk in 2006. Under Buddhism, I could continue my studies and learn to maintain positive thoughts. I always remembered my grandma's inspirational words: 'If you want to meet your parents, go to school.' Her words became a small voice reminding me to never give up on education. That's why I committed. 'No matter what happens in my life, I must graduate.' When I studied in primary school, I wanted to graduate high school. After high school, I wanted to graduate from university but now I dream even bigger, I want to finish a master's degree.

After being a monk for 11 years, I finished high school in 2017. Then I decided to leave the monkhood because I wanted to experience and explore new things. Even though I left the monkhood, I still lived in the pagoda, because I did not have enough money to rent a room to stay in. When I was a monk, I was very quiet. I could not make eye contact and felt nervous when I talked to someone. I wanted to destroy my cowardice and nervousness, and explore more things in life, so I left the monkhood to experience life. After leaving the monkhood, I was still quiet and I was not confident enough to do the things I wanted. I applied for many jobs such as receptionist, English teacher, waiter, and server to earn money to support my studies. Unfortunately, I always got rejected.

I started my first term at university with only one subject. I had no money to support my education so I forced myself to drop out of school.

While I was jobless, I helped a woman, who treated me like I was her young brother. I looked after her shop and took her son to school and back from school. In return, she gave me breakfast, lunch, dinner, and also a $30 to $40 allowance per month. I saved this allowance to pay for my school fees. After a few months, I paid for two more subjects at the university.

I walked slowly but I never stepped back because I believe in education. Education is a tank to crush all defeats.

In 2017, I applied for the CRST scholarship, but I failed. Then in 2018, I applied for the CRST scholarship again, but I still failed because my basic English was not good enough. I almost gave up because I faced so many defeats. However, whenever I felt like giving up, the small voice of my grandmother was always in my head: 'Go to school, go to school!!' This voice is my motivating power to continue my journey. I believed that one day, I could join CRST and would have access to my studies. I kept my persistence and a never-give-up attitude and pushed myself to improve my English. Finally, in 2019, I applied for the CRST scholarship again, and I was selected. Thanks to me for believing in myself and never giving up.

CRST always provides opportunities for every student to improve their skills by allowing them to work, volunteer, and find their passion. I am also given opportunities. I have two roles in CRST. First, I am an assistant marketing manager of Project R. Project R is a plastic education program in which 'R' stands for 'refuse, reduce, reuse and recycle' plastic. It empowers people to reduce single-use plastic. Second, I am a member of Project V, in which 'V' stands for 'volunteer'. 'Project V – The Volunteer Experience', is about exchanging cultures and experiences between foreign guests, students and local people in Cambodia. Through these roles, I become more confident and responsible. Moreover, I can also find my passion, and what I want to be in the future.

Besides these two roles, I am involved with other projects as well, such as 'Project G – Empowering Girls'. Project G empowers girls and women in Cambodia by teaching lessons about the reproductive system, human trafficking and basic self-defence. We also distribute sustainable menstrual hygiene kits to rural high school girls, so they can continue coming to school while having their period, instead of missing a few days of school each month – often missing too many days and just giving up on their education. We also teach boys about their role in supporting girls and women to be all they can be, so we can have a more equitable and empowered society. Through this project, I learn how to help vulnerable people, especially girls and women.

Joining CRST is amazing to me. I feel like I am having a new life. CRST is changing my life and providing the best education at university, health care, school supplies and a living allowance. Besides all of this support, I am also taught how to help other people while I am still poor. Through the CRST activities, I can get involved in helping others in community service activities, volunteering and teaching. Every month, I join house-building activities for poor families in rural areas and I volunteer in other NGO projects. Excitingly, I can also share what I have learned with other students. I used to think that I could not help others because I am poor. However, CRST exposes me to the understanding that helping others does not depend on how much I have but on how much I can and wish to do. Since I joined CRST, I made the commitment, 'I must share what I have learned with others, I do not wait until I get rich. I will never disappoint my supporters.'

I am grateful to my parents, who gave me birth and made me see this beautiful world. I am grateful to my grandmother, who is the most inspirational woman in my life. I love and always miss her. I am grateful to Cambodia Rural Students Trust, the Palti family, sponsors, and everyone for trusting me and being a part of my life.

I hope I can inspire you to join our journey as we create our society's future leaders by breaking the poverty cycle through education. Thank you so much!

*Ang was one of the most beloved and respected members of our NGO, New Student Selection team and leadership team. Our students saw him as a wiser older brother and he loved everyone with an open heart. He's now working in Phnom Penh, bought his first motorbike and getting ready to study his MBA.*

Much of the success of CRST can largely be attributed to our diligent recruitment process. Rhinestones are much easier to find, but finding diamonds in the rough is worth the effort – they will last longer and shine brighter, leading the way for others to follow.

## Building student integration

In addition to a transparent, efficient and effective recruiting process, we tasked the leadership team with developing a new student integration process. All our new students come from the countryside, where they live with their families, life is simple and they know their neighbours. Living in town can be daunting and stressful as the students adjust to living without their families, in an unfamiliar place, with people they've only recently met.

Our integration program is called The Empowered New Me, affectionately known as TENME or 10ME. It includes finding rooms and NGO roommates for new students, taking them to local markets and shops, leading bicycle rides around town to gain familiarity, and learning about traffic lights and one-way streets. We also introduce the new students to their new high school or university and facilitate tutorials and introductory classes. To support them emotionally, each new student is buddied up with one or two senior students, and they have access to our social worker.

The work of the 10ME team begins from the moment a new student is invited to join the NGO – they, and their families, need reassurance and confidence-building to step over the wide schism that divides rural and urban Cambodia. From extreme poverty, malnutrition and lack of electricity, water and sewerage, the students will find relative wealth, as much food as they desire, 24-hour electricity, clean water out of every tap and toilets. In their villages, they would have seen a lot of bicycles, some motorbikes and few cars – in town there are cars all around, tuktuks at every turn and countless motorbikes.

## Bridging the divide

On our early trips to Cambodia, we found it challenging to reconcile the poverty of rural Cambodia with the numerous Lexuses, Mercedes and Range Rovers we saw in town. A mere 20- to 30-minute drive away from the mega-villas surrounded by 3-metre walls, massive gates and luxury cars in the driveways, were malnourished rural Cambodians living in huts, chicken coops and cowsheds.

As is the case in many developing countries, the wealthy don't necessarily see social equality as a priority. With the fall of the Khmer Rouge and the ensuing civil war, much of the wealth was often redistributed among the winning armed forces and elite families – the wealth was generally real estate holdings and opportunities, which increased in value exponentially as Cambodia started to develop. As happens in many societies, people who understood the leadership's infrastructure development strategies were in prime positions to profit by acquiring real estate assets that made them the new social elite in a few years.

With their new-found wealth came better education, more opportunities and luxury lifestyles – the wide economic and social divide between urban Cambodians and rural Cambodians cannot be overstated. Many rural Cambodians genuinely believe they are not as good as urban Cambodians – and that they will never be as worldly, never have the same opportunities and never be able to bridge the social canyon they face.

## Cementing the transition

Allowing their kids to come and live in town, the big place that they know so little about and feel so uncomfortable in on the rare occasions they need to visit, is a big decision for parents. Families of girls are particularly anxious and we go to great lengths to reassure them. Our female NGO students visit the new students' families, sharing their experiences of the support and respect they receive.

We invite (and pay for) all our new students and their families to join our Integration Day and take them to the high school, university and some students' rooms. Our team arranges a presentation about our NGO's departments and projects, and every team member introduces themselves, stating which village/commune/district/province they're from, how long they have been in the NGO, what they're studying and the roles they hold in the NGO. Parents of current students speak of the incredible changes they have seen in their children since joining CRST, and new parents share their feelings about their children being selected to join the NGO.

The new students and their parents are often overwhelmed by the comradery and professionalism of our team, and the parents start to understand that their children are in safe hands. After a communal lunch, we invite all our new students to share a little about themselves and receive their CRST T-shirts.

To further cement the transition from the student selection phase into integration, our New Student Selection (NSS) team morphs into The Empowered New ME (10ME) team. Many of the students who lead the selection process and formed those early bonds with the potential new students and their families are now the NGO students who help integrate the new students in to the NGO and reassure their families that their kids will be looked after. Integration must dovetail the selection process – these formative weeks and months lay the foundation of empowerment for our new students.

### October 2018

*Yeat was selected to travel to Philadelphia to represent CRST, speaking at community and business gatherings. This is his ambassador presentation:*

Good afternoon ladies and gentlemen, my name is Yeat. I come from Cambodia and today I would like to tell you about the power of education and how it changes my life!

I see my parents work so hard every day just for little money. They live with no electricity, no clean water and they go to the toilet in the field.

If I give up my education I will be like them or worse, but if I continue I can help them in the future.

I did not go to school until I was 10 because I was having fun playing in the fields. But my brother explained that school could help me be something other than a farmer, so I went and I found that I loved learning.

One night at the end of grade 9, I overheard my mum talking with my dad. She did not want me to continue studying. My dad said nothing, as he understood the value of education. He used to be a monk for three years during the Pol Pot regime and he could read and write, but my mum could not. However, she had more power than my father because she earned the money. My dad had a serious ox-cart accident when I was four. His ankle was completely crushed, and he was never able to work as hard as before. Mum had to work harder to feed our family of seven children.

And my mum believed in the Khmer saying that a duck cannot live in the chicken's house – that means that a farmer cannot get a job in town. In the end, I would just be a farmer, even if I could study, so it would just waste my time and their money.

My eyes filled with tears because I really wanted to continue to study even though my parents could not afford to pay. I saw my four older sisters, who could not even read or write because my parents did not send them to school, and now they have limited choices in their lives. Today my sisters really regret their lack of education and they don't want their children to make the same mistake as them.

You know, in the Cambodian countryside, for girls it's enough to be housewives and people say they don't need to get an education. But I have a different belief from them because one of my teachers told me that if he didn't study, he could not stand in front of me and teach. He made me passionate about education. Recently I told my parents that I will support my youngest sister to stay at school and they supported my idea and encouraged her to continue her studies in grade 10.

When I was 19 years old, my brother took me to live in a pagoda 30 kilometres from my hometown. A pagoda is a religious place for monks to live and learn about Buddhism. Boys who want to be monks and poor students who can't afford to pay rent or want to get an education sometimes stay there as well.

I slept in a big hall with 15 students with no electricity, no clean water to wash or drink and a toilet in the field. We got up every morning to prepare breakfast for the 30 monks and then went to school. I did that for two years.

To study in grade 12, I needed to move to Siem Reap which was 80 kilometres away. It was a huge challenge because I would have more expenses and my parents did not want me to continue studying. I said to them, 'Mum and Dad, I have only one more year to go, and I will finish high school. Then I can find a job to support myself and pay you back.' And they agreed!! I was over the moon and felt like I had a new life. They sold a cow for $250 and gave me $100 and I expected it would last for one or two months. They said they would give me only $25 every month. $25 is a very big amount for my parents because together they earn less than $60 per month.

When I arrived in Siem Reap, it took only one week and the $100 had gone, and I could not afford food, or extra classes for the rest of the month.

On one hand, I was so excited to be in Siem Reap for the first time and to see Angkor Wat, but on the other hand everything was hard. So, I needed to find a pagoda to live in again. The third pagoda I went to, the monks allowed me to stay. And I still live there today!

I needed to find a part-time job, but it was hard for me because my English was terrible. Finally, I got a job in a small shop for four hours a day, 28 days a month and I earned $35 a month. Imagine working every day for four hours, school and extra classes for 10 hours and then homework. I was so tired, and I could not concentrate on the lessons so my results went down and I had to leave my job.

During that time, I started to look down on myself and I thought about what my parents said in the past might be true – a poor farmer's son will grow to be a poor farmer. I felt disappointed and embarrassed in front of my classmates. Some days I had no food and when I got hungry, water was my best friend and then I would get sick. I asked myself why I was so unlucky when I saw my classmates with parents who took them to school, and gave them food, money, nice clothes and motorbikes. I lived far from my home, in the pagoda and rode an old bicycle to school every day. I had nothing and felt lonely and homesick.

Years later I learnt the quote, 'If you are not willing to learn, no-one can help you, but if you are determined to learn, no-one can stop you'. And I was determined to learn!!

Near the end of my high school studies, I heard about the Cambodia Rural Students Trust scholarship. I applied, and I was accepted. Then my life completely changed. The NGO sends me to the best university in Siem Reap, which has an English program with highly qualified Cambodian and foreign teachers. We also receive a living allowance and full health care. I never thought that I could continue past high school and I'm now in my second year at university in a business administration degree.

I think I am so lucky to be a part of CRST. Even though I am from a poor family, I know that I am not really poor because I have an education. I know clearly in my mind that I will have a job with a good salary that will support me, my parents and my future family to live a great life.

Besides education, CRST has given me an opportunity that opens my heart to my people through community service. We often go to the countryside to build a house for poor families and provide food supplies to some families as well. We do it from our hearts because we come from the same background, and we understand their situation. And it has shown me that there is no need to wait until I have everything to help others. I can do it now. And I believe in Ronald Reagan's words that 'We can't help everyone, but everyone can help someone'.

In 2015, our NGO's founders started an educational social enterprise called 'Project Y – Frozen Yogurt'. Their idea was to mentor the students on how to run a business and then we could apply what we learnt to our everyday lives. Every six months, we rotate through six different business departments, and now I am the finance manager and assistant store manager. 100 per cent of the profit from our educational social enterprise remains in the NGO so we can select more students every year, and our NGO's university students receive an incredible hands-on business education.

It is hard to believe who I am today, because I nearly turned my back on education forever when I was 10, before even stepping into a single classroom. But today I can stand and speak to you all in English and represent CRST.

The power of belief in education has changed my thinking from impossible to I *am* possible. I have changed my parents' belief that education would waste my time and their money, and now I am the one who inspires my older sisters to send their children to school because they saw how my life has changed and how I overcame the challenges. I became the hero of my village because there are only three people in my village going to university, but none go to the best university like me!! I believe in the wonderful Nelson Mandela words: 'Education is the most powerful weapon which you can use to change the world'.

If you would like to join us on our journey in breaking the poverty cycle through education, I'd love to meet you today!!

Thanks for your attention and kind support.

*Yeat became the general manager at Project Y and, after graduating from his bachelor degree, went on to graduate with his MBA. He is now a CRST role model, with a successful real estate business in Phnom Penh. Before moving to Phnom Penh, I remember telling him, 'Remember where you came from.'*

*'I will never forget,' he replied. Yeat is a shining example of education breaking the poverty cycle – he bought his parents their first mobile phone, their first motorbike and their first ever holiday. He is paying his younger sister's tuition at a private school in town and sponsored a family in CRST's Family Support program. At 24, he bought his first car – a new red Toyota Prius.*

# FOUNDATIONS OF LEADERSHIP TAKEAWAYS

- Where you start is not relevant; the steps you take will determine your journey and next destination.

- Everyone is someone; believe in them and support them until they believe in themselves and support themselves.

- Rhinestones are plentiful, diamonds are not – as a leader, be selective about who you invest in to get the best return on investment.

- Education is a process, not an event – plan the journey, take action and be patient; constantly correct and continue.

- There are no mistakes, only learnings; 'sharpen the saw' as you go along.

- Supporting your team at their lowest points is more valuable than celebrating their wins because you are laying the foundations for their future success.

- A team member who has walked the journey is the best advocate to promote your vision and impact – you may have given them the shoes, but they've walked in them.

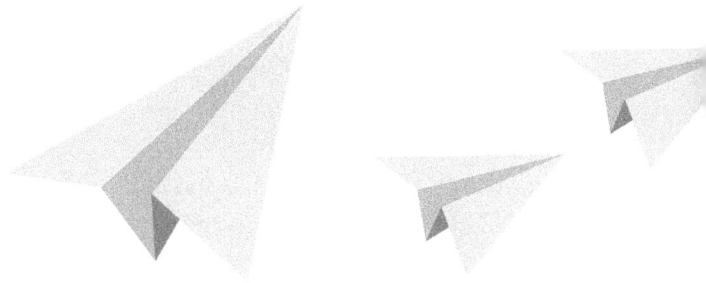

# Chapter 11

# When you give up on others, you give up on yourself

It's impossible to mentor young adults and not want to give up from time to time. Impossible.

The frustrations are immense, often due to a clear disconnect in life experiences and values, all the more so when the young adults are from a different culture and background. What seems obvious to me is not even on the radar for them.

Our students are bright and eager, but they are not experienced enough in life to be life-thinkers – yet. Priorities and timelines are esoteric terms. To take on a mentorship role requires not only quality experiences and the balance of heart and head, but also patience. I lack the third virtue, in spades – an Aries trait.

Some of the times I feel like giving up are when students give up on themselves. They get addicted to social media and fail school, or they get an idea in their head that they want to do something else and therefore drop NGO activities. They 'fall in love' and need to spend time with their girlfriend or boyfriend, so they go into hibernation until we give them a wake-up call.

## Losing a star

I hit the deepest melancholy when quality students want to quit or do quit the NGO. I carry the depression for days, sometimes two to three weeks. To be clear, when an NGO star like Norn tells us he's leaving, I feel I personally failed. I failed to embrace him enough, appreciate him enough, share the vision enough for him to see that dropping out of the NGO is like dropping off a slow-moving train. You will survive, but you will take a long time, if ever, to reach your destination.

Norn had a girlfriend. He 'loved' her, she 'loved' him – they were 'in love'; all the while the definition of 'love' is illusive. Yes, you may enjoy someone's company, think you are friends, compatible for a lifelong relationship. But 'love' has so many aspects and definitions and I doubt that any late teen or early-twenties young adult can actually grasp the full meaning of 'love'.

Let's start with the fact that many of our students had challenging parental love. I grew up in a home where telling your parents you love them was matter-of-fact. Deep hugs, kissing on the cheek – 'normal' stuff. My father grew up in a home where the word 'love' was rarely uttered – both his parents, who divorced when he was 13 and then remarried to other people, were warm 'loving' people. But no-one ever said 'I love you'. When my grandmother was 91 and my father was 68, she told him for the first time that she loved him. She passed away four years later – all those wasted years.

My grandparents on my father's side grew up in Germany – they had a formal, strict upbringing and 'love' was not in their families' vocabularies.

My mother's parents came from Russia and Poland – they had warmer, more embracing upbringings and 'love' was in their families' vocabularies. To this day, my 85-year-old mother gives me long hugs, stroking the back of my head as she whispers 'I love you, I love you, I love you. You will always be mine.'

When you grow up without love, you don't know what it is. You most likely see it in other families and you very likely crave it, as does every human I've ever met. But what it means, what it takes, what it gives – these are experiential for many.

Norn was an orphan, raised by family members. When he told me he and his girlfriend were 'in love', the piece of the puzzle fit the picture very snugly. He assured me she was so very nice, had a very nice family (another craving) and they were very compatible. She was supporting him to study and wanted to see him graduate from university. Call me a cynic, but I've heard it all before.

## Thinking big

I still remember calling Rith late at night when I was in Siem Reap and asking him, 'What the hell are you doing Rith?! Do you want to go back to working illegally in Thailand?? Meet me for breakfast at 7 am tomorrow – don't be late!!' He knew instantly what I was talking about – his grades had dropped at university and he had even failed a class. He'd 'fallen in love' and his girlfriend rang him at all hours of the night saying she needed him and if he didn't have time for her, she'd leave him. Of course, he had less time for his studies and his grades told the story.

When he walked in to Jaya House for breakfast, he was wearing his shy smile, knowing he'd done wrong. We greeted each other politely and I motioned for him to sit. He'd already eaten, but ordered an orange juice.

'So, Rith, what's new with you?' I asked with a fake smile.

Rith is a gentle soul and his life passion is his education. He joined the NGO while still a monk and left the monkhood soon after, because he felt isolated, wanted to be more sociable and eat after midday (in Cambodia monks only eat between dawn and midday). He was bright, inspirational, aspirational, warm and loving – a good catch for anyone. Before he joined the NGO, his dream was to be a teacher, so he could help change his country. After a few years in the NGO, he decided to be a businessman, make enough money and build a free English school in his hometown – now, that's a big thinker. Why settle for being a teacher, when you can have a whole school?

*October 2017*

*Rith was selected to travel to New Zealand to represent CRST, speaking at schools, community and business gatherings. This is his ambassador presentation:*

When I was 18 years old, I spent time in a Thai prison after being caught for being an illegal worker.

I was shocked at the conditions – there were children, women and old men, and people were sick, crying and starving.

It touched my heart very much. That was my third time in Thailand as an illegal worker and this time we were caught without passports or permission and were sent to prison.

My first illegal trip to Thailand was when I was in grade 6. I was 15 years old and gave up school. My father and brother had been very sick and my parents owed a lot of money to pay for the medical expenses. We sold our house, our cows, our land, but it was not enough, so we decided to go to Thailand where the wages are higher. I still remember the day we left home at dawn and got to the Thai border at 6.30 at night.

Everyone was preparing quietly, quickly and nervously. I asked my father softly, 'Why does everyone seem very nervous and scared??' And my father said, 'Son, we don't want the Khmer police to see us. If they see us, they will not allow us to go to Thailand and they will fine us because we don't have passports or permission.' And he said, 'Son, we are about to cross the border very soon and to cross the border, we have to swim across this river and run across a Thai road into the forest very quickly. So now what you have to do is to eat rice so you have enough energy.'

I remember some parts of the river were deep and some were not. The sky was a terrible colour and dark, and the water was flowing very fast. While we were swimming across the river, I had a problem with my left leg. The muscle of that leg did not work properly and I nearly drowned by the force of the water. Fortunately, my father saw me and grabbed me very fast. And that night we reached the workplace safely.

That first time in Thailand, we cut sugar cane. My father wanted to get more money so he carried sugar cane to put in the big trucks. He worked for only 15 days and then he got sick so I had to work harder to get more money to pay for medicine and food. After three months, I had only $5 in my hand. Just holding that money, the tears dropped out of my eyes. That is life with no education. Working so hard but no money left.

We gave up and came back to Cambodia. But life was so tough – there was no work and no food, so my mother and I returned to Thailand illegally to harvest rice. My mother only worked for one month, and then a grain of rice jumped into her eye, so she could not work.

Walking to work, I saw Thai students going to school very happily. Staring at them walking to study, my heart was beating very fast.

The curiosity of going to school was getting stronger and stronger. It became a burning desire in my heart and soul. I thought to myself, *How can I get an education if I have no money and my family is so poor? And if I can't help even myself to have a better life, will my family always live in miserable conditions?* My mother and I returned to Cambodia with no money.

After a few months, my brother, sister and I returned to work in Thailand to pick papaya and chilli, and cut sugar cane. This time I thought of education strongly because I was bored of the tiring work and I was getting sick. I was only small but I was doing the same work as the adults to get equal pay. We were caught and sent to prison as illegal workers, before being deported back to Cambodia.

I asked my parents if I could become a monk because I could gain education through the Buddhist school and learn about Dharma and general knowledge. They agreed, so after becoming a monk, I started to study in grade 6 again when I was 18 years old. I studied in the Buddhist high school for 7 years until I finished grade 12.

Besides studying at school, I studied English at places that were free for monks. I walked four kilometres to the class and after coming back, I taught the children in my village what I had learnt.

One month after finishing grade 12, I came to visit my parents and told them that I received a scholarship from an NGO called Cambodia Rural Students Trust, which is a non-government organisation with the vision of breaking the poverty cycle through education. It sends all scholarship students to private high school and private university and provides English and computer classes, and health care as well.

You know when I told them I got this scholarship, they were so delighted for me. My father gave me a big smile and said, 'Congratulations!', and my mother of course was so very happy and cried a lot. I felt extremely excited because finally my dream for a better education was coming true.

The boy who usually worked in the rice field, and went to Thailand without a passport or permission and was put in prison, is now standing in front of you doing a speech in English with confidence. And now I am a second-year student at university.

Last year I was selected to be the education manager for CRST. This year I was promoted to be the operations manager at Project Y, our educational social enterprise. It has given me clear direction to know who I am and what I can become. I can say that my life would not be able to get to this level without CRST.

I have been in CRST since 2015, and my life has completely changed. Before joining CRST, I was nervous and afraid. I can say my soul was in a dark place and I could not find the light or the way out. What should I do and where should I go? I could not afford to keep being a monk and go to university; but if I left the monkhood, I would have had problems because my English was very poor, I could not use a computer, and I didn't have money to buy clothes, food, a bicycle, rent a room, or pay for school fees. My life was so conflicted at that time.

After only two years with CRST, I am much more confident and have more knowledge. I use the computer every day, and my English and my communication skills are much better because CRST sends me to the best private university in Siem Reap.

Our NGO also has volunteering and community service activities for us to share our knowledge with poor students and families in the countryside. Every month we build a house for a poor family in a rural area. Since joining CRST, I have participated in building over 25 houses for single mothers, the elderly and the intellectually less-abled. I love doing community service very much because I can see those people have a big smile and so much gratitude and happiness, and my heart feels very warm.

In the future, I want to be a businessman and professor. I want to have the chance to work with students every day, so I can inspire, motivate and encourage them to lead their lives the right way, and to live peacefully in our society. And mentor them to never give up.

I want to help the poor people in my country to have a job with a proper salary and also be a good role model for the next generation. I want them to give up the concept that 'We are poor, we cannot do it' and show them that 'If I have done it, so can you'.

I believe that by changing one soul, we will change one life; by changing one life, we will change one family; by changing one family, we will change one village, one society, one country and the world.

Aviv changed my life through his vision and kindness, so now I change my mindset. Before I just wanted to have a good job with a good salary and live very happily with my family. That was enough for me. But now I don't think like that because 'the beauty of life does not depend on how happy you are but how happy others can be because of you'.

So here is my favourite quote: 'Life plus hope equals change; life plus hope plus education equals a greater change'.

Breaking the poverty cycle through education – it's a simple concept and I am proof of its reality. I invite you to join us on our journey.

Thank you so much!!

*After representing the NGO as an ambassador to New Zealand, Rith went on to study his MBA in Phnom Penh, and is now working as a highly successful real estate agent.*

By the conclusion of our breakfast meeting, Rith and I were on the same page. His head was back leading his heart and he soon got his grades to the As and Bs we'd come to expect from him – he had the guts to tell his girlfriend that his studies came first and she learned to respect that.

## Learning from the losses

By the time the team alerted me to Norn's predicament, he'd already left Siem Reap for his hometown. We spoke briefly via the Telegram app and he kept breaking down. We switched to Telegram messages and he shared what was going on. He and his girlfriend were in a room – nothing had happened, but her family wanted them to get married so her honour and their honour would be protected. A few more days of conversations to explore some options and Norn was gone.

We lost a star – a bright inspirational star, who would have left deep footprints. I was crushed. All the love, the time, the effort, the energy, the money – and the tree was uprooted before it even knew it was a tree. I took the loss pretty hard and told the students I'm going to back off from the NGO for a while and reassess what went wrong and where I failed Norn. They were shocked. I explained that when a student leaves needlessly, that's going to leave a scar – not because I'm weak, but because I'm human.

Jess and the senior students in Phnom Penh stepped up to ensure the NGO was well led and managed by the leadership team. The students, however, were all on tenterhooks to see what would happen next.

After two weeks I emailed them and set a task – the senior leadership team had to come up with a process to identify which students were vulnerable to leaving and may need early one-on-one big-brother or big-sister mentoring. Jess or myself mentoring from afar was pointless; they needed someone who innately understood the culture, the pressures, the options and the extensive support the NGO could provide. Most importantly, they needed someone who they saw as family to show them where they have come from, where they are, and that their destination is so, so close.

The Empowered New Me (10ME) team took on the task and came up with early warning indicators and a multi-level support process, which included NGO leadership team members, our counsellor and the Senior Student Group (SSG) from Phnom Penh. Jess and I would be alerted early, but not be part of the process unless it was felt our input was going to sway the result.

Norn got a job working nightshift at a restaurant and when he got married, most of the guests at his wedding were our NGO students, his NGO family. He's now doing administration work at a real estate agency and at least they respect him for his potential. He wrote us a touching email on the eve of his wedding, respecting all he's received, grieving all he's given up, owning who he is and setting a goal to put himself through university in the coming years. He said he knows education has changed his life; he's just taken a detour.

## Getting caught in other ways

Being a monk in Cambodia does not require a lifetime commitment. Many boys become pagoda boys and junior monks so they can be educated for free at schools for monks only. They live in the pagodas for free, while cooking and cleaning for the monks. At certain times in their lives, some boys and men become monks for a short period as well – for example, after a momentous event in their lives or the passing of a close family member. But other religions can be less open minded.

Churches of all persuasions sent missionaries to Cambodia and set up shop to 'save' the people of Cambodia from themselves by offering food, education and community in exchange for baptisms. To put it simply, money was often weaponised to create self-serving spheres of control.

One of our students, Sotheara, was lured by the Jehovah's Witnesses. She'd graduated from high school and was already attending PUC, but we noticed an unusual number of class absences and she also asked for permission to skip some NGO activities. So on my next trip to Siem Reap, I asked for a meeting. She sat across from me at the coffee shop and I asked her my standard opening questions: 'How's life going, Sotheara? What's new?' I find this 'blank canvas' is a secure conversation opener, allowing the other person to paint their picture, while enabling me to see things from their perspective before adding my framing.

Sotheara told me that she was really happy with life – and she did look happy and healthy. I asked her whether there were any challenges she was facing that we could assist with, and she said no, not really. 'So what's with all the skipped classes and NGO activities, Sotheara?' I asked with a disarming smile.

'Well ... I have many activities at my community and sometimes I can't manage my time so well,' she replied.

Knowing that rural communities have pretty much no demands on people's time other than family weddings, funerals or a few religious ceremonies, I asked Sotheara what community she was referring to. It turned out that Sotheara was helping 'foreigner friends' at a new 'community centre' and she really loved spending time with them. They treated her with respect, offered plenty of food and companionship, and even had some lessons they took together. It didn't take me long to work out she was attracted by a Christian organisation and I asked which one it was – 'Oh, they are Jehovah's Witnesses,' she replied with confidence.

I explained to Sotheara that we were not here to judge or coerce, that we loved and accepted our students for whoever they are. We didn't own our students; we were here to give them a hand up, not a handout. Our way of doing that was through providing the best education possible and teaching them life skills that would empower them for the rest of their lives and inspire others to follow. In exchange for our support, we only asked for three things – do your best in your studies, contribute to leading the NGO and participate in NGO and community service activities.

'None of the three things we ask is for our benefit, did you notice that? That's called "unconditional giving" – it's giving with the expectation of no personal gain in return. It seems to me that the Jehovah's Witnesses church who are your new friends are giving you food and friendship but, in return, they also want to control a part of your life. If they are not supporting you to go to university and participate in NGO or community service activities, that means that they want to control you – they don't want other ideas in your head, just their ideas. So you will need to make a really important decision – be in control of your life or be controlled by others.' Sotheara left CRST shortly after, with our unconditional love.

Of course, the Jehovah's Witnesses are just one Christian group who ply their trade in Cambodia – there are countless others, including some Korean 'churches' that skim 10 per cent of their impoverished followers' income. I have nothing but contempt for despicable 'church leaders' who prey on some of the world's poorest people and rob them of their meagre earnings with promises of a better life after death.

To be sure, some wonderful Westerners and organisations provide much needed support with integrity. Rather than pretend to be better than the Cambodians, they help raise the tide, so that everyone benefits. Natasha, our former English teacher, Christian from Jaya House, Sara and Paul from Haven and Susan from Honour Village Cambodia were some of the inspirational expatriate stars we found.

## Local failings

Sometimes I feel like giving up when Cambodians fail to help their own. Like the time the director at Future Bright International School (FBIS), the private high school our students attend, told me that the school's owner would no longer let our students study there because when they join in grades 10, 11 or 12, they may fail their national exam and lower the school's reputation. Their policy moving forward was that high school students needed to join in grades 7 or 8, which was way too young for an NGO like CRST.

I looked across the table at Mr Seng and outstretched my left arm while pointing at it with my right hand. 'Mr Seng,' I said, 'as you can see by my skin, I am not Cambodian. I do not live in your country – I'm a foreigner. Tomorrow I will be on a plane to my comfortable home. If you don't educate your country's future leaders, who will? Our students come from poor families, but they are not dumb – we have had students finish in the top 500 students in Cambodia. None of our students has ever failed grade 12. How can you tell me that it's okay for a foreigner to love your kids more than you do?'

Mr Seng was a pedagogue, the ultimate professional educator. Small in stature, large in presence; his small eyes had depth. He was wise and he was kind.

'Mr Aviv, you are right. I have already told the owner all that – how can we, Khmer people, care less for our own poor people than the foreigners who come to help us? But he said he won't change his mind; we won't be able to accept your students here again,' he said softly.

I stood up and told Mr Seng that in all of my family's activities in Cambodia, I had never expected that Cambodians themselves would shut their hearts to their own children. 'What is the point of us spending our energy and money if Cambodians are not prepared to partner with us for the benefit of the next generation?' I asked him. And I left.

The following week our leadership team advised us that FBIS would make an exception only for CRST students – they could join the school in grades 10, 11 and 12.

## Steps forward – and back

I also almost give up when confronted by out-of-date, out-of-heart, out-of-touch organisations expecting us to jump through antiquated process-hoops to request funding. Rotary International is working to reinvent itself as a progressive organisation that provides in-country capacity-building, not merely benevolent volunteering that leaves a skills void when the volunteers return to their home countries.

So when the Rotary Club of Glen Waverley applied for a District International Grant for 165 bicycles to be distributed through CRST's

'Project B – Bicycles for Education', their district celebrated the in-country community needs assessment and project implementation Project B provided. They endorsed the idea that the Rotary Club of Glen Waverley would support and account for funding and any needed mentoring, but the implementation would be done and reported by the CRST team in Cambodia. Instead of short-sighted, short-term colonisation by Western volunteers, they supported accountable in-country leadership that would ensure sustainability.

The forward-thinking Rotary Club of Keilor East also provided vital support for Project B, donating $3000 in seed funding. However, when they applied for a Rotary District International Grant to collaborate with CRST on the installation of water filtration systems at four rural high schools, their district's Foundation Committee took a different view. The project was worthy, but it needed the Keilor East Rotarians to be 'actively involved in delivering the project' – a Rotarian with the right expertise had to be in Cambodia to conduct the community needs assessment and the implementation.

Too bad they couldn't travel to Cambodia for three years during COVID-19, and what exactly was the 'right expertise' they required – considering we had a very experienced in-country organisation who we planned to use to install the water filtration systems? Water-testing lab reports showing the water from the wells was unfit for consumption and professionally drawn site-installation plans didn't tick the Rotary Foundation Committee boxes in that district; it had to be Rotarians who did these jobs. So the 2250 students and surrounding families would continue to drink water that made them sick, boil their water or not drink water at all – at least the interpretation of The Rotary Foundation's rules in that district would supposedly be upheld.

We ended up negotiating with the Foundation Committee in that district and common sense finally prevailed. The collaboration led to the installation of four water filtration systems and eleven toilets in four rural schools in Siem Reap, benefitting thousands of students for years to come. That proof-of-concept project led to much greater impact.

I talk more about Project B and 'Project W – WASH for Education', and Rotary's involvement in these projects, in chapter 14.

We give people a hand up, not a handout – we never ask for money, we ask for money with a purpose. We have the track record, transparency, accountability and sustainability that attract practical sponsors and collaborators. You can get as involved in the project or remain as hands-off as you like – but please don't get in our way trying to look like you're the hero who saved the day. That role is already occupied by our students.

---

### FOUNDATIONS OF LEADERSHIP TAKEAWAYS

- Walking away is often easier than working through issues, but if we all walked away, what would be achieved?

- Letting someone into your life and out of your life should be handled in the same way – with respect.

- You can lead a horse to water, but you can't make it drink – share your vision, inspire and support; the rest is up to the team member.

- People only tell you what they want you to know; learn to read between the lines and ask the right questions.

- Add value and express respect and gratitude *during* the relationship; it's often too late when it's over.

- As much as possible, leave the door open when people leave your life – you never know when they may walk back into your life.

---

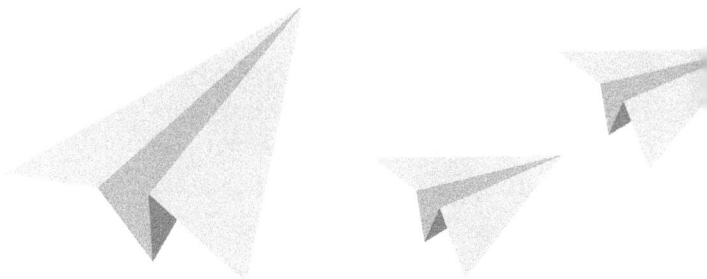

## Chapter 12

# Find your teacher, learn to walk, then run, then fly

Over the years, more than 20 of our students have had the opportunity to travel to Australia, New Zealand, the United States and Thailand as part of our Ambassador Program. Without exception, each of their lives has been significantly impacted by the opportunities to travel and experience life in developed countries. You can see what life can be like in developed countries in the movies, and you can read about it in books; however, when you walk in clean streets, see drivers respecting the road rules, walk through a mega-shopping centre or stand at the base or on top of a 50+ storey building, you have now seen and touched what's possible. And without exception, they all wanted to bring that progress and development back to Cambodia – the fuse was lit!!

Whether it was at schools, business meetings or social gatherings, our students also left an impression – of educated and life-engaged young adults. They exuded empowerment and inspiration as they shared how they overcame life challenges, which are now overshadowed by their education, community contributions and their responsibility to help inspire the next generation of Cambodian students.

## Next stop, Philadelphia

I walked through Hong Kong airport to our agreed meeting place next to gate 15, and there they were, all on their mobile phones using the free Wi-Fi to connect with Cambodia. You'd think they were born to fly and were in and out of airports all their lives. Sompeas looked up and said, 'Hello Aviv', and then they all jumped to their feet to greet me. The students had flown on their own from Siem Reap and we were all about to set off on the biggest trip of their lives – Philadelphia, here we come!

Months earlier our Philadelphia-based supporters Steve and Liz (who I introduced in chapter 6) had suggested that we arrange an ambassador trip to the United States.

'Maybe just three of the girls,' Liz suggested. 'They can stay with us and we'll show them around and the four of us can do some girly things to make them feel special. What do you think?'

I thanked Liz for the generous invitation, but explained to her that wasn't how the Ambassador Program worked. The students needed to earn a spot as a CRST Ambassador; we didn't discriminate by gender. It was a program open to all who were prepared to commit to this life-changing opportunity – a journey that would support them to dive into past traumas when they were growing up in the countryside and write down their life stories through the lens of an empowered young adult.

The purpose of the Ambassador Program trips was both to expand our students' horizons to see what's possible, as well as to share some of the work we do with potential donors. So Liz's invitation was great, but we would still need to work on the ambassador students' selection and trip content.

'Well, I want some girls – it's high time we gave them extra support,' Liz replied.

And Liz was right, in rural Cambodia many girls were culturally undervalued – boys were deemed worth educating because they would need to work and earn money for the family, but girls – that's a whole other story. They could drop out of school at any age and help in the fields or around the home – after all, they would just be told who to marry, have kids, cook, clean, work in the fields and hang around the village; educating girls was not a priority.

But that's not how it was in CRST – our girls were valued and respected. We had spent time educating our students that it was their generation who needed to exemplify gender equality. This was their responsibility – not to talk about it, but to live it. The boys had the responsibility of supporting the girls to do anything they chose, whether it was sawing and hammering the mainframe of the houses we were building in our community service activities, or playing football. The girls had the choice of stepping outside cultural norms to do whatever they now felt empowered to do, and the responsibility to find their voice.

## Finding empowered girls to lead the way

It took us a few years to increase the number of girls in the NGO because fewer girls were applying to join, and some who did get accepted had their families change their minds and deny them permission to leave the village and come to town. We knew what we needed was a core group of empowered girls to lead the way and set the example, so we ensured that despite having fewer girls than boys in the NGO, girls were still given 50 per cent of the leadership positions. We encouraged the creation of a girls football team and we appointed one of the girls to be the Girls' Affairs Manager so she could be the voice of our girls. We also created 'Project G – Empowering Girls', to specifically address taboo subjects such as the reproductive system and menstruation, normalising girls getting a period and educating boys about the support role they had in creating an equal society for all. Although it took us nine years to appoint Srey Leab as the first female NGO Manager, we knew it would be futile to elevate anyone, boy or girl, to that position until they were sufficiently empowered and inspirational.

As of 2020, we have 65 per cent girls in our NGO – and they are without a shadow of a doubt, all social-change leaders. We didn't intend to have 65 per cent girls, but over the preceding years, the number of girls applying to join CRST had far exceeded the boys, their commitment to education was palpable and their families supported them. During the same period, many of the rural boys dropped out of high school and left for Thailand as illegal migrant workers, to try to earn some money for their impoverished families.

(See the next chapter for more on our equal opportunity efforts.)

## Star performances

'Liz, I completely agree! We will absolutely continue to elevate our girls and support them, giving them every opportunity we can,' I said.

She seemed happy with that, and we agreed that Steve and I would coordinate the details, with the aim of an ambassador trip to Philadelphia in October, about six months away.

So there we were in Hong Kong airport – Sinuon, Sompeas, Doeb and Yeat, our US ambassadors. Two girls and two boys – four of the best.

They were pretty excited when we landed at Newark Airport after our 15-hour flight, but very nervous US Immigration would trip them up with questions about their visit. I reassured them there was nothing to worry about – their visas meant they had already been qualified to travel and they just needed to answer any questions from the Immigration Officers truthfully and simply. I let them all go ahead of me in the line so I could ensure they were all processed smoothly, and shortly after we were met by Liz and Steve. We piled into Steve's SUV and drove the hour and a half from Newark Airport to Philadelphia, stopping along the way to allow Sinuon to get over her motion sickness. (Our students were not used to travelling by car for long distances.)

We spent the next week living at Liz and Steve's home, experiencing the Western lifestyle we take for granted. On the first day, we went shopping for some new clothes, so our students would feel comfortable as they met new people and represented themselves, CRST and Cambodia. We saw highlights of Philadelphia while riding the open-top hop-on hop-off bus, we visited the zoo and Steve took the students to a Philadelphia Eagles football game.

We met with some partners and associates from Saul Ewing Arnstein & Lehr, the legal firm that did all the pro bono work to register the Cambodia Rural Students Foundation USA Inc. as a tax-exempt organisation in the United States. Setting up this organisation was crucial in allowing us to raise funds from US-based donors, and our CRST Ambassadors expressed their gratitude as they presented and chatted with our hosts in the firm's conference room. We were also hosted on tours of software company SAP's headquarters, Villanova University and Temple University, where Steve was an Associate Professor of Finance at the Fox Business School. These visits, and the numerous people we met through Liz and Steve, allowed our students to absorb the magnitude of living in a developed country.

Without a doubt the highlight of our visit to Philadelphia was the CRST Ambassadors' lunchtime presentation at the Union League of Philadelphia. Founded in 1862 and occupying the same historic building since 1865, the club epitomises American heritage and entrepreneurial spirit. Liz and Steve sponsored a lunch for over 60 of their friends and associates at the club, giving Sinuon, Sompeas, Doeb and Yeat the opportunity to share a little about their background, their love for education and their passion to bring sustainable change to Cambodia.

The night before our presentation, Liz and Steve shared the seating plan with us and we agreed that we should all be split between the tables so we could connect with more guests over lunch.

'As you all know, we only get one chance to make a first impression,' I reminded our students. 'By remembering our guests' names and some key details about them, you will be memorable and professional.' We sat at Liz and Steve's round dining table reviewing photos and bios for the key guests who would be seated at each of our tables.

We followed that by reviewing each of their presentations and the images that would be shown behind them as they spoke, so they could be more at ease and hopefully get to enjoy this remarkable milestone opportunity.

Liz also requested that we have a full dress rehearsal to ensure everyone looked great – Steve loaned neckties to Doeb and Yeat and I had to change my pink checked shirt to a more conservative red-white-blue checked shirt. Personally, I liked my pink shirt, but of course the red-white-blue check shirt was 'safer' and had the added benefit of representing the flags of the United States, Cambodia and Australia.

At the club, the students were extremely nervous, feeling the significant pressure of this presentation more than any other. Liz, Steve and I took great care to stay close to them, facilitating introductions and starting conversations, even though this was also my first time to meet the guests. The guests themselves were well-accomplished professionals, and they were warm and interested in the students and their stories. As lunch started, we split up among the tables and each student came to the front of the room in turn, to deliver their eight-minute ambassador presentation.

They were a hit, connecting with the guests at their tables and inspiring everyone in the room when they shared their backgrounds and achievements. Many guests lingered a little longer after the event concluded and we were then escorted by the executive chef on a tour of the massive kitchen.

That afternoon, we returned to Steve and Liz's apartment in town and just before heading to the Philadelphia Zoo for an afternoon of decompressing, Steve received a text message from two of the guests at the lunch. The guests advised Steve that they wished to make a five-year pledge to CRST for a six-figure sum. I still can't describe my gratitude and love for these social change-makers whose contributions make our efforts possible, empowering the legacy of change that will be felt for generations to come. The support from these two guests absolutely helped shape our NGO, giving critical financial support and the confidence that we were on the right track and must keep going. I will always remember this humble couple who never sought any form of recognition – they supported us because they could and because they knew they were leaving a legacy. After five years they renewed their pledge for a further three years!!

## Supporting more success

Steve and I have become good friends over the years and he was instrumental in registering the Cambodia Rural Students Foundation USA Inc. as a 501(c)(3) tax-deductible charity in the United States. This enabled us to expand our donor base, support more students and create more social impact through our projects.

Steve's engagement with the students at our Business School was also inspirational as he connected with them on a professional, yet personal basis. He identified the students who grasped the financial concepts he was teaching faster than others and embraced our Business School methodology of having a 'buddy system', placing students in clusters so no-one was left behind.

Following one of the later Business School sessions, Steve asked Sreng to lead a part of the class with him on the following day.

'Oh, I'm not sure I can do that – I'm not a professor,' Sreng said humbly to Steve and me, with a big grin on his face.

'Sure you can, Sreng,' Steve said. 'You're as good as me when it comes to explaining the reasons, logic and processes of financial statements. What do you think, Aviv?' Steve turned to me.

'I'm really looking forward to class tomorrow, Professor Sreng,' I said with a laugh. Sreng was indeed bright and diligent; he was also a true leader, loved and respected by all, and was hardworking and humble. The next day, speaking in Khmer, he led part of the class with clarity and passion, making extensive use of the whiteboard, answering questions and setting mini-tasks for our students to work through in their clusters in class.

'He's pretty good,' Steve leaned over to tell me.

'No, Steve,' I replied, 'he's brilliant. The full package. And to think that just two years ago he was putting himself though high school working as a waiter, without any prospects of further studies. You know his GPA is 3.67?'[5]

'Wow!!' Steve exclaimed.

The following year Sreng relocated to Temple University in Philadelphia to study his bachelor degree majoring in management information systems. Imagine a 25-year-old Cambodian student turning up in a foreign country with no family, no friends, no familiar food, in below freezing temperatures and a foot of snow. He was way out of his comfort zone but we knew Sreng had resilience. I spoke with him frequently to ensure we didn't lose him to any mental health issues – I encouraged him to have a regimented daily routine, starting with a gym session each morning, and then cooking his favourite Cambodian breakfast food at home. His study routine was just as important – revise the day's upcoming classes each morning, always sit in the front row of the class, and revise the day's classes at the end of each day. I also suggested to him to do his revisions in a variety of places, of course including his room, but also the university library, public areas and outdoors when the weather was good. This would always give him something different to look forward to and allow him to feel in control of his studies.

Liz and Steve sponsored Sreng for his studies and living expenses and were also a great support to Sreng. Steve met with him on campus to ensure he had all his classes under control and Liz took Sreng shopping to make sure he always had whatever he needed.

Sreng returned to Cambodia at the beginning of COVID-19 and completed his degree online from Phnom Penh – due to the time zone difference, he studied his classes between 1 am and 6 am. Sreng graduated with a GPA of 3.82, 'magna cum laude' (an academic

---

5   Grade point average (GPA) is a calculation of a students' average grade or result. This can be calculated on a yearly basis, or for the course as a whole, and is calculated using a scale of 0 to 4.

award that translates as 'with great praise'), in the top 5 per cent of his year! Through James and Zed, a couple of our long-time Australian sponsors, we connected him with KPMG, one of world's four largest accounting and advisory firms. He joined their IT Audit Department and on my next trip to Phnom Penh, I told Sreng that our family would like to sponsor his MBA at the American University of Phnom Penh. His eyes welled up.

'Aviv, you and your family have done so much for me and my family already,' he said. 'Maybe you can save that money and invest it in some of our other students.' He agreed to accept our offer, provided he could be an active mentor and contributor in the NGO. Two years later, Sreng graduated from his MBA with a 3.8 GPA. By that time, he was working as a senior IT auditor at KPMG and he was approached by the Ministry of Economy and Finance; his interview lasted 15 minutes and he was hired. They knew gold when they saw it.

'I spoke with my boss at the Ministry,' Sreng told me a few months later. 'He's agreed to support me to teach at university on the weekends. Can you please speak with PUC and ask if I can teach there?'

'Sreng, PUC is in Siem Reap and you're living and working in Phnom Penh. How do you plan to do that?' I asked him with my eyes wide open. (The drive between the two cities takes about seven hours.)

'It'll be a little hard, but I can do it – I'll take the night bus on Friday and teach on the weekend, and then return on the night bus on Sunday,' he said with conviction. 'I really want to help the next generation and inspire them. I know I can help them, like an older brother – and I have so much to share. You always teach us that education is for us, so we can share it with others.'

Sreng and I agreed that it may be best to continue developing his career for now and he may revisit the opportunity of teaching at university in a few years. Always full of gratitude and humility, living the CRST mission of 'breaking the poverty cycle through education by educating future leaders', Sreng is very special to us.

*December 2023 – May 2024*

*Sreng wrote us these emails after completing his MBA studies:*

**From: Sreng Sokh**

Sent: Tuesday, December 12, 2023

Dear Aviv, Michelle, Jess, Aaron, and Steph,

I would like to share with you this special day for me – the day I have finally submitted my last assignment to AUPP class!!!!

I have now completed everything and only need to wait for my final score to be released on the 16th of this month!!! Finally, I have graduated with another degree – the MBA!!!!!

The title 'អនុបណ្ឌិត' is very special in Cambodia and well respected by many!!!! Those with this title, especially back in my village, would be highly respected. 'អនុ' refers to pre- and 'បណ្ឌិត' means doctor. This big milestone is achieved, again, under the support from CRST ... and, of course, ALL OF YOU!!!!

I would like to take this opportunity to thank you for all the education you have given me. This will become a weapon I hold with me for the rest of my life fighting toward success and improving my country!!!! Thank you for giving me this powerful weapon!!! THANK YOU!!!!!

My graduation ceremony will be on Saturday May 4th, 2024. I will invite my mother, my step-father and my sisters to be there. If you all could be there, that would BE MY GREAT HONOR!!!!

Again, thank you so much, Aviv, Jess, Michelle, Aaron, and Steph as always!!!!!!!!! THANK YOU!!!!

Best,

Sreng SOKH

**From: Sreng Sokh**

Sent: Tuesday, 19 December 2023

Good morning Aviv, Jess, Michelle, Aaron, and Steph,

Just some additional information. The final results are out:

Global Management – I got an A–.

Capstone – I got an A.

So my overall GPA is 3.8 – could not be happier with this result!!!! 😊

I have attached my overall grades. 😊

Best,

Sreng SOKH

*These were our replies:*

**From: Jessica Palti**

WOW!! CONGRATULATIONS SRENG! How exciting and you have a fancy new title too. 😁

We will take a look at our diaries to see if we can be there for your 2nd special day. 😊

Jess

**From: Aviv Palti**

An incredible milestone Sreng and we are so proud of you!!! 🎉🎉🎉 🎉🎉🎉 We may have provided you with the opportunities, but the commitment, dedication, effort and brain are all yours!!!!

Congratulations to you and your family and thank you for being the extraordinary leader and role model that you are. 👨‍👩‍👧‍👦🎊🎊🎊👨‍👩‍👧‍👦

Love you always ❤️❤️❤️ Aviv

*Sreng sent us another email after his graduation:*

**From: Sreng Sokh**

Sent: Tuesday, 14 May 2024

Good morning Aviv, Jess, Michelle, Aaron, and Steph,

I would like to take this opportunity to share with you some of my special days – I think this is the end of my academic life!! 😊

As you are aware my graduation ceremony was last week on the 4th. The day before the graduation, my mother and my sister came to Phnom Penh to prepare for my ceremony and for my mother to see where I live and how I live in PP. In the evening, I also had a chance to bring her to Aeon Mall – that was the first time for her to actually be there. We had some dinner and then did a little bit of shopping.

On the graduation day, due to my mother's health, she decided not to go to the event but joined me to take some photos at the garden near the royal palace. Rany accompanied me to the event while my sister took care of my mother. The event ended and we headed back home and then went to the royal place together with my mother and sister. We took some photos there and I showed my mother around a little bit – the last time she was in PP to the Royal Place was many years ago. My mother then went back to Siem Reap.

Originally, I thought I was going to spend the next two days in SR but then decided to do that the week after. So last week, I went back to SR to be with my family to celebrate one last time. The first day we bought some food, cooked and ate together. We discussed a lot of things afterward. The next day, we went to Angkor Wat together.

These two days meant a lot to me – not only that I could spend time with my family but, recently, I started to realise even more that life is too short and I've got to spend more time with them when I can. And not only to spend time at home but also do something meaningful together. My stepfather fell off the bed when he was back home and now has to be brought back to the hospital. His condition now has been even worse than before. During my two days visit, I was hoping to be with him at home showing my achievement – the achievement he has contributed to. But I could not show him that. I hope that he recovers soon!!!

Aviv, Jess, Michelle, Aaron, and Steph – the big three academic achievements (my BA from PUC, BA from Temple, and MBA from AUPP) are all possible because of CRST, because of your support – both financially and emotionally. For the past 11 years – since 2013 – there were many times that I wanted to give up some for very stupid reasons, some for financial reasons, some for family reasons, some for personal reasons ... But you have never given up on me, and continue to give me chances. Now I have achieved more than I could imagine.

When I was in Japan last month with my team, as we were walking down the road to a Japanese University, my friend (who introduced me to the Ministry and is also from a poor family) told me that he was the only person in his family who had chances to travel abroad and stay in a very nice hotels and got to enjoy time in Japan. I reflected on that to myself and feel blessed that I have come so far. Opportunities are always there but if we are not ready to catch them, they will be gone. CRST has made me ready for these opportunities.

Thank you for being in my life, giving me confidence, and teaching me how to fish. ***Now it is time to give back!!!!!!***

ALSO VERY EXCITED TO SEE YOU IN MELBOURNE IN A FEW WEEKS!!!! ☺

Best regards,

Sreng SOKH

## Developing our Business School

Our Business School program over the years has included insightful mentors who are passionate business leaders, drawing on their practical life and business experiences. In addition to the CRST university students attending, we're always joined by non-CRST university students, including ones from the National University of Management, who come all the way from Phnom Penh to join us for the week in Siem Reap.

Over the years we've covered some incredible topics, leaving our students inspired and empowered by our international mentors:

- *Business Planning for Success:* From the big picture to the detailed plan, we covered finance, operations, HR, sales and marketing – culminating in all students preparing and presenting their own business plans!

- *Leadership Fundamentals:* Topics covered included developing the characteristics, skills and habits of successful leaders, the steps to leadership and developing your inner circle.

- *Keys to Peak Performance:* Topics included hierarchy of needs, effective communication, emotional intelligence, body language, and the habits and secrets of highly successful people.

- *Project Me – Life Skills that Lead to Success:* Putting down your baggage, using your moral compass and the power of your magic book.
- *Personal Financial Management:* Creating a financially secure future starts today.

During COVID-19, our international guest mentors were unable to travel to Cambodia and we pivoted our Business School program into a Business Class program, which is now a permanent activity. These half-day classes are held one Sunday each month, with our alumni returning from Phnom Penh to Siem Reap to share knowledge and experience from their lives in 'the real world'.

## Far-reaching benefits of the Ambassador Program

While the CRST Business School program exposed our students to visiting business professionals who shared their knowledge, our Ambassador Program exposed our students to all that a developed Cambodia can look forward to. As they visited Australia, New Zealand, the United States and Thailand, they saw all that was possible – and they understood that it was their generation who had the responsibility of developing Cambodia.

'What's that metal thing sticking out of the ground?' Sreng asked us when we were having coffee one morning at Starbucks on his first visit to the United States as a CRST Ambassador to San Francisco in 2017.

'That's a street light – you have these in Siem Reap too, Sreng,' I replied, a little bewildered by the question.

Sreng chuckled and said, 'No, not that tall pole, the short one next to it.' He pointed towards the footpath outside the window.

'That's a parking meter,' Jess replied, and patiently proceeded to explain to Sreng, Sompeas and Nak what parking meters were, why we have them and how they work. That 2017 trip to the United States helped shape the rest of Nak, Sompeas and Sreng's lives – that's no exaggeration; they could see what was possible, and they went after it with both hands!!

'I can't believe all these tall buildings,' Yeat remarked on another ambassador trip, this time to New York in 2018.

'There's a lot of money in real estate,' I replied.

'Yep. That's what I want to do – I want to be in real estate and make a lot of money. What do you think, Aviv?'

'I think you'll be *great* in real estate, Yeat!! You make connections with people very fast, you're genuine, you're super-friendly, you have the million-dollar smile and you can *sell*! That's why you're the best sales person at Project Y – Frozen Yogurt!!' I thought a career in real estate would be an incredible life choice for Yeat. That trip changed Yeat's life. He returned to Cambodia full of the vision of what was possible, finished his BA, studied his MBA and developed his real estate agency business and joined Cambodia's middle class.

The Ambassador Program allows us to have a unique voice, by enabling our students to share our impact from their perspectives. While our supporters experience our impact through our students' eyes, our students experience all that is possible through education and development.

I have no doubt that each of our students who had the life-changing opportunity to become a CRST Ambassador was enriched. They experienced developed nations, and they could see and touch what was possible; as Cambodia's future leaders, they could now work on bringing some of that back to Cambodia.

### March 2024

*Our Business School has also sustainably impacted our students' lives in so many ways, and they in turn have been able to share the ripple effect of empowerment with their families.*

*Alumni Sineang and Barang married after graduating from their bachelor degrees and moved to Phnom Penh to work and study their respective MBAs. They recently emailed us to share an exciting addition to their lives:*

Good morning Aviv, Michelle and Jess,

Not knowing if you all had a good night's sleep, but this is supposed to be the good morning email and just if you are about to do something, please finish reading this first before doing that thing you wish.

Remember the sentence in my previous email about personal good news? Here we are, and as I said it was because of your support that greatly impacted our personal financial plan.

For the last two years besides family and work, and while continuing to study our master's degrees, Sineang and I have saved and managed to buy a few plots of land in Siem Reap. Of course, all these will be remaining as our future investment and/or business purpose once we are able to create our own opportunities.

Moreover, the good news is: Our birthdays and wedding anniversary were jointly celebrated, and we gave ourselves a lovely present – a family-friendly SUV Highlander. A C-A-R! A CAR! A dream that I myself would always wish to come true. Of course, we are as happy as could be imagined when a dream comes true!

For rich people, this car is nothing compared to the money and assets they own, but for us (and our families) it is a tangible achievement. We drove our families around for a few days in a few provinces with some blessing ceremonies. We would also like to drive you all around Phnom Penh as well, and maybe in Siem Reap – please visit us any time soon.

We are sure you do not mind that we are sharing such personal matters, but because we are so happy and grateful for it and we would like you to be proud and happy too. Every second of our success, we sense the result of your support and LOVE. Sharing this with you is the same way we did with our parents and you all receive the same RESPECT from us as our parents and family too. Please also personally account this success, life-changing result, and happiness as a part of all your efforts so far.

Last but not least – Good Morning!

Sineang and Barang

## FOUNDATIONS OF LEADERSHIP TAKEAWAYS

- Empower others to amplify your voice as your ambassadors.
- People know what they see – show them more and widen their perspective.
- Teams reach further and create greater impact; ensure your team is well trained.
- Public speaking, networking and effective communications are learnable and critical life skills – learn them early and start reaping the rewards early.
- Leaders catch their team members before they fall.
- Leaders cast shadows; make sure you stand in the correct position to allow plenty of sunshine for your team to grow.
- Reframe manipulation into collaboration.
- If someone else has done it, so can you – and once you've done it, help others do it too.
- When out of your comfort zone, create 'a new normal' with routines and habits that will support you.
- Always look for the next leadership opportunity.

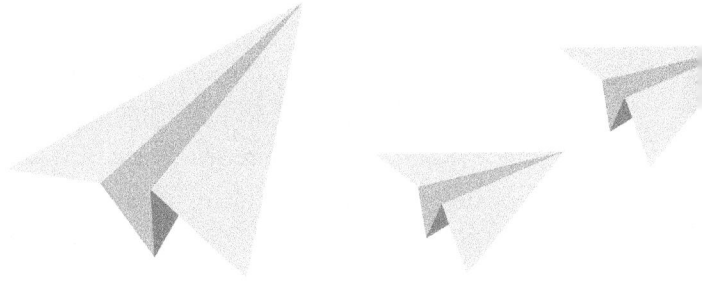

# Chapter 13

# Gender equality is not a concept; it's a set of actions

Gender equality is a global hot topic. Not a day passes by without some sort of gender-based rhetoric in the media. Whether it's related to domestic violence, discrimination, access to jobs, promotions, leadership or the basic human rights of dignity and respect, 50 per cent of the world's population has to struggle to be heard and valued.

I grew up in a home where gender equality was never discussed – it was a fact of life, our 'normal'. My parents were also products of gender equality. My father's parents were educated professionals with intelligent and articulate world views – and an appreciation that having an opinion came with an equal measure of allowing others to be heard and respected. My mother's parents definitely had gender-based domestic roles, but both worked hard, cared for their kids and encouraged my mother, her sister and brother to be ambitious as they sought further education beyond high school.

My mother graduated from teachers' college when she was 22 years old and was a school principal by the age of 27. Driven by the power of education and the role of teachers in shaping the society we seek, her career included tenures in special education schools, government schools and private schools, before culminating as a professor at the University of Melbourne.

My father is a computer engineer-turned-entrepreneur. His work never distracted him from his focus on family and his passion for effective communication, including 25 years as a volunteer journalist on community radio. I've never seen my parents' marriage as anything but an equal partnership. The mainstream media, however, showed us that our 'normal' was not universal.

## Building up the lives of girls

In the early years of the NGO, we were seriously challenged to reach gender equality, with far fewer girls than boys applying to join CRST. We also had to be honest with ourselves and recognise that the girls who applied were nowhere as passionate about their education as the boys. Due to social gender biases, girls were seen as weak and an extension of the household, not the co-foundation of the household.

Many girls dropped out of high school before graduating – their gender meant they were far more likely to be consigned to a life of domestic servitude rather than social leadership. With home pressures to help the family earn an income, girls were encouraged to drop out of school at younger ages than boys. The prevailing view in many rural Cambodian families was that girls didn't really need an education – ultimately, they would get married, have kids and look after the house; if they weren't going to get a job, they didn't need an education. Boys, on the other hand, were going to be the breadwinners, so they were more worthy of an education.

Whilst this was the prevailing view in rural Cambodia when we founded the NGO, it's incredible to see how regional political realities and a new generation of young educated Cambodians are realigning the social norms. With Cambodia's more active participation in ASEAN, the Association of Southeast Asian Nations, came the urgency to develop a nation that would be based on successful commerce, with reduced dependency on unreliable income from agriculture. What better way to stimulate a country's economy than to grow the middle class by refocusing on education – and universal education for both genders? And with a new generation of girls encouraged to stay at school, graduate and continue on to university, for the first time many rural girls had role models exuding knowledge and independence, not a lack of opportunities and dependence.

Our NGO student membership is currently skewed 65 per cent in favour of girls – not because we're biased, but because in recent years the girls applying to join CRST have been so much more passionate about their education than the boys. It seems that the government's and society's new focus on the importance of educating girls is showing green shoots – we are now receiving many more applications to join CRST from girls who are dedicated to their studies and committed to forging an empowered future.

## Tackling period poverty

Celeste Mergens founded Days for Girls International (DfGI) following a trip to Africa, where she learned that countless girls were missing school while experiencing their periods. Whether it was period shame, a lack of feminine menstrual products or social ignorance, girls isolated for a few days each month, amounting to a few weeks missed over the course of a year. They missed so many school days that often it became simpler to drop out rather than constantly catch up or put up with the social stigma of having a period.

Celeste and a core group of volunteer friends took a pragmatic approach – they set out to tackle period poverty from both an educational and informative perspective, as well as the practical and sustainable angle. They developed educational modules for both girls and boys, focusing on the reproductive system and the natural beauty of menstruation, which enables all people to develop in a healthy and nourishing womb. The girls' education includes self-love and appreciation; the boys' education includes their responsibilities to support girls so that society as a whole will benefit. The DfGI team also experimented and developed a beautiful and sustainable menstrual hygiene kit that girls could use for three to five years.

## Connecting with Days for Girls International

In line with our focus on gender equality, we were seeking to create a project that would allow us to celebrate and empower our girls, and allow all our students (girls and boys) to inspire other rural students to experience that gender equality and female empowerment were facts of life, not mere catchphrases. The universe put the US-based Days for Girls International organisation (DfGI) in our path and we connected with them.

The DfGI program was exactly what we were looking for – it combined the incredible power of education, with the empowerment, value and love we wanted to show our girls.

'This is bigger than our girls, Dad,' Jess said to me. 'We need to speak to DfGI about becoming one of their registered enterprises. Can you imagine the impact of making and distributing thousands of kits in Cambodia every year? Can you imagine the impact of our girls educating other rural girls? And our boys educating rural high school boys? This is BIG!!'

Jess was super-excited – and I didn't need to be sold on the idea.

Over the next six months we set up our second educational social enterprise, 'Project G – Empowering Girls'. Jess took on the key mentorship role as our students prepared a business plan using the knowledge they had acquired at our Business School. Our product was 'girl empowerment', and our target market was rural high school students in Siem Reap province.

Jess announced to our students that the first Project G general manager would be Sinuon; she was shocked and emotional. Much as Sreng did when appointed the general manager of Project Y, she said she couldn't do it, and that she didn't have the knowledge, the confidence or the magnetism a GM needed. Jess reassured her: 'You know we selected you because we know you can do it, right? Because when you show everyone how great you are as a leader, so many other girls will look up to you and will want to be like you. Leaving footprints, Sinuon – just remember you're leaving footprints for more girls to follow.'

Sinuon, like practically all our NGO students, experienced trauma in her earlier years, but was determined to graduate from high school, go to university and get a rewarding job that would allow her to look after her mum. She was less than five foot tall, of nervous appearance, with self-doubt never far away. But she had a voice – all we did was help her find it.

### October 2018

*Sinuon was selected to travel to Philadelphia to represent CRST, speaking at community and business gatherings. This is her ambassador presentation:*

Hi everyone,

A girl without education is like a bird without wings – happiness is not always with you all the time. I am Sinuon. I am 20 years old and today I am very happy and confident to share with you the story of my life, what challenges I have faced and what I have achieved to become a role model for my family and Cambodian people.

When I was in grade 1, my family was considered middle class. We had enough food, clothes, a better house, and all children went to school happily. My dad brought me to school every morning and waited in front of school when I finished my class. Every day after dinner, my parents always told us jokes and we would all laugh. There was very great love and these are unforgettable best memories in my life.

My parents were in a serious traffic accident when I was in grade 2 and happiness disappeared in a minute. My dad became a disabled person for eight years and he could not eat, walk, talk, and even recognise his children. My mum had to stay home to take care of him every day by using body language even though her head was very painful after the accident. Dad got angry easily, and he just cried alone because he hated himself that he could not do anything.

My mum spent a lot of money and sold all our property to cure my dad, but my dad did not get better. My three siblings decided to drop out of school to work in town as construction workers to help cure my dad and support the family. They earned just $20 per month. That was not enough. We did not even have rice to eat – how can my mum afford for all her children to go to school? She forced herself to let my first sister live with my uncle in town to continue studying. There was only my older sister and me who could stay in school because we were too young to work.

It was a very painful day when I was 13. I looked at my dad just laid on the bed and could not eat anything. His tears came out and he caught my hand very strong with love. Even though he could not talk to me, I understood that he was very ashamed that he could not support me. He died with open eyes. Everyone and me just cried and cried to lose him. You may understand the feeling to lose someone who you love the most in your life. To me, it was very painful to lose my hero. After the funeral, my family situation was very bad because we lost all our property and my mum was still recovering from the traffic accident with my dad.

I remember one day that I came back from school in the evening. My mum did not have food, so she swapped some banana flowers for 500 grams of rice for six members of our family. Because I did not have enough food, I was unconscious in front of my mum, and she took me to the health clinic due to serious low blood sugar. The doctor said I was very lucky that my mum took me to the clinic on time; otherwise, I would die in 10 minutes. My mum cried, but she was glad when I started to open my eyes and talk to her. My mum is my hero because she gave me a beautiful life, love and care. Back to my studying – my results at school were very bad and I was discriminated against by my classmates. I was so embarrassed and so stressed. I could not accept the change in my family situation that was so quick.

I got a serious headache and I didn't know what was happening to me. I always thought a lot about my mum's health, my siblings and my health. Then, I decided to commit suicide two times but I could not do it because I was thinking that my mum would be alone if I die. I was very quiet, I was alone and I could not find someone to be my good listener. I had no friends, I was so isolated.

When I was 16, I still could not get away from my issues. I tried to commit suicide again. I always kept myself in a silent place, cried and asked myself, 'How many times do I need to cry and how many times do I try to kill myself?' I was reminded that my mum gave me birth, love and care. So, I told myself that I have to stand up; otherwise, my mum would die with me.

I did my best to face all the issues, and I committed to become a strong and lovely child for my mum. I continued going to school and volunteered to teach Khmer language to small kids in a free school in my hometown. It was a very good place for me to reduce my stress when teaching them. I really enjoyed what I was doing. To help my mum, I also sold some souvenirs, vegetables and Khmer cakes, and I earned only $1 per day.

In 2013, I heard about a scholarship opportunity from Cambodia Rural Students Trust and I applied but, unluckily, I didn't pass because my English was very poor. I didn't give up; I went back to school to study even harder. I asked my teacher if I could study English for free. When I came back home, I volunteered to teach English for free to kids in my village. After tremendous practice, my English got better and better.

At the end 2014, I applied for a CRST scholarship again, and I was accepted. My new life started to change when CRST sent me to the best private high school and university in Siem Reap. I study with professional teachers who always encourage me to be my best and I study with both Khmer and English native speakers. CRST provides full health care, monthly allowances and three meals per day to high school students. Social workers and the leadership team in CRST play an important part to consult and encourage me not to give up when I am stressed. Now I am completely better and enjoy what I am doing.

Throughout the challenges I faced in life, CRST played a big part. Now, I love being who I am and feel really proud that I could overcome those challenges.

Besides education, CRST gives me the opportunity to help people through community service. I love doing these activities because I have been in that situation. We usually build houses, paint schools, plant trees, and many other activities which benefit our community.

In 2015, I graduated from high school. My mother was so proud of me. I was then promoted to be the sport and health manager in CRST. It gave me a great opportunity to learn what life is supposed to be and it has taken me out of my comfort zone.

In 2016, I was selected to work at 'Project – Y Frozen Yogurt', our educational social enterprise that was started in 2015 by CRST's founders with the mission of teaching our students how to run a profitable business and raise money to support more poor students. Team members are mentored by Aviv, Michelle and Jess and rotate through six business departments every six months. Throughout the one and a half years I have been working at Project Y, I have learned how to work as a team, communicate effectively, practise my English with many guests, build more confidence and understand more about business.

Project G is our new social enterprise. The 'G' stands for 'girls'. We are partnering with Days for Girls International to provide safe, beautiful, washable, and long-lasting menstrual kits, along with vital health education. Our mission is to 'Empower Cambodian girls and women with sustainable menstrual products and health education'.

I am proud to say that I am the general manager for this project and my team and I are all university students.

We have been endorsed by the Ministry of Education, Youth and Sport to run our workshops in rural high schools around Cambodia, to educate and empower the next generation. We also distribute our kits free to all high school girls who join our workshops! Our kits are made of materials that will last up to five years, and being chemical-free, they are great for our environment!!

The kits are sewn at our social enterprise sewing workshop in Siem Reap, which employs women from high-risk situations including human trafficking and domestic violence. The women are taught sewing skills and are empowered to become a pillar of their families and an inspiration to their children. We believe that Project G will help lots of Cambodian girls, boys, women and men to understand more about their health and the vital role women have in society.

I am now in my second year of university studying international relations. My goal is to work in the Ministry of Human Rights because I want to promote and encourage people to raise up their voice when they get abused by others. My dream is to create a women and children centre to help people who have mental health issues to consult and encourage them to overcome their issues in their lives and don't think in the short term like I did!!

I could not imagine how much my life has been changed through CRST. Not just me but there are more than 60 students who are supported by CRST. We aim to help more poor students to get the best opportunity every year because our vision is to break the poverty cycle through education.

Thank you so much for your time to listen to my story today. I believe that only education can help me and of course other poor children in rural areas. If they have an opportunity to be supported by CRST, we can turn those poor kids into a great leader like me and our students. If you are interested in helping break the poverty cycle with us, we would love to have you join our journey.

*Sinuon is now studying her MBA in Phnom Penh and works as a project officer at the Reproductive Health Association of Cambodia. She is also a member of the UN Youth Advisory Panel in Cambodia.*

## Developing our DfGI partnership

The Project G team includes both girls and boys – gender equality had to be the foundation for empowering girls. Much like Project Y, the general manager is supported by an assistant GM and they lead several departments, including education, production, human resources, finance, marketing and operations. Each department has a CRST student as manager and additional students as team members.

We set ourselves the target of becoming a DfGI-qualified enterprise within six months. We knew this was an incredibly ambitious timeline, but we set it to both challenge our team and allow us to become DfGI's first enterprise in Cambodia. The tight time frame meant we needed to plan and deliver a fully operational sewing workshop producing DfGI-approved kits with a fully certified DfGI team of educators. Each department got to work on their part of the plan – Sinuon and her assistant general manager, Khean, had their hands full with coordination and communication. Khean was one of our male university students and he took great pride in his leadership role in Project G.

'We'd love to help – what can we do?' Penny asked Jess on the phone. A few weeks earlier, Jess and I had met Karin and Penny from Perth at a DfGI training event in Melbourne. Jess told them we were working on setting up a DfGI enterprise in Cambodia and they were very excited. They told us they were experienced DfGI chapter leaders and would love to support us – although, frankly, I wasn't sure what they could do from Western Australia, which of course was nowhere near Siem Reap.

'Well, we were wondering if Karin and you might consider flying to Cambodia to train our sewing team?' Jess replied.

'Wow, that would be great. We'd love to!!' Penny replied. Jess told them that of course we would pay for their travel expenses, but we wouldn't be able to pay them for their time.

'Absolutely out of the question!! We have our own little fund for these sorts of opportunities – you keep the money for your amazing work in Cambodia and we'll pay all our own expenses,' Penny replied. Jess and I were shocked – and there was more to come.

Penny and Karin arrived in Siem Reap a few weeks later and trained our sewing team – three ladies from the local community who were already experienced sewers. After spending a week together, we had the basics all under control and sent photos of the sample kits to DfGI for approval.

During the week Karin and Penny spent with our team, they assessed what else we needed and gifted us an overlocker machine – their generosity and spirit are still creating an impact for thousands of rural girls in Cambodia. We now have five sewing ladies, Mom, Neang, Sopheak, Heang and Kimhon, who have sewn thousands of DfGI kits as part of the Project G production team – they are an inspiration to their families and their community.

Samach and Doeb, our senior students and former health managers, took on the roles of senior educators. They studied and trained on the DfGI online platform, and became DfGI-qualified educators. They then set up training workshops for the rest of our Project G educators. Over the next few months, 26 of our girls received DfGI's Ambassador of Women's Health accreditation and 14 of our boys became Men Who Know educators. The Project G education team translated the DfGI teaching material into Khmer and prepared flip charts, ready to share the knowledge with thousands of rural students in Cambodia!!

With the kits passing all quality control checks and a team of qualified educators, Project G became DfGI's first enterprise in Cambodia. In 2019, the team was honoured to host DfGI's inspirational founder, Celeste Mergens, in Siem Reap, and in 2021, Project G received DfGI's highest accreditation as a Gold Standard Enterprise. Also in 2021, the Project G team began researching and writing *Empower a Girl, Inspire a Nation*, a book about gender equality in Cambodia, the teachings of Days for Girls International and the social impact of women in society. Celeste and Leyla from Days for Girls International wrote the forewords, along with Maria (the former Days for Girls Country Representative for Cambodia), Jess and me.

Since 2018 we have educated over 20,000 girls, boys, women and men in rural Cambodia about the reproductive system, menstruation, gender equality and basic self-defence for girls. Our team has distributed over 16,000 beautiful and sustainable Project G–DfGI kits to girls and women in rural Cambodia, and the Project G team now educates over 7000 students and distributes over 5000 kits every year.

Social media enables the rural high school girls we teach to maintain contact with our Project G educators, so they can ask questions at any time and continue to follow the path of education and aspire to be like their CRST role models. We have also added modules about human trafficking to our workshops, to educate rural students about the trap of human trafficking and provide them with a list of emergency contact numbers.

## FOUNDATIONS OF LEADERSHIP TAKEAWAYS

- The most impactful way to add value is to ask people what they need, help them get it and support them.

- Empowerment means helping people to help themselves.

- Help people be the best they can be and then support them and inspire them to be better.

- Start with a need, develop a plan, take action, evaluate and improve.

- If you don't add value, you're not valued; if you're not valued, you're dispensable.

- Relationships are measured by mutual benefits.

- Make a habit of regularly asking team members what else you may support them with; even if you can't give them what they want, you can certainly learn more about their needs and create ways for them to feel more valued, appreciated and respected.

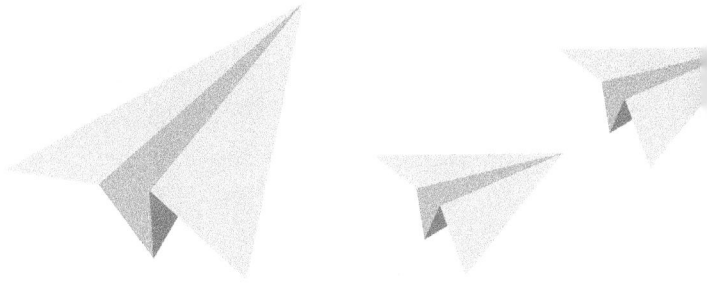

## Chapter 14

# We all have responsibility – 'response ability'

Cherrie has been sponsoring Somey since the first CRST Ambassador trip to Australia in 2017.

She rang me one evening and said, 'Aviv, the Rotary Club of Keilor East would like to support a project with CRST in Cambodia – do you have any new projects coming up?'

We normally have a buffet of projects and activities requiring funding, so our potential supporters can easily choose the purpose that best suits their mission. Whether that purpose is education, health, nutrition, gender equality, plastic pollution, clean water, alleviating poverty – and the list goes on – we have a project that focuses on it. In fact, we are ticking 14 out of the UN's 17 Sustainable Development Goals – not that we set out to do that, but here we are.

'Great timing, Cherrie!!' I instantly replied. 'We're looking at a project that will supply bicycles to rural students, to support them to stay at school rather than drop out. You know, right now many of these students need to walk for an hour each way to get to school – in the searing sun or pouring rain, two hours a day, there and back! Gifting them a bike, and helping them to maintain that bike, will make a massive difference to their education and their ability to graduate and help their families. Would this be something you and the club members might be interested in, Cherrie?'

## The (seemingly) simple gift of a bicycle

Two months later, the Rotary Club of Keilor East donated $3000 as seed funding for 'Project B – Bicycles for Education'. It often takes one visionary to walk the first few steps before others see what's possible and follow. With additional funding from other Rotary Clubs, private donors and corporate sponsors, we now distribute several hundred bicycles to pre-qualified rural students each year. Our Mobile Bike Mechanic (MBM) program repairs hundreds of bicycles for rural students every year, enabling them to continue going to school.

Project B is entirely managed by the CRST students. Our first Project B general manager was Saoly, one of our university students who previously was the NGO's health manager and assistant GM at 'Project V – The Volunteer Experience'. Leading a team of students who manage a variety of departments including finance, operations, marketing and education, Saoly infused the balance of heart and head that CRST has become known for.

Our team regularly visits high schools in Siem Reap province, meeting with the school directors, teachers and, ultimately, students, families and village leaders. Our student-qualification process is vital – we only gift bicycles to students who are committed to their education and whose families are too poor to be able to buy them a bicycle. While the process takes a number of school and village visits, the results are sustainable and the impact long-lasting.

When schools were closed during the COVID-19 period, the team couldn't follow our process of visiting schools to assess which students needed bicycles, so we started our popular MBM program. We contracted a local bicycle repair workshop in town to come to our campus and train all our students on the basic elements of bicycle repairs. After learning and practising on their own bikes, our students were ready for action!

The Project B team visited villages and assessed what bikes needed fixing, allocating a number to each bike assessed. Back in town, they bought the necessary parts to repair the bicycles and, on the agreed Sunday, all our NGO students travelled to the selected village and 'set up shop'. The team divided into groups of four to five students, each group laid a tarpaulin on the ground and invited their allocated bike owners to bring their bicycles over for repair. On any given Sunday, the CRST students repaired over 100 bicycles, supporting rural Cambodians' daily lives. As the schools reopened after the COVID-19 closure, we switched the MBM program to schools and now repair hundreds of bicycles for rural students each year, supporting their education.

Our CRST students become role models, exemplifying the power of education and the benefits of remaining at school. Our team especially love visiting some of their own old schools, talking with their previous teachers and taking great pride in telling the current students that they were students at that school just a few years ago! Now, after graduating from high school, they are at university and are already able to come back and help others. As they share the empowerment of education, the next generation can see what's possible – educate, empower, inspire.

## Finding more Rotarian support

'Hi Aviv.' David, friend and advisor to our company's board, was on the other end of the phone.

'Good morning, David. How are you?' I replied.

'I'm great!! Listen, I spent the weekend with this lovely guy and his wife – they came up to the farm. Anyway, turns out that Gwyn is a member of a Rotary Club in Glen Waverley, and he wants to know if you can present at their club and tell them what we're doing in Cambodia,' David said enthusiastically.

A few weeks later Jess, David and I joined the members of the Rotary Club of Glen Waverley at their weekly meeting and dinner at the Village Green Hotel in Glen Waverley.

'Welcome! You must be the people from the Cambodia Rural School,' said Michele who greeted us at the door.

'Right,' I replied, 'from the Cambodia Rural Students Foundation. Thank you for the invitation to join you tonight, Michele,' I replied, reading her name badge.

Michele smiled broadly, introduced herself as the Club's International Service Director and handed us our name tags. 'Tony, would you be able to take our guests from Cambodia in with you?' she asked another club member. Turns out that Tony was the club's previous International Service Director – Rotary Clubs rotate roles every year, similar to CRST. 'Actually, we live in Melbourne, Tony. Our organisation is based in Cambodia,' I clarified for Tony.

'I thought so – Michele got a little excited,' he replied with a grin.

Everyone was super-nice and very welcoming as we stood around chatting with the members filtering in to the room. David introduced us to Gwyn, who was very gracious in connecting us to his Rotary Club, and who seemed to already know a fair bit about our work in Cambodia, likely thanks to David. We sat at round tables of eight or so and chatted for a while and then the waiter arrived with the alternating offer of lamb or chicken for dinner. I found a willing volunteer to swap my lamb for their chicken, but before I had the chance to finish my meal, Tony stepped up to the lectern to introduce me.

'We have some really special guests here tonight – they are from the Cambodia Rural Students Trust but, to be clear, they live here in Melbourne. And we are very grateful to Gwyn for introducing these wonderful people to us – Aviv will share with everyone some of their outstanding activities and contributions to society.' Polite applause followed Tony's introduction and I stepped up to the microphone as Jess took control of the laptop to scroll through the PowerPoint presentation, which included photos of NGO students and activities, to project behind me as I was presenting.

For the next 20 minutes I introduced the origins of CRST and the work the NGO does. I outlined much of what I have already covered in this book, talking about our first visit to Siem Reap, and then our development of CRST as an NGO with the mission of 'Breaking the poverty cycle through education'. I highlighted that we sponsored bright students from poor rural families to study at the best private high school and university in town, provided them with a monthly living allowance so they could afford to live in town, and mentored our students to become future leaders in society. I also ran through our students' volunteering activities, noting all our students contribute to society regularly.

My passion for the cause was obvious as I concluded my speech:

*The ripple effect we create reaches far and wide as our students inspire thousands of other rural students to see the power of education. 'Stay at school, sister; stay at school, brother. In just a few years you will be like us and education will change your life, like it's changing ours.' That's the message our students spread through rural high schools around Siem Reap province.*

*I would love to share more with you, but I want to be respectful of our time together and allow you to ask some questions. So I'll stop here – and again, we sincerely thank you for inviting us to share a little about the Cambodia Rural Students Trust NGO with you tonight. I'll be happy to take any questions.*

The club members clapped enthusiastically, and many murmured to those seated at their tables. From the expressions on their faces, they were mesmerised by what they'd heard. After I answered some questions, Tony stepped back to the microphone and was super-excited. 'Aviv, this was one of the most interesting and inspiring presentations we have heard for a while. We're just so pleased you joined us tonight. Look, we normally don't do this, but our International Committee would like to tell you here and now that we want to partner with you. Let's meet after tonight and discuss how we can support the great work you do.'

A couple of weeks later, the Rotary Club of Glen Waverley donated $3000 to CRST, for our community service program in Cambodia. We used those funds to buy materials to build houses for five rural families! Jess and I returned to the club when the houses were built and shared photos with the members. When Sinuon and Roeun visited Australia a few months later as CRST Ambassadors, they also came to a club meeting to express their personal gratitude for the support.

'It's been our sincere pleasure to partner with you on building houses in Cambodia, especially as we know that your organisation is so wonderfully led by your students. We are so proud to know you – you are truly inspirational!' the Club President said. Sinuon and Roeun cupped their hands in gratitude as the club members applauded.

The power of gratitude is a life value often overlooked; sincere appreciation is a key foundation in relationships.

The following year, I received a call from Angela who had recently taken over as International Service Director at the Rotary Club of Glen Waverley. 'We're ready for another project, Aviv. What should we do?' she asked over the phone.

Following a successful District International Grant application to the Rotary Foundation Committee in their district, the Rotary Clubs of Glen Waverley, Monash and Wheelers Hill donated 165 bicycles for us to distribute through our Project B program.

Jess and I were delighted to be invited back to the Rotary Club of Glen Waverley to express our gratitude to the club members for facilitating the empowering outcome of Project B, and the club subsequently sponsored Lita for a number of years as part of our student sponsorship program.

## Making the relationship even stronger

'How would you like to join Rotary?' one of our students' sponsors asked me one day.

'No, I think I'll pass,' I replied. 'Thank you for the offer, but I travel too much to make the commitment to attend weekly meetings and, as you know, I already have so much on my plate.'

'No, this is a different type of club, Aviv. It's a Rotary Passport Club and we meet online, so you can Zoom in from wherever you are in the world. Also, if you can't make all the meetings, that's okay; our members just need to commit to 30 hours of community work a year and I know that you and Jess do a heck of a lot more than that!' She was persistent.

The sponsor and her family were sponsoring a couple of CRST students and the new club's Charter President was Maria, who we had met on several occasions in her capacity as the Days for Girls Country Representative for Cambodia. Jess and I discussed the opportunity and thought we'd give it a go.

A couple of months later, Jess and I were inducted as Charter Members of the Rotary Passport Club of Melbourne. I joined Rotary because my research showed me the organisation had a great online learning centre and not knowing what I don't know, I'm always keen to gain knowledge. I also wanted to be in the company of like-minded people, who use their energy and resources to help others. Jess joined Rotary because I did – she liked the idea, but didn't love it.

Rotary is an international organisation of 1.4 million people in over 200 countries – that's more countries than members of the UN. It was founded in 1905 by Chicago lawyer Paul Harris to enable professionals with diverse backgrounds to exchange ideas and form meaningful, lifelong friendships. Soon enough the group's work extended to humanitarian service and expanded across North America and into the rest of the world.

Headquartered in the United States, Rotary International now has over 46,000 member clubs facilitating grassroot community projects. Needless to say, it's the largest community service organisation in the world with an incredible network of diverse Rotarians.

One of my early impressions of Rotary was on one of our CRST Ambassador trips to New Zealand. As I stood up to introduce Roeun, our CRST Ambassador student, at the lunchtime meeting, I noticed the elderly Rotarian in front of me fully asleep, head slumped forward on his chest. As I sat down and Roeun stood up to present, I told him to just ignore that man and look at everyone else. I could imagine Roeun bursting out laughing at the sight of the elderly man asleep just five feet in front of him, and then giggling right through his presentation. From other Rotary clubs we spoke at, I concluded that this was an organisation for retirees to get together for a meal and a chat once a week, do a little fundraising at BBQs at Bunnings and Officeworks and spend their money on small-scale community work.

I was wrong.

Within a year and a half of joining the Rotary Passport Club of Melbourne (Rotary Passport Melbourne), I was elected Club President and Jess continued to hold the role of Club Image Director. Being such a diverse organisation, we have met an incredible variety of people from all over the world and quickly learned to separate the rice from the chaff. Some were from the old Rotarian mould, comfortable in their ways and fellowship; others were bright sparks, driven by the prospect of creating sustainable change in many corners of the world.

## WASH for change

A couple of years after providing the seed funding for Project B, Cherrie rang me again. 'OK, we're ready – the Rotary Club of Keilor East is ready for another Cambodia project. What can we help with?'

'What about a new project to bring clean drinking water to rural high schools and communities in Siem Reap province?' I replied.

'Sounds good – does the project have a name?'

'Project W – Water for Education,' I replied. 'Cherrie, this project will also be entirely led and managed by our students – we have another great project team trained and ready to go.'

'That's why we love what Jess and you are doing,' she replied. 'You're teaching people how to help themselves – that's why we love you so much!!'

Cherrie, Deb and their generous club members, together with Rotary Passport Club of Melbourne and The Rotary Foundation, ended up donating over $35,000 to fund clean water stations and two toilet blocks at four rural high schools. Thousands of students and hundreds of families had clean drinking water for the first time in their lives.

A fifth Cambodian high school's water filtration system was co-sponsored by the Interact Club at St Albans Secondary College. Interact Clubs are Rotary Clubs for high school students, and this particular high school's Interact Club is supported by the Rotary Club of Keilor East. How incredible that an Australian high school raised funds to provide clean water for a high school in Cambodia – that's empowerment and inspiration!!

These five schools became the critical proof-of-concept for a much larger project, as 'Project W – Water for Education' became 'Project W – WASH for Education'. WASH is an acronym widely used by NGOs and aid agencies for water, sanitation and hygiene, linking critical elements to reduce disease and sustainably improve health, wellbeing and productivity. Our Siem Reap team identified that 54 out of 97 high schools in Siem Reap province didn't have clean water for their students. Over 20,000 students and 30,000 families would benefit from water filtration systems, as well as toilets in many of the schools. Supported by the generosity of Barbara and John, the Rotary Club of Keilor East, several Rotary Districts including Rotary District 9800 and The Rotary Foundation, plans were developed to install clean water filtration systems and toilets in dozens of schools in Siem Reap province.

The CRST Project W team also prepared to run WASH educational workshops at the schools, teaching about the importance of clean water to our health, and providing vital information about nutrition, sanitation and hygiene. Once again, our student team focused on identifying a community need, working on sustainable solutions with local schools and communities, and developing a business plan (including a budget), an empowering educational curriculum, implementation plans and an evaluation plan.

As the title of this chapter suggests, we teach our team that we all have responsibility – response ability (and my gratitude to Steph for sharing this terminology with me). While many in society may wait for governments or other organisations to do many things, we the people, can already do so much to help our communities. When we see opportunities to contribute to society, it's our response ability that supports our governments and social leaders to achieve much more, bringing sustainable empowerment and inspiration to our fellow citizens.

Over the ensuing years we continued to build toilets, water filtration systems and incinerators in rural schools across Siem Reap province. We've received support from the Embassy of Canada in Cambodia, The Funding Network in Australia, Rotary International and Smart Axiata, Cambodia's largest telecommunication company.

## FOUNDATIONS OF LEADERSHIP TAKEAWAYS

- Build your credibility and your brand.
- Do what you say and say what you do.
- Dream big, plan, act, correct and continue.
- Be transparent and accountable, always.
- Be of service to others and they will be of service to you.
- Collaborations create greater impact; never go it alone.

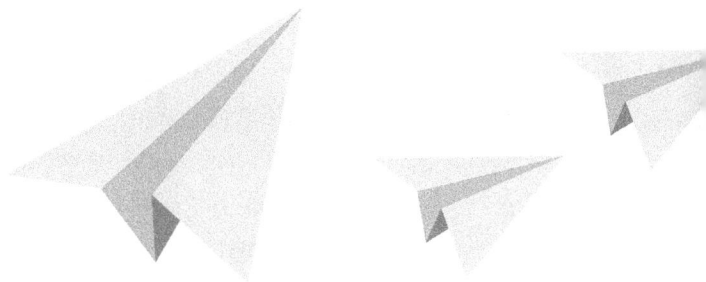

# Chapter 15

# Money can't save your soul

'You know, if you want to build something in someone else's backyard, it's best to let them know. It sure would be great if you could meet with some of the leadership team from District 3350,' Mark from The Rotary Foundation advised me when we were chatting about the potential Rotary Global Grant for a WASH project in Siem Reap. District 3350 is the Rotary International District that includes a part of Thailand and the whole of Cambodia, Myanmar and Vietnam.

'Let me get you the name of their District Governor, Governor-Elect and Rotary Foundation Chair,' Mark offered.

## Meeting the neighbours

A couple of days later, Dale, our own District Governor in Melbourne, emailed the District 3350 leadership team to introduce me. Governor-Elect Iida, Governor-Elect-Nominee Wichai and experienced Rotarian Jay met with me at the St. Regis Hotel in Bangkok a few weeks later. Iida was a Japanese businessman living in Bangkok and was the epitome of Japanese respect and thoughtfully crafted sentences. He was clearly a critical thinker and spoke quietly and deliberately. He had a wry smile and a friendly demeanour. Wichai was a little older; he was a Thai businessman who had a sparkle in his eyes and proudly told me he has not missed a Rotary weekly meeting in 27 years! He clearly knew the Rotary processes, networks and personalities and had been involved with projects and club charters for many years. Jay was a Korean businessman who had been living in Bangkok for a number of years, and had supported and led some extensive high-profile Rotary projects in the region.

I took an instant liking to them all as we chatted and I spoke about what brought me to Rotary. I also handed each of them a CRST booklet introducing our work and impact in Cambodia, by this time reaching over 10,000 beneficiaries annually. They were blown away that a student-led organisation was able to deliver sustainable projects in Rotary's areas of focus, including basic education and literacy, women's health, the environment, growing local economies, and now WASH.

'What's the Rotary involvement with these projects?' Wichai asked. I replied that we'd had collaborations from several clubs in Australia even before I'd become a Rotarian, and that now we were looking at scaling up our impact by partnering with more clubs and Districts, to create greater impact. I outlined our ambitious plan to bring clean water and sanitation solutions to 54 rural high schools in Siem Reap, and that our pilot project of four schools was already underway.

'So you will apply for a Global Grant?' Jay asked. Global Grants were large-scale Rotary projects that saw The Rotary Foundation contribute funding alongside club and District funds.

'We're looking at that possibility, Jay. What do you think?' I replied.

'Jay is an expert on Global Grants,' Wichai replied without hesitation. 'He's raised hundreds of thousands of dollars and has a lot of experience. It would be very good to work on this together.' It seemed Mark was right – if you're going to build something in someone else's backyard, it's best to let them know.

'Your projects are really amazing,' Iida said. 'Congratulations to you. We want to support you, so please tell us what we can do.'

## Checking in with CRST university students

I next met with the CRST university students and shared with them some background on Rotary, and its values, achievements and impact. I shared that I had joined Rotary for their excellent online Learning Centre and the incredible network of like-minded people all over the world.

'Did you say you joined because you could learn more from their Learning Centre?' Sokal asked, genuinely surprised.

'Right – I don't know what I don't know and I'm always happy to learn more!' I replied. The students found that amusing. 'You can also join Rotary. They have a level of membership aimed at young adults like you. You can gain so much new knowledge and, of course, meet so many new people who will come to Siem Reap. If you like, I can email you some details on Rotary and Rotaract[6] and some links and you can see if that's of any interest to you,' I said.

It turned out that more than 50 of CRST's university students were interested in the possibility of joining Rotary.

## Getting the students involved

At one of our meetings a few months later, I asked Governor-Elect Iida whether he thought it would be a good idea to charter a Rotaract Club in Siem Reap.

'Do you think there will be any interest? We have two Rotary clubs there, but they are both not so active. We could really use an active club in Siem Reap. Who would join such a club?' he replied.

I explained that on my previous trip to Cambodia I had met with CRST university students and more than 50 were interested in joining.

Iida was very excited – chartering a new Rotaract Club in Cambodia during his year as Governor would be very impactful.

---

6    Rotaract stands for 'Rotary in Action' and is a Rotary-partnered service club for people ages 18 and older.

'You will need a sponsor club, or maybe even two sponsor clubs,' Wichai offered. 'I suggest that maybe an in-country club such as the Rotary Club of Phnom Penh Metro may be interested. And I can also introduce you to the President of the Rotary Club of Bangkok. Their President, Vasana, is an excellent person.'

Steve was a retired American doctor living in Phnom Penh and as the President of the Rotary Club of Phnom Penh Metro, he was very used to collaborating with Rotarians and Rotary Clubs from all over the world. He wore jeans and a polo shirt, had slightly ruffled hair and a couple of days' stubble. We chatted at the sky bar of the Rosewood Hotel in Phnom Penh, overlooking the sunset and the smog, as we traded stories of the deep satisfaction we shared at being able to create sustainable impact in so many people's lives. I raised the possibility of chartering a Rotaract Club in Siem Reap and Steve loved the idea.

'Yeah, I know you guys already do such an awesome job with so many projects, may as well bring them into Rotary, right?' he asked rhetorically. He said he was sure his club would love to be a co-sponsor of the Rotaract Club of Siem Reap.

A few weeks later, Wichai introduced me to President Vasana from the Rotary Club of Bangkok at the magnificent high-ceilinged lobby of the Anantara Siam Bangkok Hotel. We had coffee surrounded by oversized colourful flower arrangements and gem-coloured velour seats, making the lobby feel rich and opulent. Vasana was humble, and clearly intelligent and accomplished. She had worked in the United States for a few years and had an easy communication manner.

'Wichai told me a lot about your work in Cambodia and I'd be happy to propose to our board that we co-sponsor the Rotaract Club in Siem Reap. Would that be helpful?' she asked politely.

'That would be absolutely great, Vasana,' I replied. The Rotary Club of Bangkok was chartered in 1930 and, as the oldest club in the region, had sponsored many other clubs previously. Its members included well-respected professionals from many nationalities and

HRH Princess Maha Chakri Sirindhorn, the King of Thailand's younger sister, was an Honorary Member.

'As I shared with Wichai, we are planning an opening ceremony for the new CRST campus on August 6th. We'll be hosting many Cambodian government representatives, including the Secretary of State from the Ministry of Environment, His Excellency Neth Pheaktra. We'll also have over 30 overseas guests, including many Rotarians. Do you think we may be able to have a Charter Ceremony on August 7th, while all the guests are in town?' I asked.

'I can't see why not – we have enough time to do the paperwork, don't we Wichai?' Vasana replied.

'Sure. Let me follow-up with Governor-Elect Iida – I'm sure we can arrange that,' Wichai said.

## Encountering a bump in the road

As happens all too often in large organisations, it's not all butterflies and rainbows. Ugly politics and controlling personalities are always lurking in the background, ready to take the sunshine away for their own self-gratification.

And so it was that I received an email from Johnson, a Past District Governor from District 3350, summoning me to a Zoom meeting. Also on the Zoom meeting was Governor-Elect Iida, who apologised for being off camera as he was attending a memorial service for a Rotarian who recently passed away. He said he wanted to be in the Zoom meeting because it was very important, but requested our understanding that he will stay off camera and not say much. The others joining the meeting included District Rotaract Chair Supachai and Rith, the President of the Rotary Club of Battambang who was also the Rotaract Chair for Cambodia; I hadn't met Johnson, Supachai or Rith previously.

'I'm not going to beat about the bush, Aviv,' Johnson said. 'What's the purpose of this club you want to charter in Siem Reap?' he asked with what seemed to be an aggressive undertone.

Johnson was a Singaporean living in Bangkok, and an experienced Rotarian – and he sure had no hesitation in letting you know where he stood.

'Well, Johnson, we have over 50 CRST students who are happy to join the Rotary family so they can gain new knowledge and create a wider network. That would enable them to create an even greater impact in society and of course promote Rotary's vision.'

'And what else?' he asked impatiently.

'That's pretty much it, Johnson. Should there be anything else?' I replied.

Johnson went on to quiz me about CRST's activities in Cambodia, then his real agenda emerged.

'We understand that you want to charter this Rotaract club for your own benefit, Aviv. And we won't allow that. You have your own organisation, your NGO, and you can't use Rotary to pay for your activities'.

'I'm not sure I'm following you, Johnson – my family and our supporters fund the NGO and the projects; we receive no material benefit in return. We don't own the NGO, no-one owns the NGO – it's a student managed and led organisation for the benefit of society. So what exactly is the benefit to me??' I started getting a little aggressive myself.

'Come on Aviv, let's not play games here. You need to follow a process and we will not approve this club just for your benefit so Rotary will pay for your NGO!!'

Their argument was just nonsensical – our NGO was fully-funded and of course Rotary does not fund NGOs. For the next 15 minutes I felt like I was at my own trial – and the other meeting participants seemed to be in on it. It seemed they wanted to flush me out, pressure me to crack, and to admit to some self-interest in proposing to bring our Cambodian students into the Rotary International family. They challenged my integrity and sincerity, without any evidence of wrongdoing.

I knew I'd have to stand my ground, get more assertive, throw it all back at them and let them stew on the shame of their unfounded accusations. Quite honestly, if they didn't want our CRST members, and others who will be inspired to follow, they could stick to their conspiracy theories and we'll continue our sustainable social impact irrespective of their support. At that point I also realised that Rith, Supachai and Iida had said very little so far.

'Iida, did I not introduce myself to you at our very first meeting as the President of the Rotary Passport Club of Melbourne and co-founder of the Cambodia Rural Students Trust NGO? Was I not up-front, open and transparent about our activities, our funding, our achievements and our impact?' I asked.

'Yes, you were very truthful, Aviv, and we still think you and your family and organisation do such an amazing job,' Iida replied quietly.

'So why do I feel like I'm on trial here? What's the evidence you have that chartering a Rotaract Club in Siem Reap is of any personal benefit to me?'

'No, you're not on trial here, Aviv. We just need to understand fully what your intention is!' Johnson replied.

'Well, I'll tell you what, Johnson – frankly I don't need this headache. The CRST students who could become Rotaractors would do Rotary proud! They already deliver impact and sustainable outcomes and Rotary could be a part of that. But you don't think that's good enough; you think there is an ulterior motive. So let me end this meeting now by saying that I know the Rotary Four-Way Test. I know that I pass that test on each and every point, to the highest standard. You can continue your trial without me and just let me know what you decide,' I concluded.

At that point Iida came on camera, wearing a black tie at what appeared to be a public memorial service venue. 'Johnson, you called this meeting and we all heard what was said. Aviv has been truthful from the start and as Governor-Elect I endorse the charter of the Rotaract Club of Siem Reap. I will be in Cambodia on August 7th to charter the club, my trip is already booked.'

### Rotary International's Four-Way Test

One of the world's most widely printed and quoted statements of business ethics is the Four-Way Test, which was created in 1932 by Rotarian Herbert J Taylor (who later served as Rotary International president) when he was asked to take charge of a company that was facing bankruptcy.

This 24-word test for employees to follow in their business and professional lives became the guide for sales, production, advertising, and all relations between dealers and customers, and the survival of the company that faced bankruptcy in 1932 is credited to this simple philosophy. Adopted by Rotary in 1943, the Four-Way Test has been translated into more than a hundred languages and published in thousands of ways.

The questions that make up the Four-Way Test are as follows:

- Is it the truth?
- Is it fair to all concerned?
- Will it build goodwill and better friendships?
- Will it be beneficial to all concerned?

This wasn't the only time that Past District Governor Johnson tried to bully me into 'confessing' that a Rotaract Club in Siem Reap was of personal benefit to me. But the facts were clear: CRST was willing to support the Rotaract Club of Siem Reap and receive absolutely nothing in return. Rather than celebrating community support for Rotary, Johnson was looking for malpractice and self-interest – he never found it. CRST is transparent and accountable, and our activities and financial statements are a matter of public record; we contribute and receive no material gain in return.

## Hitting the ground running

On 7 August 2022, District Governor Iida chartered the Rotaract Club of Siem Reap. The club was co-sponsored by the Rotary Club of Phnom Penh Metro and the Rotary Club of Bangkok, and supported by the Rotary Passport Club of Melbourne and CRST. The 54 Charter Rotaractors were all CRST students and they planned to introduce their external friends to the many projects they would undertake, as they continued to grow the club.

Since that time, CRST's projects have been carried out by CRST students, many of whom are also Rotaractors. That's easy for us to do because we don't own the projects – we just facilitate, support and provide opportunities. And of course we don't own our students either, so it doesn't matter to us whether they wear the CRST T-shirt or the Rotaract T-shirt. All that matters is the quality person inside the T-shirt and their quality community impact. The projects remain focused on social needs and continue to benefit thousands of rural Cambodians.

In May 2023, the Rotary International Convention was hosted in Melbourne, Australia. Representing the Rotaract Club of Siem Reap and CRST were five Rotaractors, including Lita and Phanich, with Doeb also joining the trip as CRST's mentor-in-residence and executive director.

During the last two weeks of May, the team put in countless hours sharing, connecting and inspiring hundreds of people from all over the world to see the empowerment of education in action. They presented at high schools, community events, business gatherings and at 12 meetings of Melbourne-based Rotary Clubs. They also hosted countless Rotarians at the dynamic Rotaract Club of Siem Reap display at the Conventions' House of Friendship.

They also saw all that we take for granted in a developed country, from wide roads, to organised traffic, clean streets, parks, letterboxes, skyscrapers, public transport, massive retail stores and supermarkets with almost-endless aisles.

Lita, Phanich, Doeb and the team were able to exemplify the next generation of Rotarians as 'People of Action', proud of their achievements and passionate to share their empowerment with society. I'm not sure how many other Rotaractors and Rotarians can say their club reaches over 20,000 beneficiaries in a year.

*June 2023*

*Phanich summed up her life-changing trip to Melbourne in an email to her sponsors:*

Hello Kevin and Liz,

I trust you are doing great. To me, I am good!

I would like to share with you about my 3 week trip in Melbourne last month. WOW!! I was so excited and right now I still miss everything there. It was such a long trip for our 5 ambassadors in Melbourne, from the 14th of May to the 2nd of June. My deepest THANKS to the Palti family for supporting us for everything on this trip and giving us an incredible opportunity to travel and explore the real world 😊🙇❤🖤🙇

I left Cambodia on 14th of May and I had good wishes from my family. They also came to the airport to say goodbye to me with the CRST family as well. That's an exciting day in my life ❤😊. And my mother was delighted and cried during that time when I left. There were 5 ambassadors including me and we went directly to Singapore Airport. As it was my first time on the plane, I felt nervous when the airplane took off, but I was still in control. We had 8 hours at Singapore airport and I had more time to explore at the airport with my team as well. It was our first-time trip and first time exploring Singapore airport. WOW!! It's a very big airport.

We left Singapore airport around 11 pm and flew directly to Melbourne airport. I felt more comfortable on the big plane and not nervous like when I left Cambodia. I had some food on the plane as well because I really wanted to know how food in the sky tasted. This was the greatest experience in my life on the plane. We arrived at Melbourne airport around 9 am and we had a very warm welcome from our founders, the Palti family 😊❤🖤👫

We had a busy schedule. On our first day, our founders took us shopping for some warm clothes in order to protect us from the cold weather. We really enjoyed shopping.

Our big purpose of the trip was to attend the 2023 Rotary International Convention and to present at 12 Rotary Clubs in Melbourne. I was so curious to tell you about my highlight activities while I was in Melbourne. First, I was so impressed about the Rotary Convention and the way they organized the whole event; it was so amazing and there were so many inspirational speakers from different counties to share with us. 'The House of Friendship is a true festival of Rotary, showcasing the organization's fellowships, action groups, and community projects from around the world.' The convention made me feel unforgettable experience, cultural attractions, and so much more. Together we can create a better world for the next generation by contributing to society. I met so many Rotarians from many countries all around the world. It was a fantastic place where many people gathered, networked, and learned about programs, products, or services from each other. I was so happy to make new friends and many Rotarians look forward to connecting and collaborating with our sustainable and impactful projects. It was an amazing event that I have never seen before and I was able to connect with thousands of fellow Rotary members from around the world and have access to hundreds of Rotary project booths to see what they do.

It was such a wonderful time to take part in meeting with 12 different Rotary Clubs, and I learned from those people and made great conversations with all of them. It was a great chance for me to build up my public speaking skills and be able to connect with many Rotary members from different clubs and share our amazing projects with all of them. I extremely enjoyed all the activities as well as the presentations. This amazing life-changing trip really opened my eyes to see a different view of the world and learn new experiences from many successful people around the world. During this trip, I have learned and gained a lot of experience in my life. Increase networking from day to day when communicating with many people and I was so proud to share our impactful projects in Cambodia with many Rotarians from different clubs. They are helpful people and they contribute to the community from their heart. I could see how different Rotary clubs work and run their clubs effectively.

Second, University of Melbourne, WOW!!! ☺ It is a huge university and has outstanding education facilities. There were a lot of different buildings for students to study depending on their major. For example, if students are studying IT, they can go to study at an IT building.

It was completely different from the university in Cambodia. Students just come to study only. But University of Melbourne is the place where students come to study, research, have group discussions, self-study, group study, relax, make connections with friends and has a unique library. More than this, there are coffee shops, gyms, swimming pools, a football pitch and so on. This university is a truly unique environment, designed to make students feel more comfortable to study. I will take all the information that I learned and what is the difference to share with the students in my country.

Third, Parliament House is the meeting place of the Parliament of Victoria and makes decisions for the state. We were generously hosted by David Southwick who is a Member of Parliament and the Deputy Victorian Liberal Party Leader. He explained to us that Parliament's main roles are to debate issues, pass laws and hold the government to account. The most interesting part was about making laws for the state of Victoria. Every proposal for a law must be initiated in the form of a bill. And a bill can be introduced in either House but must be agreed by both Houses as well. The government must receive Royal Assent to the bill before it becomes law. I also went to visit the library, WOW!! ☺ It was amazing and there were so many kinds of documents and all parties can come to research before debating to create the laws. I noted that there was a big book from a hundred years ago that was stored in the library. This library provided modern information and research service to members and staff and has an extensive digital collection.

Fourth, Moonlit Sanctuary is another amazing place for me and an unforgettable experience with Australia's diverse wildlife. Honestly speaking I knew only two kinds of animals such as kangaroos and koalas, but the reality I have explored the bushland while feeding kangaroos and wallabies, petting friendly koalas and enjoying encounters with wombats, dingoes, and beautiful birds and many other animals. And a special show by some animals and birds as well. I noted that in Australia, they take care of all animals as a people, especially the way they train some kinds of birds in order to perform for all the visitors, so they can be ambassadors to care for the environment. I used to study related kinds of animals and I did research to find those animals. But last month, I experienced it and I had a chance to take many photos of my favorite animals that I wished to see for a long time. It was a great experience to see many different animals and birds.

Fifth, I had a great chance to take the train to watch a game of AFL – Australian Rules Football. Everything is my first time and a wonderful experience on the train as well. There were so many people who spent their time relaxing and watching Carlton play Collingwood. We sat on level 4, the top level and it was a bit crowded, and when I looked at the other level, I saw people were so small. Most people there were big fans of this football game and their shirt and scarf had the logo of Carlton or Collingwood on it. Back to our team, we were fans of Carlton, but a bit sad we lost the game. However, we still had an amazing and fun time together 😊☺️❤️. I used to see this game through social media and magazines and I do not know how they play this game, but after seeing the real picture and sitting in the big stadium of 100,000 people, I could understand some rules because I had good explanations from Jess and Aaron. It was a wonderful experience to participate in watching this game with thousands of people in Melbourne 🌏☺️

Sixth, we flew to Sydney for one day, then we went to the train station, which is under the ground at the airport. WOW!! Another amazing experience again and the train was so clean and very quick from one station to another station. Many people there take a train to work or school because it saves time and money rather than taking a bus or taxi and it is very helpful to reduce traffic as well. We spent around 20 minutes to arrive at Circular Quay and we walked along the waterfront and had extremely beautiful views of Sydney's iconic Harbour Bridge and Opera House. These were amazing structures which many people around the world identify with Australia. I never believed that I could be there and see the real beautiful view with my eyes. I was so impressed with the Opera House with the amazing design. I could not express how excited I was that I had the opportunity to visit this amazing place in Australia. Next, we took the ferry to Manly Beach, just WOW ☺️ when I got on the boat and looked at the fresh view and I felt I was in a dream because everything was so amazing for me and full of water and fresh sea air and taking in the extremely beautiful beach.

Finally, I would like to take this opportunity to pay my gratitude and big THANKS to the Palti family ❤️👪 who always support us, giving us their valuable time, energy, love, support, encouragement, and motivation while we were there. Without all of them, I might not have had a chance to be there to visit many places and stand in front of so many people to share my life story and our impactful projects that we are doing in Cambodia to help society. I never imagined myself being able to travel outside Cambodia, but the Palti family made my dream come true. And thank you so much for believing in me and the other ambassadors as Cambodia's future leaders to inspire the next generation. All what I have learnt from the 3-week trip, I cannot wait to share both my knowledge and experience to my juniors and community as well.

I have a lot of photos I want to share with you too 😊😎🙂

Best Regards,

Phanich

## The speed bump becomes a roadblock

Sometimes very educated people behave with great ignorance. These are the most dangerous people in the world – the ones who don't know what they don't know.

In August 2023, the Rotaract Club of Siem Reap and the Rotary Passport Club of Melbourne applied for a Rotary International Global Grant to provide more rural Cambodian schools with WASH infrastructure and WASH educational workshops. CRST agreed to be the cooperating organisation to provide logistical and operational support to the Siem Reap Rotaract members, who of course were all university students.

Johnson took exception and once again accused CRST of attempting to derive some benefit from Rotary. I explained yet again that CRST was supporting the Rotaractors and the project without any benefit – without receiving any of the credit or publicity or passing on any costs. Our only interest was to empower Cambodia's future leaders to create sustainable social impact and we wanted nothing in return.

I took the matter to Rotary International, which came back with their position: they congratulated us and acknowledged 'the win–win' in the relationship between CRST and the Rotaract Club of Siem Reap, creating sustainable, impactful social development as we educate future leaders 'who become brand ambassadors for Rotary and Rotaract'.

Johnson wasn't satisfied with that and a couple of weeks later we were advised by Rotary International's Grant Officers that our Global Grant Application was 'full of conflicts of interest'. I found it interesting that they used Johnson's exact words and copied him on their email. When pressed to advise what perceived or real benefits CRST was deriving from the proposed project, they provided no explanations; instead, they replied with a simple, 'We encourage you to find other funding sources for this project'.

The Rotaractors and we were despondent – over the preceding six months we had been mentored extensively by a Rotary-appointed specialist. Past District Governor Lindsay was instrumental in almost 20 (!!) Global Grants and by the time we were done, he gave us a reference letter stating that our Global Grant Application was one of the best he'd seen!

Jess and I concluded that providing clean water and toilets to thousands of rural students in Cambodia was more important than continuing to justify the integrity of CRST. The beneficiaries didn't need to go without just because certain people couldn't be bothered doing their due diligence. With agreement from the Rotaract Club of Siem Reap and the committee from the Rotary Passport Club of Melbourne, we removed CRST as a cooperating organisation for the Global Grant. This left a greater burden on the Rotaractors, but they agreed that the endgame was to bring clean water and sanitation solutions to thousands of rural students, even if it added to their workload.

Our Global Grant Application was then ignored by District 3350's Rotary Foundation Committee for another three months, after which they advised that they had 'no confidence' in the members of the Rotaract Club of Siem Reap. It seems that despite the team attending all the required Rotary and District training sessions and already delivering projects to thousands of beneficiaries, they were still not good enough for Rotary. Managing and reporting on five previous WASH projects also counted for nothing – it was clear that some of their District leadership members were simply intent on not supporting them.

The Rotaractors were devastated and wrote to the District 3350 leadership team, inviting them to Cambodia to see for themselves the incredible sustainable projects they were leading; they were ignored. With heavy hearts they agreed to withdraw from the Global Grant Application they had put months of work into, so the Rotary Club of Phnom Penh Metro could become the host club, enabling 11 rural schools to receive WASH infrastructure and educational workshops.

District 9800 in Australia, as well as other Rotary Districts, clubs and generous Rotarians in Australia, Canada, France, Hong Kong and New Zealand, continue to support the CRST students and Rotaract Club of Siem Reap members to implement numerous projects. Each year scores of Rotarians also visit and volunteer with the team in Siem Reap, experiencing first-hand their energy, passion and impact.

Despite being devalued and disrespected by some influential Rotarians in their District, so far they have managed the installation of WASH infrastructure and delivery of WASH educational workshops at over 30 (!!) rural schools in Siem Reap, supporting over 10,000 students to continue their education and impacting thousands of local community members.

We have grown to accept that irrespective of its ideals, the Rotary organisation still harbours deep biases among some of its members. To me, Rotary is about bringing positive changes in the world; it's not about power and manipulation. We've had to learn to sideline and ignore the control freaks within the organisation and invest our time and energy with the countless other like-minded people who focus on creating the kind of society we want to live in. The grassroot Rotarians,

Rotary Clubs and Rotary District leaders who volunteer tirelessly and contribute their resources generously are the champions of Rotary.

We've been blessed to be able to surround ourselves with hundreds of incredible humanitarian Rotarians, who collectively add to our sunshine.

## FOUNDATIONS OF LEADERSHIP TAKEAWAYS

- Articulate your vision clearly.

- Everyone has an agenda, and that's normal – leadership is aligning someone else's agenda with yours, or knowing when to respectfully walk away.

- Leverage is availing yourself to someone else's knowledge, experience and reputation, and allowing others to avail themselves to your knowledge, experience and reputation.

- Have the facts on your side; opinions may vary, but facts are indisputable.

- Often those who challenge you have done much less themselves.

- Focus on the bad behaviour rather than the person.

- Always remember you are a leader; others are watching and will follow your lead. How you react in the face of a challenge is just as important as your reactions when faced with success.

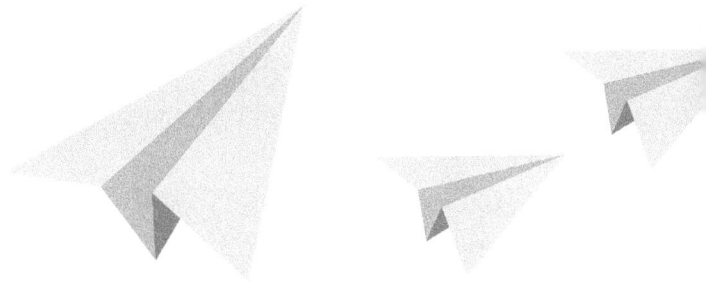

# Chapter 16

# Use your gifts to fill the gaps

On one of my trips to Siem Reap I met with Heng at Jaya House. After joining CRST in grade 10, she was now in her second year at university and had just been selected to travel to Australia as a member of our next ambassador trip.

'I'm sorry, Aviv,' she told me sadly, with an embarrassed wry smile, avoiding as much eye contact as possible. 'My family want me to get married now. I won't be able to travel to Australia and I will need to give up my studies. My grandpa is old and they want to make sure that I will be okay before anything happens to him. They want me to drop out of university and get married in the next few weeks,' Heng told me, by now getting a little emotional.

'And what would you like to do, Heng?' I asked her.

'I'd like to continue my studies until I graduate, but they won't listen to me.'

We spoke a little about the dynamics of Heng's family – she lived with her grandparents, aunt, uncle and cousins. Grandpa was the ultimate decision-maker, but Grandma had a voice and Aunty was a power broker.

'Hmmm,' I said to Heng. 'I'd like to meet your family, would that be okay?'

Heng looked at me very surprised; she knew I rarely met with our students' families, preferring our students to be the heroes of their life stories.

'You want to meet Grandpa and Grandma and Aunty??' she asked incredulously.

'Sure. Please ask them if tomorrow afternoon will be okay with them and it will be my pleasure to visit your home and meet your family.'

'And what will you tell them, Aviv?' Heng asked nervously.

'I'll tell them how important you are, Heng. I'll ask them to support us to continue to support you by allowing you to travel to Australia and graduate from university,' I replied.

## Making our case

The next afternoon I travelled by tuktuk to Heng's family village on the outskirts of Siem Reap. Veun came along to translate and, on the way, we stopped to buy a slab of 24 bottles of Pocari Sweat (a Japanese sports drink). I figured it would be impolite to visit empty handed and I had learnt that Grandpa enjoyed these energy drinks. Besides, I knew that a thoughtful gift was significantly more valued than a thoughtless gift or no gift at all.

Heng's family were most grateful for the drinks and thanked us profusely, saying of course they were not necessary. Veun and I were invited to sit on red plastic chairs and were offered some cans of soft drinks as we made some chitchat, with Veun translating for me and Heng adding some words here and there.

I asked Grandpa how his health was, and then about Grandma's health – I thanked them both, as well as Aunty, for supporting Heng's education for so many years. They cupped their hands in gratitude, thanking me for our family's support that enabled Heng to graduate from a prestigious private high school. I replied that it was our family's sincere pleasure to support Heng, because she was an extraordinary young woman. She understood the importance of education in her life, for her family's future and to Cambodian society. I shared with them Heng's responsibilities and accomplishments as a leader in our 'Project G – Empowering Girls' enterprise. They looked at Heng with admiration and said that she had changed so much since joining CRST and they were so proud of her.

I then told Heng's family that, as they knew, she had been selected to represent the NGO on a trip to Australia. We understood that they were worried about her going away from them, especially to travel overseas for two weeks. They nodded anxiously and explained that Heng was very special to them and they had a big responsibility to look after her.

'I have two beautiful daughters and I know how precious our girls are,' I told Heng's family. I assured them that Heng would live with our family, in our home, for the whole time she was in Australia. She would live with us, and we would love her and take care of her like our own daughter. She would be able to speak with them on the phone every day and of course they would be able to follow on Facebook all that she did. In fact, as we had thousands of followers, including many Cambodian students, Heng would inspire countless people as she gained new life experiences while representing Cambodia in Australia.

Grandpa looked at me and thanked me again for being so respectful to come and visit them; he said he knew that I was very important and very busy and for me to take the time to visit them was so meaningful to them.

'I'm really not that important, Grandpa,' I said respectfully. 'Heng is important; she is important to your family and important to Cambodia. That's why we're supporting her education and that's why I've come here to respectfully ask you and Grandma and Aunty to support Heng's opportunity to travel to Australia for two weeks, and then continue her education at university until she graduates. She has her whole life in front of her. I am asking you to help me and my family to support Heng's education,' I said cupping my hands. Grandpa was looking at me intensely as I paused for Veun to translate.

'And when she has graduated from university in just two or three years, she will be able to marry and be secure and happy for the rest of her life. This trip to Australia will open her eyes to what's possible and the rest of her university education will set her up for a lifetime of success. Please support us in allowing Heng to travel and finish her studies before she gets married,' I concluded.

Heng looked at me with tears in her eyes. I don't think she had ever experienced the intense love we have for all our students. Grandpa looked at her, then at me, and then at Grandma. His eyes welled up and he said, 'We are so proud of Heng. I support her to travel to Australia and then finish her education.'

### April 2019

*Heng represented CRST and Cambodia in Melbourne and Sydney, speaking at schools, community and business gatherings. This is her ambassador presentation:*

Hello, my name is Ry Heng. I trust all of you are great today. I would love to share with you a little about my life.

Eighteen years ago, my mum gave birth to me. And just one year after giving birth, she had a traffic accident and died. After the death of my mother, life was incredibly difficult for me. My father started to let himself down and lost all responsibilities, so he ended up leaving me with my grandparents and my aunt.

Everything that we had in the family was sold to pay back a loan because when my mum was alive, she borrowed some money for her small family business. I never had the chance to call anyone in life 'Mum' or 'Dad', and all I have are my grandparents and my aunt. Although they are not my parents, they give me the love only a family can give.

When I was in grade 6, my family's situation was getting worse and I felt guilty that I could not do anything to help them. So, I decided to get some vegetables to sell in the market to earn some money for my family. My aunt and especially my grandparents never let me stop studying even though we needed the money, and they said to me, 'We do not have anything to give you besides education for your new life.'

But, even with the love I received from my relatives, the feeling was never the same as my own parents. When I was about 16 years old, my memories came flooding back, and I could never share this with anyone. I was wondering why my father left me, and why he did not love me.

One day, my grandpa told me, 'My grandchild, you are a very special girl. You can live without your mum or dad until now, why don't you continue to make them proud?' I started to cry and said, 'I miss my mum so much. I feel that the world is so empty.' My grandpa smiled at me and said, 'There are reasons for you to keep going in your beautiful life. Your mum loves you more than anything in the world. You must still have hope and believe in yourself and continue your life.'

Today I believe that I am independent and confident enough to share this whole story with you because I want to let you know that no matter what happens in life, do not give up. Be strong, things will get better. It may be stormy now but it never rains forever. I can overcome, why not you?

I must admit that I sometimes do feel down and want to give up. I remember once there was a man saying that he could help me to go and study abroad. I was young and naive. He told me to prepare some documents and give them to him. I prepared everything myself and gave them to him and then I asked my grandparents for permission to go with him, but they told me that the man was actually a human trafficker and I must not go with him. Later I found out that my grandparents were right – that man wanted to sell me to other people for money. Without my grandparents, aunt and uncle, I cannot even imagine what my life would be like right now.

A shiny bright spot in my life was school, because my aunt and uncle fully supported me to get education. Even though sometimes I felt pressure to study, I understood that this was my responsibility. Fortunately, one day, my grandmother heard about one of my relatives who was being sponsored by an NGO called Cambodia Rural Students Trust. I was very happy and asked him about the opportunity that he had. He told me that every year, the NGO selects new students to join and the students must be from poor families and love education.

Several months later, after doing a written test, a verbal interview and receiving a home visit from the NGO student managers, I was selected to join the CRST student family. This turned out to be the most amazing opportunity I have had in my life. I was very proud of myself. I now believe that my dreams and my ambitions are very achievable, and all my relatives are so proud as they see me growing and achieving amazing new goals.

The NGO's activities have completely changed my life because I have changed the way I think and the way I do things. At first, I thought I would never have a chance to even finish my high school, but CRST sponsored me to study at the best private high school in Siem Reap. Now I'm a first-year student studying a bachelor of business administration degree at the best university – a university which students in my village cannot afford.

I understand how hard most students struggle to go to school and study English. When I was younger, I would ride my bike around looking for places to study English for free. Whenever I see kids looking for a free school to study, it always reminds me of that situation. Now I am not only a student in the NGO, but also a volunteer English teacher, helping kids who want to learn English. I love volunteering so much!!!!

Every month our community service team organises activities including building houses for very poor families who are living in terrible conditions. I love our volunteering so much because I can help people who are in such desperate situations, and help lift them up by building a house for them. I thought that my life was extremely difficult because I lost my parents – but after joining these activities, it reminds me that I am lucky. I have a big family in the NGO, my grandparents, and my aunt and uncle who always look after me and give me love. I never thought that I would be able to help anyone, but look at me now – I am helping so many people.

Last year I was promoted to be the assistant manager in one of our NGO projects. Project G, as in 'G' for 'girls', has the mission of 'Empowering Cambodian girls and women with health education and sustainable hygiene products'. Collaborating with Days for Girls

International, we are providing safe, beautiful, washable and long-lasting menstrual hygiene kits, along with vital health education. It was my first time working in an enterprise, and wow, I have learned *a lot*. My role is to assist all the departments to plan their work and do their work smoothly, and follow up with them.

After helping manage our team for about four months, I am now also the finance manager in Project G. This role is a bit more challenging for me, as I deal with finance and I have to ensure that there is enough cash for our daily operations, as well as regularly update the financial reports and ensure compliance and transparency.

Our NGO has taught me many life lessons and while I know that life can be challenging, I also know that it's my responsibility to bring out the sunshine and live in the light. I've learnt that when life gives me lemons, I can make lemonade – and share that lemonade with others by inspiring more students, especially girls, from the countryside to believe in themselves, rise up, be the best they can be and have a great life!!

I know that there are many more people out there who need our help, so I would like to invite you to join our journey in helping break the poverty cycle through education. Investing in someone's education creates life-changing opportunities for our young generation, so we can make a better society in Cambodia. Thank you for your valuable time to be part of our journey!!

## Making lemonade (again)

A few months after returning from a triumphant trip to Australia, Heng asked to meet with me again. This time she brought her long-term boyfriend, Thearak, an educated young professional who was a little shy and very respectful. He had a gentle, kind face and demeanour; I could tell the two of them had a special, supportive relationship.

'My family wants me to get married now, Aviv. My grandpa is very sick and he wants to see my wedding before he dies. I'm really sorry. I will need to leave CRST and get married,' Heng told me emotionally.

*Here we go again*, I thought to myself. I just couldn't believe we were in the same place we had been in just a few months ago.

'But didn't Grandpa say he supports you to finish your studies??' I asked disbelievingly.

'Yes, but now he's very sick. And my aunt is not happy that I just study and not help the family by working and earning money,' Heng replied.

This of course was not new to me; in Cambodia we frequently encountered the tug of war between working and earning a little money today, and studying and earning much more money tomorrow.

'What would *you* like to do, Heng?' I asked her.

'I'd like to continue my studies until I graduate, but they won't listen to me.'

'And what about you, Thearak – what would you like to do?' I asked, turning to Thearak.

'Of course I agree with Heng – we know education is so important.' Thearak said quietly. 'But Heng's grandparents are a different generation and they want to make sure she is safely married while they are alive. Her aunt is also pushing for Heng to get married; otherwise, the reputation of the family may be impacted if we have a long relationship without getting married.'

Quite honestly, I was shocked. I thought all this had already been put to bed a few months ago.

'I'm really, really sorry to hear that, Heng and Thearak,' I replied. 'Can I help in any way?'

They exchanged glances and Heng turned to me and said, 'We'd like you to speak with them. I'm sure they will listen to you more than they have listened to us. They respect you a lot, you know. And you know what to say and how to say it. Will you come to my home and speak with my family again, Aviv?'

That was a big ask. I knew that if Heng was to marry now, she would need to leave CRST and get a job. It would be highly unlikely she would ever return to her studies and would never reach her full potential.

I also knew that I had already fired all my shots at the previous meeting with Heng's family. What could I possibly add now that would convince them to allow Heng to finish her studies before getting married? What could I possibly say that would fulfil her elderly grandparents' desire to see her wedding? Or her influential aunt's need to protect the family's reputation?

'What about if the two of you got engaged now and then get married when you graduate? Do you think that would be okay with your family?' I asked.

Heng and Thearak looked at each other; they could see where I was going. Our NGO policy was very clear: students who wished to get married needed to leave the NGO because we understood that their life focus would need to change. Balancing a marriage, new financial pressures, possible family commitments, studies and community service contributions is no easy task in any society; it's much tougher in developing countries where education is seen as a 'nice to have', but not a 'must have'.

Getting engaged would be another story. Heng could delay the pressures of marriage and continue to focus on her studies. Her grandparents would have the commitment and joy of an almost-wedding ceremony and the family's reputation would remain intact.

We discussed the possibility of having a big ceremony in the village, with Heng and Thearak dressing formally and maybe even having some official photos. They could invite family, friends, their neighbours and community. Maybe they could even have a procession through their village leading to a big celebration at Heng's home, and the monks could come and bless them.

The next day Veun and I collected another slab of 24 Pocari Sweat bottles and made the pilgrimage to Heng's family home. This time we were also joined by Roeun, CRST's general manager and a university student himself – I needed the firepower to show the impact of education.

Heng and Thearak came to the roadside to greet us. They were both visibly nervous as Roeun, Veun and I alighted from the tuktuk with our gift for Grandpa. Thearak rushed over to carry our gift and he and Heng led us to the back of the house, where Grandpa was laying on a daybed, and Grandma was sitting on a large red plastic chair. Her aunt appeared from the side of the house, apologising that she was a little messy because she was cleaning the large plastic tubs the family used for transporting fish to the market. We learned that Heng's aunt and uncle were fishmongers at the local market – an arduous job with long hours.

Grandma and Grandpa were very welcoming, although both clearly had health issues and Grandpa was not very mobile. Heng and Thearak handed out some drinks as we took our seats on the large red plastic chairs. We made some small chitchat, with Roeun, Veun, Heng and Thearak translating. Heng's family were very grateful for the opportunity she had to travel to Australia, and they loved the Australiana gifts she'd bought for all of them, especially the T-shirts and the cuddly plush koalas and kangaroos.

'Grandpa,' I said, cutting to the chase, 'Heng needs to finish her studies before she gets married. I know you agree, but I can see that you may be a little unwell at the moment. And I understand that you may also be concerned that if Heng and Thearak don't get married, that may not look like good morality in your family.' I paused and looked at each of them as Veun translated.

They looked at Veun intently.

'So what can we do that will allow Heng to continue to study, while showing that your family has good morality and Heng and Thearak are in a secure and respectful lifetime relationship?' I concluded.

Heng's aunt explained that Grandpa hadn't been well and his wish was to see Heng get married, so he would know she would be looked after. I said that I could completely understand and respect the family's wishes, and my family wanted to support them all to find the way to fulfil these, while supporting Heng to graduate from university.

'What if we could find a way for Heng and Thearak to be united, show the community that they are a couple and even receive a monk's blessing for their union? Do you think such a ceremony would be valuable, Grandpa?' I asked.

Grandpa agreed, followed by Grandma, followed by Aunty.

'Grandpa, maybe we can have a big ceremony here in the village. Thearak and I will dress formally and we will have a big procession leading to our house. The monks can come and bless us – and, Aviv, maybe you and your family could join us too??' Heng did an outstanding job selling her dream, pushing all the right buttons.

'Wow, thank you for the invitation, Heng!!' I exclaimed. 'This will be *so* exciting – we've never had an engagement at CRST!!' I smiled broadly at Heng and Thearak. They still looked extremely nervous.

I was genuinely excited because Khmer celebrations are loud, epic events!

I turned to Grandpa and Grandma with a big smile on my face. 'What do you think? This engagement ceremony will allow Heng and Thearak to show their commitment to each other, so you won't need to worry about Heng, knowing that she will always be looked after. And everyone living in the village will also know they are committed to each other and the monks can bless their union. Heng will then be able to complete her studies and graduate from university before getting married and continuing with her amazing life. Do you think that could work?' I asked them all, knowing that by now the energy of the gathering was behind me.

A few weeks later Heng and Thearak had a meaningful, colourful and exuberant engagement ceremony, more like a mini-wedding really. Jess and I were joined by many of our CRST students as we celebrated our Cambodian family member's engagement and the continuation of her university studies.

Grandpa and Grandma lived on for a few more years, often falling in and out of good health. It was Heng, their university-educated granddaughter, who was by their side at multiple clinic visits and hospital stays. She was the only one who knew how to converse with the medical staff, the only one respected and respectful enough to understand what needed to be done and what medications had to be taken. Heng's grandparents' trust and belief in their granddaughter paid dividends in spades as she was their rock and angel in their final years.

## Asking questions rather than issuing directives

No-one likes to be told what to do – no-one.

So how do we engage with people to create mutually beneficial outcomes? How do we create an ecosystem for the desire to participate, collaborate and feel the personal satisfaction and recognition for setting, executing and reaching personal and common goals?

As with Heng and her family, the key is to ask them, not tell them.

This does take some practice, but the results are worth the consistent effort. The meetings with Heng's family were a series of questions seeking a common good solution. Of course, each party had their own wishes and agenda, but we also had mutual respect and the desire to reach outcomes that would reflect well on us collectively and individually.

I took great care to show respect to Heng's family, and never told them how to do anything; instead, I engaged them in reaching mutually beneficial outcomes by asking a series of questions – with the ultimate question being 'can we collaborate on this?'

That is also how we set up, lead, manage and constantly refine our NGO and educational social enterprises in Cambodia.

When people are part of the weaving of the fabric, they feel ownership and commitment. They want to do their best and do more. In addition to asking questions rather than giving directions, using suggestive words is also a great leadership trait. We use questions such as the following:

- What do you think we could do next?
- Maybe we could consider $X$. What do you think?
- Perhaps we could think about $X$?
- What about if we $X$, do you think that would work?
- Would there be any benefit if we $X$?

Empowering people means giving them the power to be all they can be, so it's critical that we allow others to engage in critical thinking to reach conclusions and not simply fast-track the process and tell them what to do. Similarly, it's important to let others show us what they can do rather than tell us what they plan to do.

Empowerment is giving people a hand up to be the best they can be, not a handout to keep them stagnant.

## Empowering based on social needs

Our projects are all based on social needs, following our three simple business steps:

1. Ask people what they need (or identify what they need).
2. Go get it.
3. Give it to them, with the added benefit of knowledge.

'Project R – Refuse, Reduce, Reuse and Recycle Plastic Education Program' came about because of the devastating impact of single-use plastic trash in rural Cambodia. Thousands of plastic bags and mountains of plastic drink bottles litter the countryside, mindlessly discarded by uneducated rural Cambodians (and tourists) and left unmanaged by the community. Understandably, trash management is not a priority when people struggle to earn an income or need to collect bushfood for their family.

The environmental damage of this trash is significant because it takes decades or centuries for the plastic to breakdown, and even then leaving nanoplastic waste to enter our food chain and waterways. There are also significant immediate health implications as animals consume the plastic left lying on the ground, and fish and birds consume plastic debris mistaking it for food. Then, of course, there is also the economic impact of Cambodia having a reputation for being a dirty, unhygienic travel destination.

The amount of single-use plastic waste in rural Cambodia is overwhelming, and was always a topic of discussion as we rode tuktuks to our rural activities.

'So what are we going to do about it?' we asked our team on one of our trips.

And that's how Project R came about. Our team, led by Phirun who was the first Project R general manager, wrote the project plan to bring single-use plastic educational workshops and management solutions to rural high schools. They then wrote the lesson plans, which they compiled into a book called *Plastic Education for Future Leaders*. The Minister for Education, Youth and Sport, His Excellency Dr Hang Chuon Naron and the Minister of Environment, His Excellency Dr Say Sam Al, both wrote forewords to the book, along with Jess and me.

We connected with Cambodia Beverage Company (bottlers of Coca-Cola in Cambodia) and Smart Axiata, the leading tele-communication company in Cambodia, and they both became local corporate sponsors. Coca-Cola placed large plastic collection bins in schools and Smart subsidised the organic cotton bags we gifted the students we educated. Our friend Shant from digiDirect, Australia's largest camera retailer, was very generous with his support and we printed 3000 copies of *Plastic Education for Future Leaders*. We gifted these to rural school libraries for students' continued reference as they put the lessons into practice.

The Project R launch was a major event, attended by His Excellency Neth Pheaktra, Cambodia's Secretary of State for the Ministry of Environment, and a busload of journalists. We made the news on television, in national newspapers and on countless online news sites. Over the next four years, our team educated over 40,000 (!!!) students in rural Cambodia about the usefulness of plastic in our everyday lives and the harmful impact of single-use plastic waste. We also provided single-use plastic waste management solutions, helping to empower a new generation of rural Cambodian students to take responsibility in managing end-of-life single-use plastic.

The power of students teaching students cannot be underestimated. The CRST students led the workshops with passion and enthusiasm, and the students they taught took that knowledge back to their homes. No-one wants to live in an unhygienic environment, and no-one wants to get sick from plastic waste or have their income impacted due to a decline in tourism. The Project R program was successful because we didn't tell people what to do; instead, we asked them how we could assist. Our team took over from there.

## Shining a light

Jess and I connected with Russell through our Rotary Club, the Rotary Passport Club of Melbourne (refer to chapter 14). Russell worked for SolarBuddy, an Australian-based NGO that distributed solar study lights to students living in energy poverty all over the world. He offered us the SolarBuddy lights for distribution in Cambodia and we took the opportunity to our team to discuss.

'We may have an opportunity to support some students who live in rural villages without electricity. We have been offered a personal solar study light about the size of a mobile phone – the lights are recharged by the sun and will enable the students to read and do homework after dark. Do you think that may be useful?' I asked the CRST leadership team on one of my visits.

'Of course!!' was the totally expected unanimous reply.

Pov offered to lead a team to write up a new project plan and went on to become the first general manager of 'Project L – Light for Education'. Pov and his team identified 350 villages in Cambodia that were still living off the grid, and set about connecting with the local school directors in those remote areas. The project plan included the distribution of the SolarBuddy study lights and much needed study materials including notebooks and pens, as well as workshops to teach the rural students about health, hygiene, nutrition and the environment. Everything from how to wash your hands and your body, brushing your teeth, a well-balanced diet and taking good care of our environment so it can take good care of us was covered.

Very few NGOs work in remote areas in Cambodia, because these areas are much more of a challenge to reach. Yet in these areas live the very students who need the most support. Our team set out from our campus at 6 am, so they can reach the distant rural schools by mid-morning. They run their workshops and distribute the school supplies including the much-needed SolarBuddy study lights.

These visits are some of the most impactful days, because well beyond supporting the rural students' education, we are providing them with inspiration. For the first time in their lives, they have incredible role models who are of a very similar age, and whose education has set them on the path to empowerment. Here are Cambodian university students, from very similar impoverished rural backgrounds, teaching valuable lessons and distributing study materials and a light by which to read and study at night! And underlying the benevolent support, the CRST Project L team exemplifies social-proof that education will change your life. The photos from these visits are incredibly impactful – the awe and joy in the rural students' faces cannot be described in words.

Project L is another example of leading a team by asking them questions, not telling them what to do. It's another example of a team taking ownership and pride in their work and the outcomes, reaching over 2000 remote Cambodian students every year.

## Using others' gifts to fill our gaps

We love collaborations – they create more meaningful impact, and often reach further, faster. They allow us to use someone else's gift to fill our gaps.

That was the case when we collaborated with Swinburne University of Technology (based in Melbourne, Australia) to sponsor some of their students to travel to Cambodia to document some of our projects and produce short documentaries on the lives of some of our students. The Australian film and media students from Swinburne received an immersive hands-on overseas learning experience, while our Cambodian students made new connections and were able to share their impact and stories. Franx and Kaylene, the two teachers leading this project for the university, are probably some of the most open-hearted and progressive lecturers I've come across. It was clear from the outset that by each of us finding out what the other was seeking, we would use our gifts to fill each other's gaps.

Another gift was given to us by Christian, the Dutch-born general manager at Jaya House River Park Hotel, our 'home' while in Siem Reap. Having lived in Siem Reap for many years, Christian's top priority while running his hotels has been to develop and empower his team. He is also deeply committed to the environment after seeing the devastating impact of single-use plastic and the uprooting of countless trees to make room for the town's expansion, while possibly giving too little consideration to regenerating the environment by planting new trees.

Jaya House is Cambodia's first single-use-plastic-free hotel, with each guest receiving a refillable aluminium water bottle and requested not to use single-use plastic bottles. He inspired us to make CRST a single-use-plastic-free NGO, and our first educational social enterprise, 'Project Y – Frozen Yogurt', followed by becoming a single-use-plastic-free store.

On one of our trips to Siem Reap, Christian and Jess started talking about planting trees – Christian had Jess at 'hello'. Jess brought the idea to the team and asked them whether they thought this may possibly be a beneficial, impactful and sustainable project. Some of our students' families had recently been relocated from the beautiful forested villages near Angkor Wat to a desolate area called Run Ta Ek as the government was working on preserving the Angkor Wat Archaeological Park. They were now living in a dusty treeless environment, with no shade and no escape from the tropical heat. And so, 'Project T – Trees for Life' was conceived, with the mission of planting thousands of trees over the next few years.

Tangly ably led the Project T team to thoughtfully select the best trees to plant and the most impactful locations, both in rural communities and schools, as well as in Siem Reap town. Planting a mix of semi-mature three- to four-year-old trees, fruit trees and seedlings, some of the Project T trees will reach maturity in just two to three years after planting, while others will take a little longer. Part of the process is to follow-up on the trees, to ensure they are fertilised and watered in the dry season and are taken care of by the schools, villages and communities with whom we collaborate.

For this project, Christian brought his gift of local vision and corporate contacts while our CRST student team brought their gift of systemic project planning, leadership and management. Together, we have been able to engage with numerous local Cambodian corporate sponsors to close the gap in this much needed environmental initiative.

Some of our students, Jess and I also met with Siem Reap's Deputy Governor to discuss the possibility of planting hundreds of trees in a designated area, which would be called the 'Siem Reap Peace Boulevard'. The Provincial Governor also loved the idea and Jess and I set about engaging with ambassadors from a number of countries to support the Siem Reap Peace Boulevard, closing the gaps of nationalities as we unite under our gift of humanity.

Project T will continue to be our joint legacy for decades to come as we plant tens of thousands of trees to regenerate the environment, using our gifts to fill this gap.

## FOUNDATIONS OF LEADERSHIP TAKEAWAYS

- Ask people, don't tell them.
- Ask people to show you, not tell you.
- Only education can change the world – those who have never experienced it, can't be expected to know it.
- Respectful collaborations fast-track success.
- The lessons are in the doing, not the learning.
- Stay humble; let others be the heroes of the story.

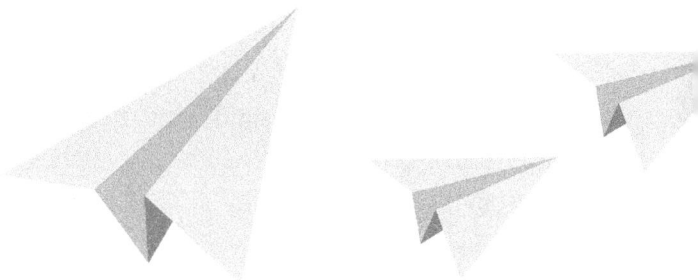

# Chapter 17

# Our biggest challenges are our biggest opportunities

Our world came crashing down in March 2020 – pretty much at the same time as everyone else's lives were being challenged by the reality that COVID-19 was not just an isolated virus, but a worldwide pandemic. There was a lack of clarity, a lot of misinformation and fear – lots and lots of fear.

I happened to be in Cambodia in early March, and we had just wrapped up the super-successful launch of 'Project R – Refuse, Reduce, Reuse and Recycle Plastic Education Program'. Following the euphoria of spending time with two Secretaries of State, and coverage of our launch on TV, in newspapers and the digital news media, some students came to me one morning and asked what was going to happen when I left.

'Nothing!!' I told them. 'The world will go on – we will adjust what we do, but the planet will continue to spin.'

I spoke in front of all the students at Green School that day – the leadership team negotiated for us to use the largest classroom they had at the school and all the students crammed in, sitting two or three to a desk. I stood in front of them and explained what a virus was, and (as much as I could at that time) where this virus started, and how and why. I shared with them the basic ways to minimise the risk of getting infected and I told them that we would survive, although things would not go back to normal for a long, long time. First, I said, many people would get sick and people would die. Then we would get a vaccine. People would start traveling close to home, then to 'safe' countries, and only after three to four years they might return to developing countries such as Cambodia. (I based this on my own reading of articles from credible news outlets and research from international experts.)

'I have no crystal ball,' I said, 'but that's my thinking – a big 'earthquake', then quiet, then life will slowly resume.' There was stunned silence.

'But the good news,' I continued, 'is that everything happens for a reason, and that reason is here to serve *you*, to make *you* better, to make *you* the best you can be!!' The students looked around at each other as if they either misunderstood or I had lost my mind.

'From next week, schools will be closed – what will you do?'

Two of the girls began to cry.

As I stood in front of the class, I used my open palm to point to the student sitting next to one of them and said, 'Riya, why is Thavry crying?'

'She's scared. She's scared that we will close the NGO and she will have to go back to her hometown and never go to school again,' Riya replied.

Thavry buried her head in her hands and I asked her to stand up. She shook her head.

'Thavry, I can wait – please stand up when you're ready, so you can see my face clearly as I look you in the eyes and tell you my message.'

Thavry wiped her face as every bit of empathy in the classroom was channelled to her, and slowly stood up, red faced and wet eyed, looking at me.

'Thavry, thank you for showing everyone the way – thank you for showing them that it's okay to be scared and emotional, that it's normal. And thank you for allowing me to share this most important sentence with you, which I want you all to write down and remember until you see my face again.'

I asked Thavry to sit, turned to the whiteboard and wrote the following in big blue letters: 'If we do this well, by the end of COVID-19, we will all be better people than we were before!!'

The students all wrote down that sentence and we discussed what it meant – it meant that we would change what we did, and we would do things differently, but better. Schools and universities would close, but we would either arrange online studies or get tutors – their education would not go on hold, life would continue. And our projects would continue. With government schools closed, for example, we wouldn't be able to run 'Project G – Empowering Girls' workshops in schools, so we would run the workshops for girls and women in the villages. Project R would also refocus from schools to villages. 'Project V – The Volunteer Experience' would combine with 'Project B – Bicycles for Education' and the students would work on a village-based program to repair bicycles rather than distribute bicycles to students. And our firstborn project, 'Project Y – Frozen Yogurt', would stay open for a few weeks, and then we'd reassess our options.

'Now is the time for leadership, not fear. Now is your time to show society the sort of leaders that you are – share your knowledge, lead by example, leave footprints. I'll be flying back to Australia in the next few days, not because I'm leaving you, but because I'm *empowering* you. We gave you shoes, you have been walking in those shoes, now you can start running – and by the time we come back here, whenever it may be, you will be flying!! You have what it takes – now is the time to walk the talk.'

The energy in the room shifted from devastation to inspiration – they had a plan, they had work to do!!

Over the next two days I met with each department and each project team and started workshopping some options. As I left Siem Reap, I told them they had until the following week to send us their revised business plans – and we may also want to plan what we, as the CRST family, were going to do to help rural villagers stay safe from COVID-19.

## Taking action and walking the talk

The business plans we received were stunning.

For the rest of March 2020, the students researched COVID-19 – including its symptoms, how it impacted the body, how to stay safe and who to contact if someone felt unwell. They wrote workshop educator notes, and prepared visual A3-size flip charts and posters. They met with District Governors, commune leaders and village chiefs. Jess, Aaron and I reviewed the material to ensure accuracy, assisted with the graphics and mentored the process. By the end of March, the COVID-19 Education Program was ready and had received approval from each District Administration.

Through April and May, our students educated over 12,000(!!) villagers in over 350 villages about COVID-19, and the simple steps the community members could take to stay safe. Instead of rumours and social-media scaremongering, they provided facts. The villagers we taught were illiterate and couldn't do their own research. Who better than Cambodia's future leaders to explain the facts to them and answer their questions? Who better to spread the incredible empowerment of education, than the very same kids who left the village a few years ago, and were now returning with their educated inspirational friends, to leave footprints?

The project teams also responded well.

The Project G team developed a business plan that allowed us to keep our three seamstresses employed, so their families could continue to receive an income. We switched from teaching at high schools, to teaching in villages – in 2020, the team reached over 3000 girls and women and distributed over 2000 beautiful and reusable menstrual hygiene kits. In 2021, the team delivered 24 online workshops to over 2000 students all over Cambodia and distributed over 1500 kits.

The Project R team also pivoted from high school workshops to village workshops, creating the Plastic Free Village (PFV) program to mentor Cambodia's first plastic-free villages. By the end of 2020, they were working with five villages, and had held educational workshops and clean-up days, appointed Environmental Ambassadors at each village, installed 'No Plastic Here' signs and, in partnership with Coca-Cola Cambodia, placed plastic collection bins (PCBs) at each village. They also arranged with the District Administration to have the PCBs emptied regularly, with the plastic taken to the district's incinerator. (Cambodia doesn't have a plastic recycling facility ... yet.)

The Project B team started the Mobile Bike Mechanic (MBM) program I mentioned in chapter 14 – instead of distributing bicycles to rural students to get to school, the team worked on repairing bicycles for community members. They travelled to villages, met with village leaders and local families and assessed who were the most needy and what needed to be repaired; from July, one Sunday a month was used for the MBM activity. By the end of 2020, they had repaired over 500 bicycles for poor rural families.

The Family Support (FS) team added four more families to the program, and the Community Service (CS) team continued to lead the NGO team in building one house a month. In November, the peak of the rainy season, they repaired and rain-proofed 23 homes.

The New Student Selection (NSS) team continued undeterred and managed to receive over 500 applications from students who wanted to join CRST for the next academic year. Instead of our regular entrance exam (refer to chapter 10), the criteria were altered to assess the applicants' most recent government school grades and current community contributions. The list of potential new students was narrowed down following face-to-face interviews and family visits, all upholding COVID mask-wearing and sanitising protocols. In August 2020, we welcomed 24 new students to the CRST family. The NSS team arranged for the new students and their families to come to Siem Reap for our Integration Day – some of our graduate students' parents emotionally shared how their teenage kids left the village just a few years ago, and today they stand next to their daughter who just graduated with a law degree from the American University of Phnom Penh, or their son who is studying an MBA in Phnom Penh and working in his own real estate sales company. The team even arranged to livestream the event – we watched it on our family room TV in Melbourne and kept shaking our heads in disbelief at the incredible event our 'kids' were leading.

All the while, our students were studying online, both at high school and university. It was an incredible adjustment and we set up Sharing Classes for the high school students and the Academic Club for the university students, so they could work with and mentor each other. By the end of 2020, all our high school students had graduated to the next grade and our university students reached an average NGO GPA (grade point average) of 3.44 – or 86 per cent.

In January 2021 we welcomed the new year with a big all-day party filled with fun, laughter, games, music, dancing and food – lots of food. I asked Ramet, our NGO Manager, to pass the following message to our students:

> *All of these achievements were possible during COVID-19 because of YOU!! Because YOU all trusted our guidance and BELIEVED IN YOURSELVES!!! Above all, 2020 has shown us the power of an EMPOWERED TEAM – a group of young adults, who work together to learn and support each other. A team of high school and university students who KNOW THEIR PURPOSE and are COMMITTED TO SUCCESS!!*
>
> *2021 will be our year to shine, to reach for the stars – we have the most NGO students we've ever had, and we will reach the most beneficiaries in society. Steph, Jess, Aaron, Michelle and I wish you a new year full of blessings, love and joy – a new year full of fulfilled expectations, success and NEW HEIGHTS!! May you all continue to shine bright and light the way for others to follow!!*

My advice from March 2020 rang true:

*If we do this well, by the end of COVID-19, we will all be better people than we were before!!*

---

## FOUNDATIONS OF LEADERSHIP TAKEAWAYS

- Being flexible, not emotional, takes practice – sometimes your plan is not 'the' plan, and being flexible will enable you to adapt and thrive, not just survive.

- When the landscape changes, get new tools to navigate the new terrain.

- If you did this today, it's old; what will you do better tomorrow?

- People's wants and needs change all the time, so stay relevant.

- Being great yesterday is of no value if you can't add value tomorrow.

- Life is a moving treadmill; when you stand still, you're actually moving backwards.

- Foster a culture of constant improvement.

- Always make your team the heroes of your success.

- There will always be change – anticipate it, plan for it, and be ready for it.

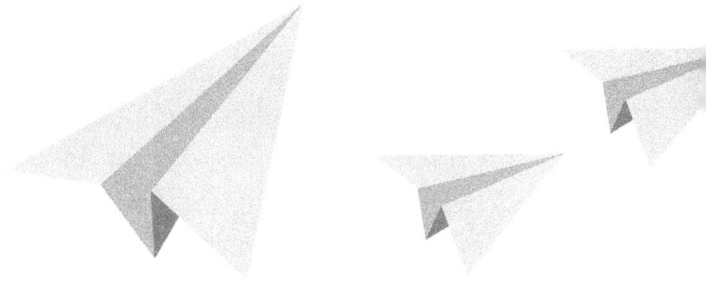

# Chapter 18

# Life is a journey, not a race

'Roni and I would like to go across the road to walk on the beach. Can you come with us?' I asked my mum.

'No, you can cross the road carefully and go by yourselves. Would that be okay?' she replied.

I was shocked! 'Ima, we can't go there by ourselves!!' I replied, exasperated.

'It's okay, this is Australia. You'll be just fine,' my mother replied, smiling reassuringly.

Roni and I went down the outside stairs of our motel on the beach at Manly and crossed the road very carefully, walked between the tall pine trees and on to the magnificent blonde-coloured sand of Manly Beach. Between the blues of Sydney's protected harbour, the glorious giant green pines, the soft sand and the light-blue heaven. We were in paradise, a world away from our past home and yet we were home. Freedom.

## My story

I was born in Cologne, Germany, in April 1964, when my parents lived there for a couple of years while my father was studying computer engineering. When I was about a year old, the four of us returned to Israel – my parents, my older brother, Roni, and me.

My primary school years were fun and uneventful but following the Yom Kippur War in October 1973, my parents made the decision that the Middle East was not the place they wanted to raise their two sons. I remember watching images of Israeli POWs arriving back in Ben Gurion Airport, many being helped down the plane's access stairs by other servicemen and servicewomen. Many were missing limbs or had bandaged heads, arms or legs. 'This is the price of war. And these are the ones who come back; others return in coffins,' my mother said solemnly. 'In Israel, every generation goes to war. Your generation will be next, I know it.' We all stared at the TV, fixated by the horrific injuries of young men just 10 or 15 years older than Roni and me.

'I'm not raising my kids here to be cannon fodder,' she said resolutely to my father.

Within a few weeks, my father, who was working with Philips Computer Systems, applied for an international transfer. I remember us sitting down for our family dinner one evening and my parents discussing their idea of relocating from Israel to another country. I was about 10 years old and Roni 12, so we were very excited by the expedition we were about to embark on. My parents, on the other hand, had a whole list of worries and considerations, including leaving behind their elderly parents, language barriers, social integration, quality of education and, of course, economic challenges. Roni and I only spoke Hebrew, and my parents only had basic German and English language skills. And while my father would have a guaranteed job, my mother's career as a school principal would come to a grinding halt, bringing with it economic challenges, or perhaps even hardship.

A few months later, Philips offered my father a transfer to one of three countries – Argentina, Australia or Iran (before the Islamic Revolution). Over the next few weeks, we discussed the options at our family dinners and read up about the three countries. Each had advantages and disadvantages, but my parents' greatest consideration was to live in a peaceful society, so that Roni and I could be all we possibly could. I remember reading books and looking at photos of Australia, including images of the green trams in Melbourne, kangaroos, koalas and beaches – it all looked like such a fairytale.

And so it was that in February 1975, the four of us arrived in Sydney, Australia. We were put up at a motel on Manly beach for a couple of weeks and then my father was asked if it would be okay for us to move to Melbourne. 'Melbourne, Sydney, it's all Australia to us,' my father replied.

To this day, each time I fly back into Melbourne after an overseas trip, I see the green paddocks on the flightpath to Tullamarine Airport and feel humbled by being so blessed to be able to call 'the lucky country' my home.

My parents were incredibly brave packing up four suitcases and relocating to the other side of the planet. For sure, we made do with very little, but we never went without. Roni and I were enrolled at a private school so we could get the best education possible – and my parents only finished paying off the loan that paid for that education two years after I graduated. I enrolled into grade 6 and one of the first tasks I had to do in my English coaching class was to list all the English words I knew – all 110 of them. I remember working diligently with my English coaching teacher, Mrs Trebilco, craving her big red ticks when I got things right, and having the school logo rubberstamped in my exercise book when I got good results on tests – with the ultimate prize being a chocolate Freddo Frog when I accumulated six school stamps.

Our first home in Melbourne was an old weatherboard in Surrey Hills. It was pretty beaten-down; my father, Roni and I took two weeks to do a reno. We painted the outside, wallpapered the inside (the walls were far too decrepit to paint) and were given someone's old carpet to put down over the broken floorboards. We were given some second-hand beds and a dining set; in the loungeroom we had cushions and a beanbag on the floor and our 'sofa' was a couple of stacks of bricks, topped with an old door, a mattress and black material. It was all so simple, humble and homely.

We rarely ate out, we shopped for clothes during sale periods and our family holidays were in caravan parks; we were happy, we were free and we lived in paradise.

## Getting started in business

I graduated from high school at 17 and started studying a bachelor degree in town planning at the University of Melbourne. Three months into the course, I knew it wasn't for me and told my parents I wanted to quit. 'And do what?' was my mother's instant reply. 'I think I'll study sales and marketing,' I replied.

My father had recently decided he wanted to be self-employed and my parents bought a photo shop franchise. So I started working alongside my father during the day and studying sales and marketing at night at Swinburne University. At the age of 19, I suggested to my parents that we should start a photo frame wholesale business and they agreed, soon travelling to Taiwan to meet with suppliers. My mother, the memory-keeper in the family, still has the telex communications I sent them, advising which factories to meet, what to look at and what to negotiate.

We kept the imported frames in the back of the shop and I started calling on photo shops and pharmacies to sell them our frames. The company name we chose was UR1 International – 'you', the customer, 'are number one'; we were customer-focused from the start. I'd make my sales calls throughout the day, return to the shop in the late afternoon, collect the frames from the shelves in the back of the shop, handwrite the invoices, and package up the frames with newspaper balls so the glass wouldn't break. The next morning I'd drop off the boxes of frames to the stores who placed orders the previous day and continue selling.

When Roni graduated with a degree in Computer Science, we bought our first computer for invoicing – a Goldstar computer with

5¼-inch floppy disks for backup. A small black-and-white TV was our screen and, in our downtime, we played Pong and Pacman. Our first team member was a young lady called Munis, who was our warehouse manager. This allowed me to focus on sales. After a year, I'd developed the Melbourne sales territory sufficiently to be able to afford to put on another full-time sales person as I moved my sights to developing the Sydney market.

Flying and renting a car was way too expensive, so I put my car on the train on Sunday night, slept on the train overnight, arrived in Sydney on Monday morning, hosed off the dust and soot from the car and started selling. At the end of the week, I put the car back on the train on Friday night, slept on the train overnight and got back home on Saturday morning. I did that one week a month for nine months until the territory was sufficiently developed to hire another salesperson. We grew the company step by step, always being hands-on and seeking to add value to our team and our retailers.

We added photo albums to our photo frame ranges and took on the Disney license, which added more value to our offer. In 1994, I met with Anne Geddes and her husband, Kel, to discuss licensing Anne's world-renowned baby photos for photo album covers. I remember them picking me up in their light-blue Mercedes from my hotel in Auckland, New Zealand, where they lived, to have dinner at a homely local restaurant. By the end of the night, I understood what was important to Anne and Kel and had committed to uphold their values and exceed their expectations.

Six months later I met Anne and Kel at the Sheraton on the Park Hotel in Sydney and Kel offered me a worldwide license for Anne's photo albums. 'Kel,' I said, 'I live in Melbourne, Australia; that's hardly the geographical centre of the world. How am I going to do justice to a worldwide license?'

'That's very easy, my friend,' was his instant reply. 'Just fly around.'

We became one of Anne's largest worldwide licensees, working in partnership with Anne and Kel for products as diverse as greeting cards, stationery, jigsaw puzzles, paper bags, keepsake boxes and more. We set up distributors in over 30 countries, and exhibited at international tradeshows from New York and Birmingham, to Moscow and Sao Paulo. I was living on planes, while Roni was overseeing our Australian business. Michelle and the girls travelled with me frequently, enabling us to teach Jess and Steph that we live in a 'global village', we are all the same and we all have a responsibility for each other's wellbeing.

I still keep in touch with Anne and Kel, who now live in New York, and when we catch up, it's as if we have just seen each other a couple of days ago. Our friendship has endured over 30 years and I will always cherish that.

## Building on success

We've come a long way in our 40-year business, reinventing it regularly and riding the ups and downs of several economic cycles. Probably our biggest success is our mantra of always adding value to our team and our customers, as well as transitioning what was a photographic-based business to a homewares-based business.

While the advent of mobile phones has meant fewer photos are being printed, people still want quality frames for the photos they do choose to print, and we've been able to take advantage of that as we added additional homeware categories. The common thread in our categories is that they are all trend-based, so the research we do forecasting homewares trends is used in our entire range offer. We then design the products, have them manufactured in Asia and ship them to our retailers. We also have our own team of visual merchandisers, who call on our retailers to ensure that our products are displayed well in stores. This ensures we're always on show and maximises sales opportunities.

By adding value in trend-forecasting, product design and manufacturing, inventory management and visual merchandising, we've become a top-tier vendor to our national retailers. We don't take that position lightly and we constantly challenge our team members to think outside the box and seek better ways to add value to our retailer relationships. Over the years we have also developed long-lasting relationships with some of the world's largest retailers, including Walmart, Target USA, Carrefour and Auchan.

It hasn't always been smooth sailing for us. Business isn't always predictable and sometimes that has the potential to destroy you. Back in 2013, through a combination of slower sales resulting in holding too much inventory, we were almost at risk of not being able to repay our business loan – and having that loan called in by the bank, and our business shut down. Through some intensive workshopping and strategic planning – and switching to a more sympathetic bank that could see the value we offered – we were able to trade our way back to liquidity, and become even stronger and debt-free.

We also add value to our team members and their families. Just as retailers have a choice of who to do business with, our team members (note we don't have employees, only team members) also have a choice – they can choose not to work with us. It's our responsibility to look after them and add value to their lives.

Long before COVID, we had team members who worked from home if they could or needed to. When their family members needed them, they could work flexible hours and days, following our philosophy that people work to live, not live to work.

## Getting (more) family members involved

Michelle and I were sitting at home chatting one weekend and she said to me, 'I think I'd like to join the company, would that be okay?'

'Well, I'm not sure, hon, I'm not the easiest guy to work with and I'm very demanding,' I exaggerated. 'I don't believe in nepotism and any family member joining the team has to bring the skill set we need and earn their own respect. Having the same surname as me is not enough; people will need to respect you for who you are and what you contribute. That would mean starting on the ground floor, learning from the ground up and adding value just like everyone else in the team.'

We sat there talking it out for a couple of hours and by the end Mich said, 'Well, you've done a good job in trying to talk me out of it, but I'd still like to join the company. So where can I add value?' Michelle joined us as a buying assistant and has become one of our most valuable team members. She is now our senior buyer overseeing all new product development and the purchasing department.

Jess also joined us a few years after studying interior design and event management; she joined as a junior designer and is now our design and marketing manager. Aaron, our son-in-law, joined us as a member of our warehouse team, before joining our buying team and then on to the export team as an export executive. Respect has to be earned; it can't be bought or bestowed.

Steph followed her passion for helping others and studied nursing, going on to graduate with a master's degree in mental health nursing. She is immersed in the much needed mental health field, with a focus on young adults and adolescents, and has developed an innovative guided holistic wellbeing program.

As a family business, we have walked the path of understanding and professionalism, allowing our team members to feel secure and valued as they continue to grow. Many of our team members got married while working with us, had child number one, two, three and sometimes four; in many ways, we've grown up together. As a family and as a business, we have been rewarded with loyalty and dedication, with an average team member tenure of 17 years; a pretty good track record for a 40-year-old business.

While Roni still manages the company's operations, I lead the 'sexy' side of the business – product development, sourcing, sales and marketing. I speak with team members regularly, commit to answering all emails within the same business day, and often ask my direct reports what else we can do to support their work, remove frustrations and add value to their lives. I also ring or email each of our team members on their birthdays and on their anniversary dates with the company. People matter, and caring for people matters.

I've been fortunate to study corporate governance and negotiation principles at Harvard Business School, as well as neuro-linguistic programming (NLP) and numerous other insightful and empowering courses. Upholding the value of being a 'student for life', I regularly stretch myself to learn more, apply more and share more.

Still, we take nothing for granted and strive to make each season better than the last, forecasting consumers' wants and anticipating retailers' needs. We're walking on a treadmill, if we stop walking, we'll fall off the back; so best to keep walking, maintain momentum and add value to our team members and retail partners.

As I've mentioned a few times through this book, business is a matter of three simple steps:

1. Ask people what they want.
2. Go get it.
3. Give it to them.

**3 SIMPLE STEPS**

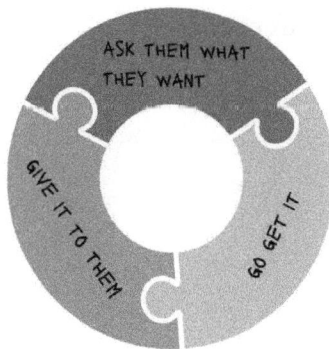

Along our 40-year history, we've had many fun times and some devastating times, we've had ups and downs, wins and losses. I take everything that happens in my business personally, which is both a strength and a weakness. It's a strength because I can learn from the experience and do it better next time; it's a weakness because I feel a sense of personal responsibility for all our team members. But I've learned that I don't need to be the 'general manager of the universe' and I don't need to oversee or manage or control all that is. I've learned to trust that whatever is happening in my life is happening for a reason, and that reason is here to support me and make me better, to make me the best I can be. And the lessons we learn, the experiences we earn and the wisdom we gain are the oxygen of life when shared with others.

## FOUNDATIONS OF LEADERSHIP TAKEAWAYS

- You are the most important person in the world – never forget it.

- Create value and add value to yourself and others.

- Take care of others and they will take care of you.

- Growth comes from flexibility.

- When faced with the abyss of the unknown, gather your 'inner-circle' and seek counsel.

- 'We' before 'me'.

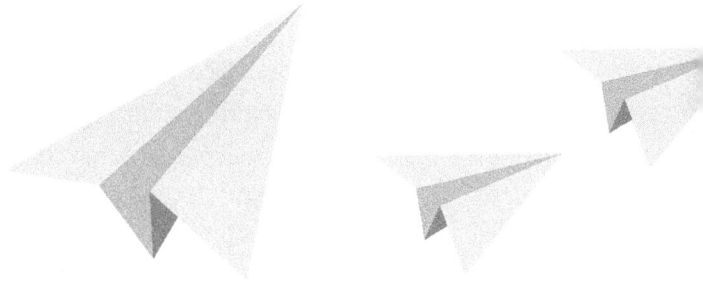

# Chapter 19

# Leadership starts with you

If you have reached this chapter in the book, you clearly understand that the Cambodia Rural Students Trust NGO is a unique, empowering and inspirational organisation. Apart from helping to break countless poverty cycles for our students, their families and many of our beneficiaries, our impact will last for generations to come. Once educated, you can't be uneducated; the value of education will not only forever empower you, but also through you forever empower all those you connect with.

While we often say that 'education is a gift that lasts a lifetime', in reality, education is a gift that keeps on giving beyond one lifetime. In developed societies, we take education for granted – everyone gets educated, that's our 'normal'. In developing societies, education is the catalyst for development for generations to come.

## Processes and systems for constant improvement

We founded CRST on the pillars of Education, Empowerment and Inspiration, but to achieve our self-renewing and replicable ecosystem, we have amassed significant 'back of house' systems. While we keep our 'front of house' clean and simple so it's easy to understand

and follow, we have developed processes and systems to ensure that we plan, create and measure the impact of everything we do. These systems allow us to be in perpetual renewal and improvement mode, making us better tomorrow than we are today.

## Start with an idea – and pressure test it

Just because you have a 'good' idea, doesn't make it a good idea. If you think it's worthy, ask your inner circle or trusted close team to hear your idea and give you 'honest friend' feedback. You don't want nay-sayers and you don't want yay-sayers – you're seeking honest feedback that will poke and prod at your idea, allowing you to 'sharpen the saw' and make your plan or idea realistic, impactful, inspirational and sustainable.

## Be flexible – nothing ever ends up as you conceived it

Use experiences and feedback along the way to change your concept to be even better than you originally envisaged it. Don't be afraid to update your vision or your mission – be in a constant mode of renewal. Windows 11 doesn't make Windows 3 wrong or stupid; it makes Windows 15 inevitable. Always seek to get better – that's evolutionary strength, not weakness.

## Leave judgement in the box – perspective is dependent on life experience

We innately need/want to be 'right', but what is 'right'? If you leave judgement behind and look at ideas, people, actions and outcomes as steps along the journey, perspective becomes a lot easier to embrace. Rampant violence, slavery, women's disempowerment and abusing animals are all 'wrong' in today's society, but were considered 'normal' not so long ago. That's perspective.

Leaving judgement in a box, we don't need to see 'right' and 'wrong', but can choose to see 'then and now' and 'now and tomorrow'. Focus on how to make things better. Ask yourself, 'What didn't I see yesterday that will create a better outcome tomorrow?' Focus on that instead of 'right' and 'wrong', because no-one ever wants to be 'wrong'.

## Start small and test – there will be less to correct

Once you've pressure tested your ideas and refined your concepts with additional perspectives, walk along the edge of the water and test your concept; don't jump into the swell. It's much easier to correct your trajectory when your feet are firmly on the ground; it's much tougher when you're already swimming and spending all your energy on not drowning.

## If you can't write it down, it doesn't exist

Writing down your vision, mission, values, plans and processes is not a waste of time. On the contrary, it's the *best* investment of your time. Writing down where you want to go has many advantages:

- Seeing the written words triggers you to own and refine the idea.
- Written words are more powerful than concepts floating in your head.
- Written words are a constant reminder, increasing focus and allowing easy refinement.
- It's so much easier to enhance or expand written concepts.
- You can communicate and share your concepts much more widely and regularly.
- Written plans are critical for evaluation and development.
- No-one ever built anything by carrying it in their head.

## Keep it simple – five easy steps

Taking effective action is a combination of dreaming, planning, acting, correcting and continuing. Here's how to keep it simple at each step:

1. *Dream big:*
   - Write down the biggest outcome or impact you can achieve with your idea.

2. *Plan:*
   - Write down all elements you can think of and need to plan for – what, why, who, where, when, how.
   - Write down your steps to get where you need to go, including what you will do, and when and how you will evaluate the outcomes.
3. *Act:*
   - Get the rubber on the road and implement your plan.
   - Be flexible – written plans are a guide, not a manual.
4. *Correct:*
   - Solicit feedback from yourself, the team and beneficiaries to evaluate your outcomes – what worked? What can work better?
   - Adjust your plans.
5. *Continue:*
   - Act.
   - Correct.
   - Act.
   - Correct.
   - Endlessly – that's perpetual improvement.

## Everyone needs to know their roles and measurables – people don't own what they don't know

Here are some simple ways to ensure your team know where they stand:

- *Job descriptions:* Keep them simple and update them regularly (ideally annually).
- *Job procedures:* Cover how, why and when.
- *Measurables:* Clearly list the key performance indicators (KPIs) so team members can measure their outcomes and constantly seek improvement.
- *Reporting:* Whenever possible use templates for reports to keep it simple and consistent.

- *Feedback:* Provide constant feedback, either casually, formally or as a team; make feedback a fun learning to be valued, not feared.

## Respect and effective communication are not negotiable

Here are some simple ways to ensure your team are respectful and communicate well:

- Call people by their name often.
- Be genuine and ask about family and life.
- Be present – look them in the eye, use connected body language, and no distractions (put away your devices).
- Express gratitude for contributions and compliment achievements, with sincerity.
- Ask them, don't tell them – use soft words such as 'perhaps', 'maybe', 'what do you think?'
- Empower and inspire.

## Share constantly and widely – there are no mistakes, only lessons

Lessons, good and bad, should be shared for everyone's benefit. Here's how everyone can learn from them:

- Set the rules and policies, and make sure everyone understands them.
- Have carrots and sticks (recognition and consequences) – shine the spotlight on the stars, and wake up and advise of the consequences for those who fall asleep.
- Hold everyone accountable but be flexible when needed – that's a strength, not a weakness.
- Measure as much as possible and share the results with the whole team.

## Celebrate your success with an open heart and a respectful budget

Take time out to acknowledge and reflect on how far you've come, and be generous with your team recognition by providing any the following:

- public acknowledgement during meetings
- snacks at key meetings
- team dinners
- cultural celebrations
- team trips.

## Tell your story to empower and inspire others

You will have noticed that I've shared stories from our students throughout this book. Here is another one – this time from Samach, who I introduced way back in chapter 3.

> ### September 2023
>
> *Samach is a first generation student who joined CRST in 2011. She was one of the first 22 students who trusted that we would support their education and help change their lives. This is her email, a week prior to graduating from her master's degree majoring in banking and finance:*
>
> Hello Aviv, Michelle, Aaron, Jess, Steph, and MJ,
>
> I trust you are well!!
>
> What a special year for me!!!
>
> It seems that 12 years is very quick. Just imagine back to 12 years ago, I was a rural girl who lived without a destination but believed that education would bring me success and break my family's poverty cycle. Luckily, you gave me the opportunity to find out who I was and you all put your effort, energy, heart, and commitment into my life in order to achieve my full potential.
>
> Of course, Cambodia has a social norm that does not encourage girls, like me, to study hard as Cambodian people believe that girls should get married, have babies, and do housework. I actually was in that

situation. Fortunately, you all inspired and empowered me to believe in myself and choose what I should do for myself. I am inspired to be who I am and to be a leader of Cambodia society. Thanks for bringing inspiration and empowerment into my life. Without your support, I would not be able to achieve so many things in my life, have a comfortable family, and understand how important it is for me to contribute back to the next generation as well as my society.

Through your mentorship and encouragement, I am able to deal with many people at my workplace and be responsible for my tasks. When I was in Phnom Penh, I was admired by my boss and he loved me so much. Even though I moved to Siem Reap, he still loves me and allows me to work in his company from Siem Reap. I just want to share that this is not a normal situation in Cambodia. This happens because of the TRUST I have built with my boss. He trusts me and gives me the opportunity to work from Siem Reap. The incredible lessons I have learned from you are very valuable. I just cannot describe enough how much it is valuable. I have never learned your lesson at school. Just an incredible lesson. Thanks for giving me the opportunity to study at PUC which is the best university in Siem Reap. It was very hard to study there but I have achieved extraordinary results now.

I cannot forget the day that I started working at Project Y. PY gave me exceptional hands-on business lessons I could use in my real work today. I still remember my first day at PY, I was a finance [team member]. I was very scared to get money from customers and exchange money for them. Luckily, you encouraged me and our team to be confident and trust ourselves that we could do it. Finally, we all overcame all challenges. It was an unforgettable experience and valuable lesson in my life. I believe that everyone who was given the opportunity to work at PY never forgets that moment. It is always in my heart. Especially, your emotional support. It was my first time learning real practical business concepts. Still, remember everyone... 💖😊

The opportunity to learn in business classes gave me the confidence to deal with my real life. I still remember our first business class. It was my first time to learn about writing a business plan, sales, and financial plan. Such amazing lessons I have learned from you all including

Steve – learning about finance. He inspired me to continue my dream of becoming a finance manager and continue to master's degree in finance and accounting.

My graduation day at PUC was my most unforgettable day ever. I could not believe my eyes that I would be able to achieve my degree. Not just finish my BA but travel from Phnom Penh to join my graduation day. Wow... Many of my friends at my school or my village friends did not receive this opportunity. It was an inspirational day for my mum and my siblings. She was very happy to see my achievement. She said to me you are an amazing daughter – I did not have money for you to study but Aviv and his family gave you a great opportunity to achieve your goal. She is very thankful to you all for the support from your heart. And of course, THANKS to Aviv and Jess for spending time on the flight to attend my special day as well as all family members from Australia to congratulate me on my special day.

Also, thanks for attending my special wedding party. Doeb and I were very touched to have you all on our wedding day. Thanks for allowing us to be your family member. You never treated us like scholarship students – we felt very warm and pleased to be a part of the family. Hope you love it and had a great experience on our wedding day!!

Amazingly, time does fly!!! I am writing to share the great news that I am going to take my final exam for my master's degree next week (8th of October). My big milestone in my life this year. I could not believe how far I have come and who I am today. Compared to my friends, I have rapidly changed both my knowledge and finances.

A master's degree will give me the opportunity to understand deeply about finance and accounting and will help to get a higher position in my current company. I am very proud to share with you that I am currently working both in Siem Reap and Phnom Penh as a Senior Finance Manager. I am responsible for the company's accounts as well as taxation. Moreover, I was recently invited by the Vannda Institute to teach finance and accounting. I have not decided yet as I am very busy with both workplaces. Of course, I never forget my goal – I would like to share my knowledge with the next generation. Maybe I will teach next year.

Lastly, I would like to say THANKS 🙇‍♀️💕 again for your support since I was in high school. Without you all, I would not be able to become who I am today and I would not be able to inspire so many lives around me to understand the power of education. Your investment in me is fruitful in my society. THANK YOU to my beloved family!!!

Samach

# The fundamentals – nuts and bolts of the organisation

Feel free to use some of our processes as a basis for your processes and systems – just keep in mind these are never perfect and are constantly updated. Make them perfect by customising them to your needs and then keep perfecting them; they are a place to start, not the end.

## The measurables – what you can't measure, you can't improve

Here's what we track and share in feedback with our CRST students:

- school/university attendance
- school/university results
- feedback to underperforming students
- monthly activity plan
- monthly activity implementation evaluation
- monthly student volunteering contributions
- celebrate and compliment high achievers for their contributions
- feedback to low contributing students.

## Set up your leaders for success – their success is your success

Here are some of the ways we recognise almost-graduated students' success, and support them in further success:

- certificates of recognition
- letters of recommendation

- introduction letter to university or potential employer
- help with preparing resumes and cover letters.

## Measure and evaluate your success – the return on your investment

And here are some ways we track and highlight the successes of our CRST students:

- alumni – where are they now?
- alumni annual salary survey
- alumni survey graph compared to general employment market
- testimonials from students who have graduated
- keeping track of students who left along the journey
- testimonials from students who left before graduating
- projects' community impact summary.

Our past shaped us to be who we are today. Our present shapes who we can be tomorrow. Make it magnificent.

## FOUNDATIONS OF LEADERSHIP TAKEAWAYS:

- How you do anything is how you do everything.

- Articulate your vision clearly.

- People follow what they understand and believe – make it simple and be genuine.

- Critical steps:
  - from an idea in your head
  - to the spoken words for sharing
  - to the written words for implementation and constant improvement.

- Leadership essence:
  - Be authentic – be you, everyone else is already taken.
  - Know that you don't know everything – develop an inner circle and a team.
  - Begin with the end in mind – where do you want to end up?
  - Think critically – ask questions, seek answers; go deeper.
  - Be flexible – you'll be amazed where you end up.
  - Be creative and let others be creative – you'll go much further.
  - Add value to all stakeholders at every step.
  - Set goals and then report and evaluate – that's the essence of continued improvement; sharpen the saw.
  - Value failings as lessons, but make sure you learn these lessons.
  - Support on the down, celebrate on the up.
  - Judge less, love more.

# Conclusion

# The end doesn't exist

Life is a journey and when we're done, our legacy continues – so make it a good one!

We didn't choose Cambodia, Cambodia chose us. We just accepted that the universe put Cambodia in our path – and then we picked up the opportunity and ran with it. I often think that Cambodia has enriched our family much more than we ever deserve. It's not often that adult children and their parents have a deep common passion that binds them closely. Normally by the time adult children reach their thirties, they're off on their own paths; yet here we are, interacting daily, still growing together, living fulfilling lives.

Life is full of choices. We all have the same 24 hours in our days, and if we live to reach 80, we will all be alive for the same 29,200 days. Leading yourself so you can have a positive impact on others is one of the most rewarding experiences any human can have, yet like many enriching experiences it takes planning, actions and constant reevaluation to get the best results. It takes determination, tenacity, flexibility and love. Leadership is a set of responsibilities and, like education, it's a process, not an event. Leadership is a privilege – your opportunity to enrich other people's lives.

Even if you've reached the end of this book, it doesn't end here, because as leaders, the lives we're impacting will continue to pay it forward, in their own lives and in the lives of those they touch – their family, friends, colleagues and society at large. Leaders have the opportunity of creating and leaving far-reaching impact; leadership is a responsibility and a privilege, and we must never forget that.

An educated parent who educates their child, who educates the next generation and creates a social norm, leaves a generational legacy of social development. The impact of the Cambodia Rural Students Trust NGO and our educated students is forever woven into the fabric of Cambodia's development. We set out to help break the poverty cycle through education in a foreign land by educating their future leaders, and we are grateful to have been blessed to enrich humanity.

To paraphrase American educator Forest Witcraft, 'A hundred years from now it will not matter what my bank account was, the sort of house I lived in, or the kind of car I drove. But the world may be a better place, because I was important in the life of a child.'

Empowered, a new generation of leaders – a legacy that will far outlive us all.

# Acknowledgements

# Nothing is achieved on our own

It's difficult for me to know where to start to express my gratitude and how far to cast out my net of appreciation.

Chronologically, I'll start with my grandparents, although I'm sure preceding generations have also affected who I am today to some degree. While my grandparents lived in very different times, they sowed the seeds of education and the work ethic to create lifetime achievements. I also want to thank my parents, Nili and Uri, who altered the course of their lives to give my brother and me a better future. Not until I became a parent did I fathom the self-sacrifice and lifetime commitment of parenthood. I'm grateful for your foresight and liberalism to allow me to be who I am, while showering me with your love and sensible guardrails.

My life-partner, Michelle, who's happy to let me be all I can be; at times surely wondering what possesses me to do all that I do. Thank you for your warmth, tender love, trust and support – I can't imagine sharing my life journey with anyone else. I love you for the home we've created, the many lives we are enriching and the lives we are living.

Jess and Steph, you are incredible humans in your own rights, at times challenged to live out of my shadow and in your own rightful sunshine. Who knows where I'll be without you? For sure, I wouldn't be on this Cambodia journey. Steph, thank you for your non-judgemental heart to help others, whoever and wherever they may be, and thank you for your kindness and wisdom; you continue to leave powerful footprints as you mentor people to own their ocean. Jess, thank you for being my partner in all we do in Cambodia – your insights, dedication and professionalism are inspirational, and the journey would be feeble without you. Balancing our father–daughter relationship, our work relationship and our Cambodia-leadership relationship, you are talented beyond words; thank you for being you. May you both continue to 'do you', laugh and love – thank you for grounding me and floating me at the same time.

Roni, MJ, Aaron, David, Jan, CRSF board members and our amazing supporters – my gratitude to you all for sharing our life-altering impact for thousands of Cambodians. Thank you for your backing and faith in our ability to break countless poverty cycles by educating Cambodia's future leaders. Thank you for your benevolence and generous spirits as together we celebrate humanity.

Charlotte, my editor, and Michael from Publish Central, gratitude for your insights and passion.

And, lastly, thank you to the amazing students of the Cambodia Rural Students Trust and your families – the heroes of modern Cambodia. It's not often we place our trust in complete strangers, yet that's what you have all done. Thank you for trusting our family, allowing us to guide you, share part of your life journey, support your education, help you empower yourselves and shine the light on you as you inspire others. You are all amazing young adults and extraordinary leaders – Cambodia is blessed to have you as her daughters and sons.

សូមអរគុណ និងសូមជូនពរអ្នកទាំងអស់គ្នាជួបតែសំណាងល្អគ្រប់ពេលវេលា!!

# Appendix A

# Where are they now?

Education and mentoring are gifts that last a lifetime. Here's an outline of where some of our alumni are on their journey, listed by the year they joined CRST.

## 2011

**Dany** joined CRST when she was in grade 11. In 2015, she was the family support manager, as well as working at 'Project Y – Frozen Yogurt'. Dany graduated from Pannasastra University of Cambodia (PUC) in 2019 and began teaching English at the Australian Centre for Education (ACE). She's delighted to share her education journey and inspire students at ACE who are studying at all levels.

**Doeb** and **Samach** joined CRST when they were in grades 11 and 12 respectively. After graduating from university, they married and moved to Phnom Penh for work and to further their studies. Today, they are back in Siem Reap where Doeb is mentor-in-residence and Executive Director of CRST and is about to commence his master of laws degree after already completing his second bachelor degree, in law.

Samach is working as an accounting and tax manager for a group of companies and as a finance advisor for CRST. She graduated with her MBA majoring in finance and banking.

Doeb and Samach deeply value education and they are sustainably and impactfully contributing to leaving a legacy of hope and inspiration for the next generation. They are also the proud parents of Thavout!

**Nak** joined CRST when he was in grade 12, and became the first NGO manager at 21 years old, while still in high school. After graduating with his bachelor degree in business administration in 2019, he went on to graduate with his MBA in marketing from PUC. Nak is running his own real estate business, is married to Theary and just welcomed their first child, Sambath.

**Veun** joined CRST when he was in grade 12 and became a member of the NGO's senior leadership team. He graduated with his BA in 2020 majoring in international relations and has graduated with an MBA in development and international studies from Norton University in Phnom Penh. Veun is working as an assistant to the executive director for an international organisation, overseeing several projects and team members. Veun is also a mentor for projects and departments at CRST.

## 2013

**Pheak** joined CRST as a university student, and while he was studying for his bachelor degree in international relations, he was the manager of the community service department. He graduated with his master's degree from PUC with honours while working at a private company in Phnom Penh. His consistency in personal growth defines him as a resourceful asset for the organisation and for Cambodia. He is currently a mentor within CRST, mentoring team members in various projects and departments.

**Rany** joined CRST as a high school student in grade 12. While studying for her bachelor degree in finance and banking, she was the health and sport manager and was a member of the NGO's senior leadership team. Rany recently graduated with her MBA in management, with honours. She is now an accounting assistant for an international NGO at the National Maternal Health and Child Centre in Phnom Penh.

**Sineang** joined CRST as a high school student in grade 11. While studying for her bachelor degree in international relations, she served as the manager of two of our social enterprises. Currently, she is pursuing her MBA while working at a French organisation in Cambodia that primarily focuses on empowering young individuals from disadvantaged backgrounds through education, helping them secure decent jobs.

**Sreng** joined CRST in 2013 and was a member of the NGO senior leadership team and first manager of Project Y before becoming the NGO manager. In 2019 he was the first CRST student to receive an overseas scholarship to study his bachelor of management information systems (MIS) at Temple University in Philadelphia. He has now graduated with an MBA from the American University of Phnom Penh and is working at the Cambodian Ministry of Economy and Finance.

**Vannak** joined CRST after finishing high school and studied the Intensive English for Academic Purposes program (IEAP) while contributing to numerous NGO activities. He left the NGO to study for an electrical vocational diploma in Thailand in 2014 and after receiving his certificate, re-joined CRST. He graduated with his bachelor degree in 2021, majoring in information technology, and is now studying his master's degree majoring in information technology. Vannak is currently working for a coding company that offers coding courses to children in both Cambodia and Australia.

## 2014

**Heng** began her journey with CRST when she was in grade 10. In 2022, she completed her studies, earning a bachelor's degree in business administration. Heng was a member of the senior leadership team and was a manager of 'Project G – Empowering Girls'. She is thriving in her professional career, working for an organisation located in Siem Reap.

**Phirun** joined CRST when he was in grade 10. After graduating from high school, he was given opportunities to work as a marketing and hospitality assistant manager and a manager of 'Project R – Refuse, Reduce, Reuse and Recycle Plastic Education Program'. He graduated from university with a degree in business administration in 2022. He is now pursuing his master's degree in marketing at the National University of Management and works as a senior production officer at a marketing agency in Phnom Penh. Phirun mentors the CRST marketing team members.

**Ramet** joined CRST in grade 11 and graduated with his bachelor degree in 2020 with a major in business administration. He was a general manager at Project Y and became one of CRST's NGO managers. He is now continuing his master's degree and working as a project officer in an NGO in Phnom Penh, which focuses on digital rights, internet freedom and freedom of expression. Ramet is a member of the CRST mentor group in Phnom Penh.

**Riya** joined CRST when she was in grade 11. She graduated with a bachelor degree in 2020 with a major in international relations. She was an assistant GM at Project Y. She is now studying for her master's degree in development and international studies at Norton University and working in Phnom Penh in an organisation that focuses on labour dispute resolution in Cambodia.

**Sinuon** was in grade 12 when she joined CRST. She was the first Project G manager and went on to become part of the senior leadership team. She graduated with her bachelor degree in international relations and currently works in Phnom Penh at an organisation focusing on health, gender equality and human rights.

**Sompeas** became a member of CRST after graduating from high school. She held a number of roles in CRST and Project Y and was a member of the NGO's senior leadership team. In 2020, she graduated with a bachelor degree in law from the American University of Phnom Penh and, in 2021, was given the opportunity to pursue a Juris

Doctor (JD) at the University of Arizona in the United States. In 2023, she graduated and then passed the bar exam in 2024, while working as a law clerk at the Pima County Superior Court, in Tucson, Arizona.

**Yeat** joined CRST after he graduated from high school at the age of 21. He studied for his bachelor degree in marketing at PUC and was selected to be a member of Project Y, and was subsequently promoted to be general manager. In 2020, he moved to Phnom Penh to pursue his master's in business management at the National University of Management and graduated with honours in 2024, receiving his certificate from the Prime Minister of Cambodia, His Excellency Hun Manet. He works in real estate and is also a financial consultant. Yeat is married to Pheaktra and they have a beautiful daughter, Athika.

## 2015

**Loy** joined CRST in 2015 as a university student and studied international relations. She was promoted to the junior leadership team in 2019, as well as a Project R assistant manager. She is about to finish her MBA in development and international studies at Norton University and is working at an NGO in Phnom Penh as a program officer and youth hub educator.

**Rith** joined CRST after finishing high school. While studying for his bachelor degree in business administration at university, he held several positions in CRST, including education manager, student selection manager, TENME manager and sales and marketing team member at Project Y. Rith is currently studying for his master's degree in marketing and is working as a sales supervisor in a real estate company in Phnom Penh.

**Roeun** joined CRST after finishing high school. While studying for his bachelor degree in business administration at university, he held various positions in CRST, including volunteer manager, community service manager, junior and senior leadership team member, and, ultimately, NGO manager. In 2020, he graduated from his bachelor degree and went on to graduate from his master's degree in marketing in Phnom Penh. He is now working as an administration and accounting manager in a real estate company.

**Synich** joined CRST as a grade 12 student, and then pursued her bachelor degree in international relations, graduating in 2021. Currently, she is furthering her education by pursuing a master's in development and international studies at Norton University, expecting to graduate in 2024. During her time at CRST, she held several roles, including education manager, public speaking manager and junior leadership team member. She is working in Phnom Penh as a project officer at a civil organisation, focused on project self-management for inclusive leadership enhancement.

## 2016

**Barang** joined CRST in grade 10. While studying for his bachelor degree in business and economics, he held the roles of finance department manager and assistant NGO manager. He graduated with honours in 2022 and in 2024 will graduate with an MBA in business administration from Paragon University. Barang works with the United Nations in Phnom Penh while remaining a CRST mentor.

**Loeurn** joined CRST when he was in grade 12 and graduated from PUC in 2023 with a bachelor degree majoring in business administration. He was a community service manager and 'Project L – Light for Education' operations manager. He is now working in a real estate company in Phnom Penh.

**Mab** joined CRST when she was in grade 10 and graduated with her bachelor degree in business administration in 2023. Mab held a number of roles in the NGO, including Project R manager. She is currently pursuing her master's degree majoring in management at the National University of Management in Phnom Penh, while working as a program manager for the first female coding club in Cambodia, Sisters of Code, inspiring more women to follow in her footsteps.

**Sall** joined CRST when he was in grade 12 and then pursued his bachelor degree in business administration at PUC. During his time in the NGO, he held several roles, including production assistant manager, marketing manager and boys education manager in Project G. He also worked as the operations assistant manager in Project R, and was a team member of the new student selection team. After graduating with his degree in 2022, he moved to Phnom Penh to work and begin his master's degree in science, information and communication technology (ICT) at Puthisatra University. Sall is currently working in a private business consultancy company as a marketing executive in Phnom Penh.

**Saoly** joined CRST after graduating from high school and was CRST's health manager, and then the 'Project V – The Volunteer Experience' and 'Project B – Bicycles for Education' manager. He earned his business administration bachelor degree from PUC in 2021 and is currently working in Phnom Penh as an account and BTL (below the line marketing) executive at one of Cambodia's leading marketing service companies.

**Sokhim** joined CRST in grade 11 and after graduating from high school she studied a bachelor degree in business and economics. She held several roles at CRST, including education manager and senior leadership team member. Sokhim is now studying a master's degree in communication and public relations while working as an employee relations officer in the human resources department in the education sector. Sokhim continues to contribute back to CRST as an education department advisor.

**Syn** joined CRST in grade 11 of high school. She joined the Project V team, hosting overseas guests during their visits to Cambodia and was also a production manager in Project G. In 2023, she graduated with her bachelor degree in business administration and she is working at East Asia Management University (EAMU) in Phnom Penh as an assistant manager for academic assessment and quality assurance.

## 2017

**Chhai** joined CRST after he graduated from high school. He was a member of the NGO senior leadership team and graduated with a bachelor degree in business administration from PUC in 2022. Chhai is currently working in the general insurance field at Forte Insurance in Phnom Penh.

**Chroep** began her journey with CRST for her final year of high school. She gained valuable experience as a marketing coordinator and a member of the NGO's senior leadership team. She completed her bachelor degree in business administration at PUC in 2023. With both practical skills and academic knowledge, Chroep works at a leading private international school in Phnom Penh – a testament to her perseverance and adaptability.

**Khean** joined CRST while studying in grade 12 and was a member of the senior leadership team and the NGO campus manager. He graduated with a bachelor degree majoring in business administration in 2023 and is now an administrator for an NGO in Phnom Penh, focusing on sponsorship, education, health, water and sanitation, income generation, and advocacy in provinces around Cambodia. He is looking forward to starting his MBA in management in 2024.

**Lea** joined CRST as a high school student in grade 12. While studying for her bachelor degree in business administration, she was the education manager of Project G and community service assistant manager. She is now working at a private school in Phnom Penh as the academic programs officer.

**Ney** joined CRST in grade 11. While studying his BA in business administration at PUC, he was the assistant education manager and a team member of the HR and operations departments. Ney now works as the assistant to the chief executive officer at Klassy Watches.

**Sokal** joined CRST while in grade 11 and excelled academically with the CRST scholarship, graduating with top honours in 2019. While pursuing his bachelor degree in business administration from PUC, he also became the NGO's general manager. Sokal now works as a grants officer at an international humanitarian and development organisation, dedicated to enhancing educational opportunities for students in the under-served rural and remote regions of north-eastern Cambodia.

Sokkhim joined CRST after graduating from high school. He was a member of Project Y as well as volunteer manager and human resource manager of Project G and Project R. At the end of 2022, he graduated with his bachelor degree from PUC and moved from Siem Reap to Phnom Penh. He is currently the human resource supervisor at Mistine (Cambodia) in Phnom Penh.

Soma joined CRST after he graduated from high school and studied his BA in international relations at PUC, graduating in 2021. While he was a scholarship student in CRST, he was the NGO's HR manager for four years. He is now working in the development sector as a monitoring and result measurement officer of an international NGO taking part in re-engineering the Cambodian market system.

Srey Leab was selected to join CRST after graduating high school and was given several opportunities to work her way up to the first female NGO manager. She earned her bachelor degree in 2023, majoring in business administration at PUC, and is currently pursuing a master's degree of communication and public relations at Limkokwing University. She works for a non-profit organisation as a project officer, aiming to increase engagement and empower young women in the public space and policy dialogue.

## 2018

Lean joined CRST as a university student and completed her bachelor degree in business administration in 2023. She was an active participant in Project G, as the marketing and HR manager. She is currently working as a business training coordinator with the Cambodia–Japan Cooperation Center (CJCC), which provides business training, services and networking to support start-ups and SMEs (small and medium enterprises) for sustainable growth and development of the entrepreneurship ecosystem in Cambodia.

Leat joined CRST in grade 11 and graduated with his bachelor degree in business administration in 2024. While a scholarship student at CRST, he was a marketing team member and manager of

Project B. He is currently working as an assistant marketing director for an international company in Siem Reap that sources and produces a variety of products for clients in the United States, China and Europe.

**Pov** joined CRST as a university student and graduated with his bachelor degree in early 2023, majoring in business administration. He was the manager of the community service department, and then became the general manager of Project W – WASH for Education. He is now working for a local NGO that focuses on empowering poor women and children living in slum communities in urban areas of Phnom Penh.

## 2019

**Ang** joined CRST as a university student and held the position of student selection manager and senior leadership team member. He graduated with a bachelor degree in business administration from PUC and is currently working as a Cambodia project coordinator at Days for Girls International to promote gender equity and empower girls.

**Langdy** joined CRST after graduating high school. While studying her bachelor degree in business administration, she was also the marketing manager in Project G and a finance department team member. Graduating in 2024, she is now working as an administrative officer at Animal Rescue Cambodia, a non-profit organisation in Phnom Penh that focuses on animal welfare and protection.

**Nath** was selected to be a member of CRST when she was in grade 12. She was an assistant education manager as well as new student selection manager. In 2024 she completed her bachelor degree majoring in business administration at PUC. Nath is a department officer working for a non-profit organisation that focuses on transforming the most impoverished children into tomorrow's leaders by delivering high-quality education, leadership training and direct support programs in Phnom Penh.

***

We're looking forward to adding many more of our alumni's journeys through life as they continue to leave a legacy of education, empowerment and inspiration.

# Our students

We are proud to share with you this list of CRST family members, Cambodia's empowered new generation of leaders.

- Ang
- Barang
- Bopha
- Bros
- Chanrong
- Chanthan
- Chantrea
- Chanty
- Chhai
- Chhaly
- Chhean
- Chhengheang
- Choeurn
- Chroep
- Dany
- Doeb
- Eam
- Heang
- Heng
- Houn
- Kakada
- Kay
- Khean
- Kimsiev
- Kimszeit
- Kongkea
- Kosal
- Kunthea
- Langdy
- Lea
- Leakhena
- Lean
- Leat
- Linna
- Lita
- Loeurn
- Longdy
- Loy
- Lun
- Ly C
- Ly P
- Lyhortt
- Mab
- Mala
- Malong
- March
- Molika C
- Molika R
- Nak
- Nath
- Neang
- Ney
- Nimol
- Nit
- Norn
- Pech
- Phanich
- Phea
- Pheak
- Pheareak
- Phirun
- Phloeut
- Pich
- Pin
- Pisean
- Poch
- Porm
- Poung
- Pov
- Rady
- Ramet
- Rany

- Reaksa H
- Reaksa K
- Reaksa O
- Reaksmey C
- Reaksmey P
- Reaksmey P
- Rida
- Rith
- Riya
- Roeun
- Rorm
- Sall
- Saluy
- Samach
- Sambo
- Samnang
- Samrech
- Saoly
- Sara
- Sarakhun
- Sarot
- Sarvann
- Sathea
- Saveat
- Saven
- Savorn
- Seyha
- Seyla
- Sievyien
- Sin
- Sina

- Sinat
- Sineang
- Sinuon L
- Sinuon P
- So
- Sokal
- Sokey
- Sokhey
- Sokhim
- Sokkhim
- Sokny
- Sokphan
- Sokrin
- Soma
- Somey
- Sompeas
- Somphors
- Somruoch
- Sophatt
- Sophea
- Sopheap
- Sophorn
- Sovann
- Sreng
- Srey Leab
- Srey No
- Sreyoun
- Sreykeo
- Sreyna
- Sreynam
- Sreynet

- Sreynuth
- Sreyoun
- Sreypeou
- Sreypich
- Sreyroth
- Sreyyon
- Syn
- Synich
- Tangly
- Tey
- Thavry
- Tok
- Tola R
- Vanna
- Vannak
- Vanndet
- Veasna P
- Veasna V
- Vech
- Veha
- Veun
- Vibol S
- Vibol T
- Vicheka
- Visal
- Visith
- Vonn
- Yany
- Yeat

# Our student- and family-support sponsors

Our gratitude to the following individuals and families, who have shared part of our journey by sponsoring our students, supporting rural families and projects at various times.

- Able Customs
- Adina
- Akash and Shavita
- Alan
- Alana
- Alena
- Angela
- Anh
- Annie and Anthony
- Barang and Sineang
- Barry N
- Barry S
- Bec, Andrew and family
- Belen
- Bella
- Betty
- Budi and Livia
- Camille
- Campbell House School
- Care for Cambodians
- Carol
- Carrie
- Castle Hill High School
- Catherine
- Chana
- Cherie R
- Cherrie O
- Cheryl, Ken and family
- Cheryl and Andrew
- Chhai
- Christina
- Christine
- Con
- Coral and John
- Damian, Anne and family
- Dan
- Dany
- David and Belinda
- David and Hayley
- David B
- David C
- David S

- Debbie and Abe
- Debra
- digiDirect
- Doeb and Samach
- Earle
- Ed
- Edna and Nachum
- Edwina
- Elizabeth
- Erin
- Georgia
- Gerald Q
- Gerard M
- Gerry B
- Gillian
- Ginny
- Glenda
- Glenn
- Graeme
- Greg
- Gus and Cherie
- Hadyn
- Harry and Silva
- Heba, Diaa and Luke
- Heidi
- Helen
- Heng and Thearak
- Henry
- Herb, Thomai and Family
- Ian G
- Ian R
- Jacky
- Jacky and Ken
- Jacqueline
- Jak and Karen
- James and Zed
- Jane and Phill
- Janine
- Jazz and Jackson
- Jeanne
- Jeannine and Bennie
- Jennie
- Jenny and family
- Jerry and Kristen
- Jill
- Joan
- John
- John and Margaret
- Joy
- Judi
- Julie A
- Julie B
- Karin
- Katherine
- Kay
- Keith
- Kelley and David
- Kerry
- Kevin and Liz
- Khemara
- Kim and Peter
- King David School
- Kristina
- Laird and Jo
- Lary
- Lea and family

- Leesa
- Leonard
- Lesley and Pat
- Lewis and Rachelle
- Lidio and Sam
- Loretta, Henry and Family
- Lorraine H
- Lorraine N
- Louise
- Louise and Adam
- Loy
- Lyn
- Lyn and John
- Manon
- Marcus
- Margaret
- Marguerite
- Maria H
- Maria J
- Marie-Claire
- Marina
- Marisa
- Martin
- Mary and Tony
- Matt
- Melissa, Fred and family
- Michael
- Michelle and Geoff
- Michelle L
- Michelle M
- Michelle P
- Mimo, Ange and family
- Mitchell
- Nak and Theary
- Nathaniel, Jeffery and Kevin
- Narelle
- Nele
- Neville
- Nicki
- Norman
- Pamela
- Paul and Jenni
- Paul N
- Penny
- Peter and Julie
- Peter J
- Peter L
- Pheak
- Philip C
- Philip T
- Rach and family
- Raman
- Ramet
- Rany
- Raymond
- Rebecca
- Rene and John
- Rhonda
- Rick and Loretta
- Ricky and Mia
- Robyn and Rob
- Roni and Debby
- Rotary Club of Balwyn
- Rotary Club of Brighton
- Rotary Club of Camberwell
- Rotary Club of Glen Waverley

- Rotary Club of Keilor East
- Rotary Club of Kowloon Golden Mile
- Rotary Club of Kyneton
- Rotary Club of Melbourne
- Rotary Club of North Melbourne
- Rotary Club of Ocean Grove
- Rotary Club of Williamstown
- Russell
- Ruth & Ralph
- Sandra B
- Sandra P
- Sall
- Sally and Brett
- Saoly
- Sarah
- Sean
- Sergio
- Shant
- Sharon and David
- Sharon P
- Sharon R
- Sina
- Soma
- Somit and Len
- Sompeas
- Sook May
- Sophea
- Sreng
- Srey Leab
- Sreynang
- Stav
- Stephanie
- Stephen and Margaret
- Steve and Liz
- Susan
- Susan and Howard
- Susie
- Synich
- Tammy
- Tara
- Taylor
- The Merck Foundation
- Tom, Kate and family
- Tomax
- Tony and Amanda
- Tony and Elizabeth
- Tracey
- Tricia
- Uri and Nili
- Vanndet
- Veronica and Tay
- Veun
- Vibol
- Vivek
- Wade and Jarrah
- Wanda, Eran and family
- Yael and Sheffi
- Yeat
- Yu Beng

# Our community and project sponsors

These wonderful organisations and people have supported our community contributions and projects over the years.

- Arden Anglican School
- Asian Outreach Cambodia
- Burgess Portfolio
- Cambodia Beverage Company
- Canada Fund for Local Initiatives CFLI
- Caprice Australia
- Celliers d'Asie Cambodia
- CEM International
- Daniel Allison & Associates
- Days for Girls International
- Designet Services
- Developing World Connections DWC
- digiDirect
- Embassy of Israel in Thailand
- Erase IT
- EXO Foundation
- Explore Foundation
- FCC Angkor by Avani
- Fella Hamilton
- Frosty Boy
- Glenvill Homes
- Global Learning Expeditions
- Grill'd Pty Ltd
- Harvey Norman
- Hindal Corporate
- Intrepid DMC Cambodia
- Jay and Peter
- Jaya House River Park Hotel Cambodia
- John McBride and Associates
- Khiri Reach
- Lifestyle Brands
- LSH Cambodia
- Mentone Grammar
- Methodist Ladies College
- Mount Scopus Memorial College
- MST Lawyers
- Nakabayashi Japan

- Olympus
- Pacific Northwest Passport Rotary Club
- Patron Foundation
- Rotary Club of Box Hill Burwood
- Rotary Club of Calgary at Stampede Park
- Rotary Club of Ellerslie Sunrise
- Rotary Club of Glen Waverley
- Rotary Club of Jerrabomberra
- Rotary Club of Keilor East
- Rotary Club of Mount Waverley
- Rotary Club Sanary Bandol Ollioules
- Rotary Passport Melbourne
- SilverChef
- Smart Cambodia
- SolarBuddy
- St Albans Secondary College
- St Leonards College
- Stockland
- Terra Ferma
- The Funding Network
- The Intrepid Foundation
- The Phillips Foundation
- The Probus Club of Glenferrie
- Travel Beyond
- ULS – Urban Living Solutions
- Winfield
- World Challenge

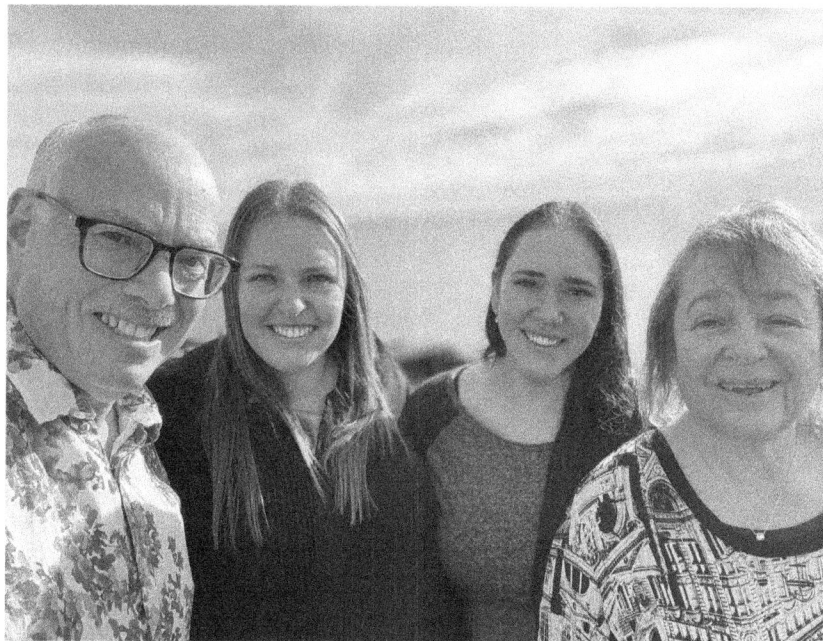

Aviv, Jess, Steph and Michelle Palti
Melbourne, Australia

For more information about the
Cambodia Rural Students Trust and the
amazing students who run it, scan the QR code.

# Notes

# Notes

# Notes

# Notes

# Notes

www.ingramcontent.com/pod-product-compliance
Lightning Source LLC
Chambersburg PA
CBHW030452210326
41597CB00013B/643